T0272470

ALSO BY RICHARD GRANT

The Deepest South of All
Dispatches from Pluto
Crazy River
God's Middle Finger
American Nomads

A RACE TO THE BOTTOM OF CRAZY

Dispatches
from Arizona

RICHARD GRANT

Simon & Schuster
New York London Toronto Sydney New Delhi

1230 Avenue of the Americas
New York, NY 10020

First Simon & Schuster hardcover edition September 2024

SIMON & SCHUSTER and colophon are registered trademarks of Simon & Schuster, LLC

Simon & Schuster: Celebrating 100 Years of Publishing in 2024

For information about special discounts for bulk purchases, please contact Simon & Schuster Special Sales at 1-866-506-1949 or business@simonandschuster.com.

The Simon & Schuster Speakers Bureau can bring authors to your live event. For more information or to book an event, contact the Simon & Schuster Speakers Bureau at 1-866-248-3049 or visit our website at www.simonspeakers.com.

Interior design by Wendy Blum

Manufactured in the United States of America

1   3   5   7   9   10   8   6   4   2

Library of Congress Cataloging-in-Publication Data has been applied for.

ISBN 978-1-6680-1102-7
ISBN 978-1-6680-1104-1 (ebook)

For Isobel June Grant

CONTENTS

A RACE TO
THE BOTTOM
OF CRAZY

*T*he Great Seal of the State of Arizona depicts the sun behind mountain peaks, a dam, a reservoir, irrigated fields and a cow. The only human is a miner with a mustache and a misshapen hat, leaning on a pick and shovel. This image was copied from a photograph of a real-life prospector named George Warren. As a boy he was kidnapped by Apaches, held captive for eighteen months and then traded to some miners for fifteen to twenty pounds of sugar.

He learned miners' vices—drinking, gambling, lying, double-dealing—and in 1877 he managed to finagle ownership of a mining claim in the Mule Mountains near the town of Bisbee. It was one-ninth of a mother lode that became known as the Copper Queen, one of the richest copper mines in history.

After a few rounds of whiskey, however, Warren got into a heated argument with his drinking companion about the relative speed of men and horses. He bet his share of the Copper Queen that he could outrun a man on a horse over one hundred yards. Once the wager was made, he placed a stake in the ground at the fifty-yard mark, believing a tight turn would give him the advantage. But he lost the race and the bet, to the amusement of the spectators, and spent the rest of his life in alcoholic penury. At one point he sold himself into peonage in Mexico, and his latter years were spent sweeping floors and cleaning spittoons.

In 1910, an old photograph of Warren in his prospecting days was hanging on the wall of a Bisbee bank, where it was spotted by one of the men designing the state seal. They needed a miner to add to the rest of the tableau, and fate decreed that George Warren would be the human figure that Arizona presents to the world.

Chapter One

GOING HOME

In my late fifties, with a younger wife and a four-year-old daughter, I decided to move back to Tucson, Arizona. I had based myself there for more than twenty years as an expatriate Englishman and traveling freelance journalist. I missed the rugged forested mountain ranges rising out of the desert like islands in the sky, the hundred-mile views in the clean parched air, hiking, camping, old friends, the chile kick in the food, carne asada grilled over mesquite coals and diced up in a flour tortilla. I missed the hummingbirds and roadrunners, the wind hissing through the needles of a sixty-foot-high saguaro cactus with its arms lifted up to the sky, the musky scents released by desert plants on the rare ecstatic occasions when it rained.

I interpreted these yearnings as homesickness, even though I'd grown up in Malaysia, Kuwait, and London, England, with no real concept of home. For my wife, Mariah, it was more straightforward. She was born and raised in Tucson (pronounced TOO-sawn) and had lived there into her thirties, when we moved to New York City, which chewed us up and spat us out, and then to Mississippi for nine years, which neither of us had expected. Now she wanted to go home and raise our daughter Isobel among family, friends and familiarity, away from the religious conservatism and social conformity of the Deep South, with easy access to wild nature and spectacular beauty.

Both of us loved Arizona, but not unconditionally. We shared the same misgivings about its rising temperatures and diminishing water supplies, its brutally underfunded and dismally performing public schools, the surly individualism and bared-teeth conservatism that prevails in large swaths of the population, and the seething undercurrents of hatred, paranoia and lunacy that bubble up into the political halls of power. "You can't spell CRAZY without AZ in the middle of it," observes Jon Talton, a newspaperman and crime novelist from Phoenix, the state capital—now the fifth-largest city in America and a vital battleground in national elections. Arizona is also a violent unruly place and second only to Florida, I would argue, when it comes to bizarre crimes.

Transience is Arizona's defining social characteristic. Although the state contains twenty-two Native American nations living on portions of their ancestral lands and some well-rooted Hispanic and Mormon communities, 60 percent of Arizona's adult population was born elsewhere. And for every three people who move to the Grand Canyon State, two leave for other places. People generally come to Arizona to get away from rules, regulations, obligations, high taxes and cold winters, to make a fresh start and reinvent themselves, or to find a refuge where they can be their weirder wilder selves without attracting a lot of judgment. Social guardrails are weak or nonexistent, the culture has almost no sense of common purpose, and this opens up plenty of latitude for outlandish behavior. You soon become accustomed to reading newspaper stories such as this one: "Father of four, 42, sacrifices family poodle in meat smoker because he didn't like daughter's T-shirt." Or this one: "A naked Apache Junction man, bristling with cactus spines, charged at a Pinal County deputy sheriff and could not be stopped with a nightstick or two superficial gunshot wounds."

Transience is the main reason why Arizona has such a thin sense of community, especially compared to a place like Mississippi, where ties to the land run generations deep and everyone seems to know each other's grandparents. Another reason is architectural. The built landscape—especially in Greater Phoenix, where 60 percent of Arizonans live—is dominated by generic suburban subdivisions that sprawl across what was recently irrigated farmland or pristine desert. Backyards are typically separated by eight-foot walls, and instead of neighborly front porches, parking garages face onto the street. This promotes privacy and security, which are highly valued, and discourages interactions with other human beings. According to a recent U.S. census report, Arizonans are dead last in the nation when it comes to spending time with neighbors. In other surveys, more than half of the state's residents report feeling lonely and disconnected from other people.

We had never lived in a subdivision and promised ourselves that we never would. Except when I was off the grid for a few years on a small ranch near the Mexican border, we had always rented houses in the historic neighborhoods around downtown Tucson and the nearby University of Arizona. A laid-back bohemian vibe prevailed in those heavily Democratic zip codes, with shady porches, cacti and succulents in the front yards, coyotes loping through the alleys, songbirds in the mesquite trees, iridescent hummingbirds feeding on the flowers. It was easy to walk or ride a bike to cafés, bars, thrift stores, record stores, food markets, live music venues and independently owned restaurants. We envisioned buying a house in one of those neighborhoods, living in a community of friends and Mariah's family members, and making frequent trips into the surrounding deserts and mountains, where we would introduce our daughter to the joys of hiking and camping in the incomparable Arizona outdoors.

So we sold our nice, comfortable, spacious house in Jackson, Mississippi, where Isobel's best friend Gray Lauderdale lived next door and the two girls had secret pathways to cross from one yard to the other, and would sometimes sit on small plastic chairs on opposite sides of the wrought-iron fence, chatting away and showing each other their favorite possessions. Gray's parents were churchgoing Republicans, kind, thoughtful, intelligent people, good company and excellent neighbors. We were not churchgoing Republicans, but that didn't stop us from enjoying meals, drinks and occasional day trips with the Lauderdales. Nor did it prevent Gray's father, John, from fixing a burst pipe under our house one night during a hard freeze.

It was hard to say goodbye to the Lauderdales and tell the two little girls they wouldn't be seeing each other anymore. And it was even harder with Louie and Cathy Thompson, our previous neighbors in the tiny rural community of Pluto, Mississippi, which we had moved to from New York City. Despite our cultural and political differences, we had become part of the Thompson family. Louie was a good-humored catfish farmer. Cathy was a labor and delivery nurse who had bought herself an AK-47 to help with stress relief during menopause, and a T-shirt that said, "Look out. I'm out of estrogen and I have a gun." She had an effusive Mama Bear personality and when Mariah got pregnant there was no question who was going to be her nurse at the birth.

Cathy secured us a comfortable, spacious suite at the hospital where she worked and made sure that all the relevant nurses and doctors knew that Mariah wanted a natural childbirth and I was there to help her. We had gone through training classes with a doula in Jackson and felt well prepared and fairly confident for a pair of first-timers. We arrived on a Friday morning with strong contractions coming at regular intervals, and Cathy took charge. She couldn't have been more efficient, reassuring or encouraging, and she was also hugely excited because she regarded Mariah as one of her daughters, which meant she was going to be a grandmother for the first time.

With the blinds closed, low lights and ambient music playing, Mariah labored all the way through Friday and Friday night into Saturday morning. She labored on the bed and she labored standing up and leaning on me. Natural childbirth meant no pain meds, and when agony overwhelmed her and she said she couldn't stand it anymore, we massaged her back and encouraged her to breathe her way through it. She labored all the way through Saturday, fully dilated, pushing with real force and determination, but progress was stalled, it was becoming clear that the baby's head was too big, and after being in active labor for more than fifty hours, she was approaching complete exhaustion.

Around midnight on Saturday, baffled that none of the medical professionals were suggesting it, I started advocating for a C-section. Mariah agreed to it after breaking down in tears. Then time seemed to speed up and shoot down a tunnel and I was in the operating theater wearing scrubs and a bouffant plastic surgical cap, watching exhaustedly from a chair as the doctors went into my wife's tented body, plucked out the bloody screaming writhing baby and handed it to Cathy Thompson, whose face beamed with joy and adoration as she said, "Oh, she's beautiful! Oh, I love her!" Once the baby was examined and cleaned up, Cathy handed her to me.

I was surprised by my daughter's strength and the force of her screams. She didn't seem fragile and helpless at all, but full of life and mad as hell. I held her and failed to comfort her as I watched Mariah spasming uncontrollably. Blood was pulsing out of her and I wondered if she was going to die. But an hour later she was stable, with Isobel on her chest. Without modern medicine in a hospital setting, both of them would have almost certainly died.

The following day it was Cathy who gave Isobel her first bath, plunging her into a sink in our new hospital room and scrubbing her vigorously with a cloth as she screamed and wailed. We had no idea you could scrub a newborn baby like that. Cathy was already referring to Isobel as her granddaughter, and in the weeks and months to come they formed a very close bond. When Mariah wasn't able to get Isobel to sleep, usually because she was stressed out about it and communicating the stress to the baby, Cathy would hug Isobel to her bosom and sit in a rocking chair. Within a few minutes, or sometimes almost instantaneously, Isobel would relax completely and fall asleep.

Even when Isobel was a baby, we felt comfortable leaving her for a night with Nonna, as Cathy called herself, and Louie, who was also great with her. As a toddler, Isobel would often stay for weekends at the Thompsons' house in Pluto and get thoroughly spoiled. Cathy was her grandmother in every sense but the genetic; when we prepared our wills, we stated that in the event of both of our deaths, Isobel June Grant would go into the custody of Louie and Cathy Thompson.

On a bleak midwinter day, we drove out to Pluto through the flat fields, deep woods and cypress swamps of the Mississippi Delta. We walked into the Thompsons' kitchen, and told Cathy we were moving back to Arizona. Her body convulsed as she broke down weeping. "Y'all are breaking my heart," she said. "That child is part of my heart." There was nothing to do but stand there and feel terrible. Cathy later described it as the worst day of her life. When we explained to Isobel that moving to Arizona meant moving away from Nonna, she went through a range of emotions—defiance, fury, sadness, despair. Then came the awful day of goodbye, with Louie and Cathy doing their best to keep things bright and cheerful, and Isobel looking small and miserable, communicating in murmurs. Cathy gave her a final hug and said, "We'll FaceTime real soon, my darling, and I'll come and visit you in Tucson as soon as I can."

We tried to sell the move to Isobel as a big fun adventure. She would see mountains and deserts and wild animals she had never seen before. Disneyland was right next to Arizona in a place called California. When she told us she felt sad about leaving her room, we promised her an amazing new room in Tucson. "You'll have great fun decorating it, and arranging all your furniture and toys and stuffed animals," said Mariah. Isobel was also sad about leaving her school, her wonderful teachers Ms. King and Ms. Robinson, and her friends Birdie and Cora. "You'll make lots of new friends in Tucson, you're excellent at making friends," I said as she stood unhappily in her room one afternoon, surrounded by moving boxes. "I don't want to go," she said in a small firm voice. "I want to stay here with my Nonna and . . ." Then she crumpled down into a sobbing heap of despair on the floor, as guilt and empathetic pain welled up inside me.

She was a strong-willed and sensitive child, which was not an easy combination for any of us. She was determined to get her way, with a deep-seated urge to test boundaries, push, argue, fight. You don't want your child to be a pushover, especially if she's a girl, but our household often felt like a battleground. Every morning without exception there was an operatic drama over brushing her teeth and hair—"BUT I DON'T WANT TO!" Sometimes she would rage against the unfairness of the family power structure and cry out for natural liberty: "What gives you the *right* to tell me what to do?" She was already slamming doors and storming out of rooms, although not at school, where she was obedient, cooperative and diligent.

This was better than the alternative—defiant at school, compliant at home—and Mariah thought it was healthy. "It's good that she expresses her big, angry, negative emotions to us. It means she feels secure, comfortable and loved." I had the urge to punish her acts of defiance and rudeness by telling her off and withholding privileges, but it only seemed to deepen the conflict and escalate the drama when I tried, and it had the side effect of infuriating my wife, who would rush to her daughter's defense and fire an insult at me: "This isn't England in the 1970s." After some lively marital spats, we agreed on maintaining a consistent set of rules and boundaries, and calmly sending Isobel to her room when she broke them. This worked fairly well. Isobel would stay in her room until the emotional tempest had subsided and she felt ready to come out. Then she would get loving hugs and reassurance.

Her sensitive side manifested itself in kindness, thoughtfulness, empathy for others, aversion to risk, and agonized meltdowns of self-loathing when she did something wrong or was gently criticized. She also had a lively sense of humor and playfulness, and was highly curious and observant compared to her peers. She loved books and was an early reader, which was gratifying if unsurprising. Her writer father and librarian mother had read to her every night since she was five months old. Like most children, she was highly susceptible to bribery, and she got to watch a lot of cartoons and eat a lot of candy and ice cream as we packed up the house and prepared for the big move, during thirty straight days of rain that flooded the backyard, the crawl space under the house, and low-lying neighborhoods all over the city.

To transport our possessions, we made the mistake of hiring Armstrong Relocation of Madison, Mississippi, who damaged our family heirloom antiques through slipshod packing and refused to pay any compensation. I loaded up the cars with computers, clothes, boxes of important files and documents, bags of toys and stuffed animals. Mariah was going to drive in her car with Isobel, and I was going to follow in mine with the dogs. Savanna, a German shepherd mix, was an aging rebel, runaway and bruiser who had finally calmed down and become loyal and affectionate after being gored by wild hogs near Pluto. Riley, a black Labrador mix, came from a feral lineage in Holmes County, Mississippi. Mariah had spotted her as a tiny pup, standing forlornly by the decaying corpse of her road-killed mother as tornadoes coiled in the sky. Riley had grown into a sweet, loving, affection-craving dog with bad breath; she couldn't understand why her advances were sometimes rebuffed with appalled groaning noises. She was enthusiastic, eager to please, and a good travel companion who curled up and slept on car journeys.

We hit the road immediately after signing the closing papers in a lawyer's office in Jackson, massively relieved to have sold the house at a modest loss in a soft market. Driving out of Mississippi, with the rain still coming down and half the landscape drowned by flooding rivers, I felt a surge of mixed emotions. I craved the dry air, warm sunshine, long horizons and cobalt-blue skies of the desert Southwest. I had had enough of Mississippi. I was tired of its obsessions with race and class, its inept and bigoted political leadership, its self-defeating stubbornness and dysfunctionality, its failing infrastructure and smothering religiosity. But I also felt an aching sadness, because I loved the place for its hospitality and bigheartedness, conviviality and raconteurship, zest for living and finely tuned sense of comic absurdity. Nowhere in

America has a richer musical and literary heritage or better independent bookstores.

I appreciated the ease and grace that Mississippians brought to social interactions. Most of them were kind, and they had a knack for brightening up each other's day with amusing remarks and acts of generosity. There would be almost none of this in Arizona, where people seemed ill-mannered, humorless and socially impaired by comparison.

Westward we convoyed through the submerged fields and sodden winter woods, with the windshield wipers going full blast. I wouldn't miss the monochromatic winter landscapes, the tornadoes and floods, or the oppressive heat and humidity of the mosquito-infested summers. But I felt mournful when I thought about springtime in Mississippi, which is as lush and gorgeous as any spring on earth. We drove past Bolton, where my writer friend Alan Huffman holds a weekend-long party in his antebellum home every year, centered around a pig roast and attracting people from as far away as New York City and Morocco. Farewell, Alan; farewell, pig roast. Driving on to Vicksburg, we crossed the enormously swollen river that gave the state its name. Farewell, Mississippi, land of paradox and tangled contradiction, representing the best and the worst of America at the same time.

*B*uckets full of human heads. A cooler full of penises. Male torsos without limbs or genitalia, stacked up like cordwood. A small woman's head sewn onto a large man's torso. These were among the intensely disturbing sights that FBI agents encountered while searching a body donation center in Phoenix in 2014. Arizona is a hotbed for the nation's cadaver industry because of its high proportion of elderly residents and an almost complete lack of regulations and oversight. Anyone can set themselves up as a so-called body broker, and unscrupulous operators abound.

The center presented itself as a medical research facility. Grieving family members were told that donating the bodies of their loved ones might lead to cures for cancer, Alzheimer's, and other diseases. In reality, the owner was running what the newspapers called a "human chop shop." He was dismembering the bodies and selling the parts to medical schools and biomedical companies, and to the U.S. Department of Defense for blast-testing experiments.

Agents found ten tons of frozen human remains, including 281 heads, 337 legs, and 97 spines. Stephen Gore, the owner of the now-defunct Biological Resource Center, was found guilty of running an illegal business and ordered to pay $58 million in damages to the traumatized family members. Two years later, one of his former employees was found guilty of dumping 24 limbs and 5 heads in the woods of Yavapai County.

Chapter Two

COMING INTO THE COUNTRY

I was a veteran enthusiast when it came to driving across America. To spend a few long days on the road was a psychological reset. It gave me a feeling of freedom and release. It soothed my restless spirit with the balm of motion. But not this time. Not with a wife and a four-year-old child in the vehicle ahead, two dogs in the back, all our possessions in transit, a massive load of residual stress from selling the house at a loss with the floodwaters rising underneath it, and a highly uncertain future ahead.

On the first day we made it to a dog-friendly hotel in Shreveport, Louisiana, arriving at dusk in cold blustery weather with spitting rain. Mariah tended to Isobel while I unpacked the vehicles, carried everything up to the room, walked the dogs, fed the dogs, and secured dinner. Then it was Isobel's bedtime. Mariah read stories and sang, and the lights were out soon after eight p.m. She was able to fall asleep next to Isobel soon afterwards, the dogs were crashed out in their dog beds, but I was a chronic insomniac, a condition inherited from my father and grandmother, and presumably passed down from their forebears in the Scottish Highlands.

I spent the next few hours sitting uncomfortably on the bathroom floor, reading and not reading, trying to relax and lay aside the nagging dread that our family relocation plan was going to be dashed against the rocks of the Tucson housing market. We had spent months poring over real estate websites, shocked at the scarcity of suitable houses in our price range. We had secured a first-rate real estate agent, an empathetic, highly efficient Danish woman named Anne who also taught in the school of geography at the University of Arizona. We had finally found a great little house and bid generously on it, only to lose out to cash buyers paying well over the asking price.

We remembered Tucson as a cheap and easy place to get a roof over your head, but those days were gone. The Old Pueblo, as the city was nicknamed (also Too-Stoned for its drugginess), had been thoroughly discovered by hipsters, investors, Airbnb entrepreneurs, house-flippers including the actress Diane Keaton, minor celebrities including the cult film director Vincent Gallo, and hordes of Californians, New Yorkers, Portlanders, Seattleites, Chicagoans and other urbanites fleeing the brutal cost of living in the big Democratic cities. House prices were going berserk in the old neighborhoods we liked, and nearly everything was snapped up within twenty-four hours of being listed, usually by cash buyers.

We had also looked through the rental listings, month after month, and found nothing acceptable that we could afford. Mariah, who had been working as an academic librarian at Millsaps, a well-regarded liberal arts college in Jackson, had applied for several jobs at the University of Arizona and gotten nowhere. We had also failed to get Isobel into a school. Aside from a storage unit for our possessions and a thirty-day temporary rental, we had nothing solid in our future. Nor did we have a steady source of income, since I was a freelancer, and our family health insurance from Mariah's old job was set to expire in two weeks.

None of this was conducive to relaxation. I tried stretching and breathing exercises, which helped a little, although sleep still felt like an impossibility. I tried lying down in bed and drinking a glass of whiskey in the dark. I was wary of sleeping pills because my father and grandmother were addicted to them their whole lives, even though their tolerance was so high that the pills barely worked. I went back to the bathroom floor with a book and another whiskey.

I had been a self-employed writer for more than thirty years. I was accustomed to financial uncertainty and doing without health insurance. As a young man I had made the decision to trade security for freedom and independence, and for decades I was satisfied with the terms of that arrangement. But now I was pushing sixty with a wife and a young child to support. More and more often, I found myself wishing I could trade my freedom and independence for a guaranteed income, good family health insurance, and some sort of retirement plan for myself instead of nothing at all.

Early the next morning, after a few hours of whiskey-induced sleep, I drank black coffee, walked the dogs and packed up the vehicles. After a quick breakfast we hit the road, hoping to make 600 miles by early evening and resigned to the fact that Isobel would watch her tablet most of the day. That afternoon, on the plains west of Fort Worth, Texas, the land turned from green to brown, the trees became scarce, the sky rose up and stretched out and turned a deeper shade of blue. We were back in the Southwest, a region defined by its aridity. I found myself looking back at the man I used to be, the one who set my life on this uncertain path. He seemed so distant now. I barely recognized him. Who was that guy?

———

In 1991, at the age of twenty-seven, I was driving across the arid plains of Texas with a girlfriend from Boston named Rebecca. I had made my final escape from England, where I had always felt out of place and claustrophobic, caged in by the low gloomy skies and persistent rain, the accent-enforced class system, the smallness of the island, and a snide, bitter, narrowhearted nastiness that was all too prevalent in the culture. I had already spent a few years traveling around America and Mexico, working occasionally as a house painter, selling my first articles to magazines, and living for long stretches of time in a dented, leaky 1969 Buick station wagon, which suited me fine because the old hulk still ran and I had no money for better accommodations.

Wanderlust was the driving force in my life. I had no career ambitions. I didn't want to be rich or successful, but I had strong aspirations to live with the maximum amount of personal freedom that was possible in the modern world. I equated this with nomadic travel on the margins of society, a hedonistic live-in-the-moment approach, and the avoidance of responsibilities and obligations. Possessions were a pointless encumbrance. Houses were traps and relationships could be too. Mainstream society was an interlocking set of scams dressed up in false advertising. I was happy drifting around in the wide-open spaces of the American West and bathing in its rivers. I needed money for beer, food, gasoline and cigarettes, but I was determined not to be seduced by the allure of money or the comforts it could bring. That would mean the end of my freewheeling independence, which was bringing me more happiness and adventure than I had ever known.

Rebecca and I were planning to spend a few months in Santa Fe, where she had friends and could get a job cooking in a restaurant, but it was January and northern New Mexico was getting hammered by sub-zero blizzards. Looking at the weather map, I said, "Let's go to Tucson. It's 75 degrees there and sunny all week. We can hang out there until the weather gets better in Santa Fe." Interstate 10 took us through the arid grasslands and craggy forested mountains of southeast Arizona, a landscape once claimed by the Chiricahua Apache. Then it delivered us within a mile of downtown Tucson, which looked like something out of a Tom Waits song.

We walked past dive bars and street bums, derelict buildings and seedy cafés, an old-time barbershop offering straight-razor shaves, a ramshackle two-story musical instrument store, a wig shop named Wigorama with cracked and sun-blistered faces on its long-necked mannequins. We checked in at the Hotel Congress. Built in 1918, it had a high-ceilinged Southwestern Deco lobby with an old-fashioned telephone switchboard still in operation behind the desk. There was a well-worn bar called the Tap Room with vintage cowboy art on the walls, a café where all the waiters appeared deeply stoned, and a night-club with a live music stage. The gangster John Dillinger was captured at Hotel Congress in 1934 after an epic cross-country bank-robbing spree, and the rooms hearkened back to that era, with iron bed frames, vintage radios and fixtures, and no televisions. It was noisy at night, with music coming up from the club and freight trains blowing their mournful horns on the railroad tracks across the street, which made it seem even more like a Tom Waits song.

As we explored the rest of the city, it seemed like an amenable overgrown college town with a lot of ugly sprawl surrounding its core neighborhoods. We liked the warm winter sunshine, the desert bohemian vibe in the thrift shops, stores and cafés along Fourth Avenue, the rich spicy Mexican food, the people we were meeting, and the ruggedly beautiful cactus deserts and mountain ranges that ringed the city. It was a paradise for hiking and lazing around canyon swimming holes, and there was good music in the cafés and clubs—a mesmerizing slide guitarist called Rainer who played over tape loops of himself and sang mournfully; an old-school country singer called Al Perry; a rocker named Al Foul; the dusty sun-damaged indie rock of Howe Gelb and Giant Sand; and fantastic mariachi and norteño bands. I loved that Mexico was less than an hour away, and Mexican culture was an integral part of the city. My two favorite countries in the world came together in the Southern Arizona borderlands, although not without friction, prejudice, exploitation and tragedy, as I would learn in the future.

One day we drove over Gates Pass in the Tucson Mountains, found a big flat rock among the towering saguaros, sat down, opened a bottle of wine, and watched the sun set in a panoramic multicolored sky. It had rapidly become one of our favorite things to do. "Tucson is so cheap," I said as the sunset faded and we waited for the stars to come out. "You can rent a small house in a decent neighborhood for $250 or $300 a month. Santa Fe is going to be four or five times that, at least, and it's still cold and snowy there." Rebecca said, "Okay, let's look for a house to rent and I'll find a restaurant job."

We signed a six-month lease on a 1940s bungalow near the university for $300 a month and furnished it from the thrift stores on Fourth Avenue a few blocks away. Rebecca started cooking and baking for restaurants. I managed to line up a few assignments for British magazines. One of them was a travel story about a rafting trip through the Grand Canyon. I bought the necessary gear on expenses, kissed Rebecca goodbye and told her I'd see her in three weeks. The trip took that long because the Grand Canyon extends for 277 miles and we were hiking in its side canyons, bathing in its hidden waterfalls, camping on its beaches under stars framed by the mile-high canyon walls. When I returned to Tucson, half-feral and utterly besotted with the Arizona wilderness, Rebecca had gone back to Boston and cleared out all the kitchenware in the house except for one plate, one wineglass and one place setting of silverware. We both knew the relationship was ending, but she didn't want me sharing a meal with anyone else.

––––––

The urge to travel was as strong as ever, but it was convenient to have an address, a Tucson bank account, and a place to keep my new camping gear and growing collection of books. Living by myself with a pre-internet attention span, I would read for eight or nine hours at a stretch. The staff at a local independent bookstore guided me toward the best titles about Arizona and the Southwest, starting with Edward Abbey's irreverent eco-crusading *Desert Solitaire* and *The Monkey Wrench Gang,* Edward Spicer's classic history book *Cycles of Conquest,* and Cormac McCarthy's gory masterpiece *Blood Meridian,* a novel based on the real-life exploits of a gang of nineteenth-century killers who were paid by the state government in Chihuahua, Mexico, to hunt Apaches and bring in their scalps. That led to history books and ethnographies about Apaches and the Tohono O'Odham who had lived and farmed in the Tucson valley and now lived on a Connecticut-sized reservation to the west of the city. I read about Tucson when it was a Spanish city and then a Mexican one. I wanted to know where I had landed and what had happened here.

One day I walked out of the bookstore with a copy of *Blue Desert* by a Tucson author named Charles Bowden. It was a mosaic of reportage, vignettes, profiles and prophetic pronouncements about the desert Southwest, written in a vivid tough-edged prose with streams of consciousness. Early on, he goes deep inside a bat cave with a scientist. Mites move up from the floor and begin crawling over his skin. Urine and feces cascade down from the ceiling in a drizzling mist. He relishes the strange intensity of this experience, and the privilege of being in the bats' inner sanctum as they prepare for the night's flight: "The sound tightens now, a shrill spike of screeches and squeaks. The mites scramble across the skin. The larvae writhe like shiny stones at our feet. We stand inside a brief island of life, a hiding place of our blood kin."

Instead of emphasizing the otherness and creepiness of bats, as one might expect, he presents them as fellow mammals with a 45-million-year history whose populations are now collapsing because of our use of pesticides. Throughout the book, there is a similar visceral connection to wild places and creatures. Arizona is depicted as a place where the land aches with beauty and the people who move here for that beauty are destroying it. Crime is high, drug use is rampant, the water is running out, the population is rootless and adrift, and "progress" is a shady euphemism for untrammeled greed and environmental ruin. It was one of those books you don't forget, because it alters the way you look at the world.

Soon after I read it, a British newspaper magazine sent me to Montana to write about smokejumpers, the wildland firefighters who parachute into remote areas to attack and hopefully contain forest fires. At their headquarters in Missoula, I met another journalist who was writing about smokejumpers for a German magazine. He was a tall, rangy, rugged figure with blue eyes that seemed to devour his surroundings, a force field of charisma, and a Chicago-accented growl. He was about twenty years older than me and heavily weathered by the sun. He said he lived in Tucson and his name was Chuck Bowden.

"I'm living in Tucson and I just read a book called *Blue Desert* by Charles Bowden," I said. "Is that you? I liked that book a lot." He said, "Yeah. Everyone calls me Chuck." We went to a bar that afternoon and stayed there for several hours in the reddish neon light under taxidermied deer and elk heads. I drank Mexican beer and smoked Camel Lights. He drank cheap red wine, smoked unfiltered Lucky Strikes and did 90 percent of the talking. I had never heard anything like it. He went from bat ecology to Beethoven's Ninth, George Orwell's political philosophy to the inner workings of the Mexican Revolution, medieval Italian scholars to twentieth-century Spanish war photographers. "Lookit," he said as he started to map out a theory that Dostoevsky was the harbinger of the alienation that defines modernity, and then, "Ya follow?" after he clinched his point.

Crooked financial tycoons were like mountain lions: "They're predators, exploiting their environment, following their instincts, scenting weakness, moving in for the kill. It's who they are and what they do. So how do you judge them?" Then he told an anecdote about an Arizona cattle rancher he had interviewed who had seen a pair of mountain lions in the act of mating, an incredibly rare sight. "He says to me, 'Which one do you think I shot first?' Well, it was the female, of course."

Chuck Bowden had once taught American history at a university in Illinois. It promised lifelong security and comfort—"my ticket was punched"—but he found it unbearably dull and stultifying. He tore up that life and fashioned a new one as a reporter for the *Tucson Citizen*, specializing in crimes and sex crimes. Then he quit the newspaper to become a freelance magazine journalist and an author of nonfiction books. The magazine paychecks bought him time to write the books, which were the ruling obsession of his life. His self-appointed mission was to chronicle his times while ignoring or exploding the conventional wisdoms and following his own intellectual instincts, which were informed by a vast amount of scholarly reading, wide-ranging life experiences, and a compulsive attraction to the dark, violent and depraved side of human nature.

"What I'm really writing about it is the future," he said, ordering a sixth round of drinks. He saw it as a collision between limited natural resources and unlimited human appetites, and he thought the desert Southwest, with its scarce water and unruly border with Mexico, was the best place to see it unfold, "the center of the future." Bowden had been a close friend of the late Edward Abbey, the Tucson-based writer, anarchist and radical environmentalist who advocated sabotage to defend the earth. He shared Abbey's views that governments and systems of authority could never be trusted, and that nothing mattered more than protecting wild places and wild creatures. "If you've got a gun and someone is about to harpoon the last whale on earth, what do you do?" he asked. Before I could answer, he said, "The only moral choice is to shoot him."

Even though we were writing about the same subject for different magazines, there was no professional rivalry. Chuck shared his extensive knowledge about wildfires and fire suppression in the Northern Rockies. He told me which smokejumpers and supervisors had given him the best quotes, encouraged me to seek them out, and recommended Stephen Pyne's *Fire in America* as essential reading. Walking out of the bar into the chill night air, we promised to reconnect in Tucson, and I watched him drive away in a small, filthy Toyota pickup that looked ready for the scrapyard.

A saguaro cactus (pronounced suh-WAH-ro) is essentially a column of water stored in spongy tissue and supported by a framework of vertical wooden ribs. A fully hydrated main stem is more than 90 percent water and weighs eighty pounds per foot. Bristly spines, up to two inches long, deter thirsty animals and cast a little shade to mitigate the onslaught of the desert sun. Gila woodpeckers excavate nesting holes high in the cactus, which seals the wound with hard scar tissue. When the woodpeckers leave, the holes are sometimes occupied by elf owls, the world's smallest owl, no bigger than a sparrow with a gnomish face.

Saguaros start growing their first arms when they are between fifty and a hundred years of age. They can reach a height of seventy feet or more, weigh up to two tons, and live for over two hundred years. In May and June they produce creamy white flowers—the state flower of Arizona—which are pollinated by bats, doves and a native bee. For the Tohono O'Odham, who harvest the scarlet fruits to make syrup and wine, saguaros have long been revered as another form of humanity. Children are taught never to throw rocks at the giant cacti or harm them in any way, because saguaros are people too, made by the god and creator I'itoi.

This view was not shared by a twenty-seven-year-old white man named David Grundman, a cook and petty drug dealer who had gone to prison for robbing his customers. In 1982, he packed two rifles and a 16-gauge shotgun and drove with his roommate into the desert northwest of Phoenix. First they riddled a ten-foot saguaro with bullets until it fell. Then, from close range, Grundman started blasting away with his shotgun at a twenty-seven-foot-tall specimen that was probably a hundred years old. A large limb fell and simultaneously crushed and impaled him to death.

Chapter Three

DESERT LIMBO

I had followed Mariah's car for nearly 1,500 miles when the first saguaros came into view. Other western states, Texas being the most egregious offender, have tried to claim the iconic cacti in their pop culture and marketing campaigns, but they grow only in Southern Arizona and western Sonora across the Mexican border, with a few outliers in California and Sinaloa—a range that corresponds closely with the ecoregion known as the Sonoran Desert. Twenty minutes after seeing the first saguaro, we came into the Tucson valley, a wide flat expanse enclosed by mountain ranges on three sides and carpeted with low-rise, low-density sprawl. A small cluster of high-rise buildings marked the modest downtown. It felt very familiar and unexpectedly disappointing to be back again. Were we really going to spend the rest of our lives in this unimpressive provincial city? Wasn't there somewhere better in the world that we could afford?

Driving around town, I was struck by the extraordinary number of smoke shops, vape shops, head shops, weed dispensaries and mattress stores. It gave the impression that smoking too much and crashing out in bed were Tucson's defining activities and an important driver of the local economy. In worse traffic than I remembered—the city had added nearly 200,000 residents while we were gone—we passed through an urban landscape of strip malls, office blocks, fast-food joints and convenience stores, barren empty lots, little patches of undeveloped desert, and two-story apartment buildings painted in poorly chosen shades of brown and beige.

The attractive historic neighborhoods had loomed large in my memory, but they formed a small portion of the spread-out city, which has a metro population of just over a million and a poverty index well above the national average. Homeless people flew cardboard signs at nearly all the traffic lights. Saucer-eyed street crazies yelled and shook their fists at invisible foes. Inflatable saguaros with cartoon faces lurched and flapped about on the forecourts of mini-malls and used-auto dealerships, and all of it looked ugly, crass and mediocre compared to the canyon-slashed mountains that dominated the skyline and had stood there for 100 million years.

Except for what we had in the vehicles, everything we owned was already in a westside storage unit, thanks to Mariah's younger brother Cody. He was able to unlock it for the antique-damaging hooligan from Armstrong Relocation, who arrived in his moving truck two days ahead of schedule, knowing that we wouldn't be there to inspect his handiwork and file a claim at the moment of delivery. Some of the antiques dated back to the eighteenth century and had been in my family for generations. I wasn't particularly attached to them or any other possessions, but they were beautiful and Mariah cherished them.

Our thirty-day rental house was in the foothills of the Santa Catalinas, the highest of the three mountain ranges and the subject of

Chuck Bowden's book *Frog Mountain Blues*. He compared the range to a "maimed stone god" and from a distance I could see it: a prostrate figure on his back. The Tohono O'Odham call it Babad Do'ag, Frog Mountain, because the front ridge of the mountains resembles a Sonoran Desert toad and the O'Odham regard toads as members of the frog family. Mount Lemmon is the highest peak, nearly 9,200 feet in a forest of spruce and Douglas fir with a ski resort, cabins and a few stores. Tucson is at 2,400 feet in the desert and in the cauldron of summer you can always drive up to Mount Lemmon to cool off, assuming you have the gas money and a functioning vehicle, which hadn't always been the case with me. Freelance journalism, especially for the first decade or so, had often felt like a vow of poverty.

Convoying through the high-income foothills, we passed gated communities and resorts with irrigated golf courses, then turned on to a succession of winding roads with Spanish names. The houses were isolated from each other on small or medium-sized plots of lands with native vegetation—mesquite trees, palo verde trees that bloomed canary yellow in the spring and were named after their green bark, agaves like splayed bundles of swords, viciously thorned cholla (pronounced *choy-ya*) cactus, ocotillos rising out of the earth in strange spindly wands like a Dr. Seuss fantasy, and big mature saguaros. We also passed some passive-aggressive scrap-metal yard art, an aspect of southwestern culture I had forgotten about. There was a western gunslinger built of rusty springs with two leveled pistols, a snarling T. rex, and a rusty two-dimensional bear with a sign that read, "What is wrong with you people? The ghettos are quieter!" Another sign, held up by a scrap-iron monkey, said, "Your leaf blower is helping spread respiratory illnesses in children. Are you really that cruel?"

We pulled up to a large white two-story house with solar panels and a small swimming pool, owned by a pair of university professors away on sabbatical. "Yay!" said Isobel. "It's fancy! It's like a royal palace!" We gained entry and explored our new temporary home. It had huge rooms, no real backyard except the pool, an upstairs kitchen and living room, and a small balcony with spectacular views to the west and south. Mariah guessed it was built in the late 1980s. After unpacking the vehicles, putting away our belongings and giving the dogs a quick walk, what the grown-ups badly needed was to collapse on a bed and do nothing. I had seldom felt so exhausted and stress-battered in my life.

What Isobel needed to do, after being cooped up in a car for three days, was to race around and play. Her favorite part of the house was the high-vaulted staircase with a right-angled turn that led down to the bedrooms. Accustomed to single-story houses, she spent at least twenty minutes scampering up and down those stairs. Then she went into her bedroom and reappeared in a dress-up ball gown and tiara, holding a plastic scepter. She was in the throes of a long princess phase that did not thrill her father.

"It's time for the royal ball!" she announced. "Everyone needs to get dressed up in their fanciest clothes and come to the grand reception in my bedroom!" My heart sank wearily and I said, "Isobel, your parents are very tired. We've driven a long way and we need to rest. Then one of us needs to go to the store and buy groceries because we don't have anything to eat." She scowled at me haughtily. "You're supposed to call me *Your Highness*" she said. "You're supposed to say, 'Yes, m'lady.' You're supposed to do everything I say, because princesses always get what they want."

One of the reasons I left Britain was to get away from the monarchy and its allegedly divine right to rule over the rest of us, demand our deference, and take a portion of our taxes, all of which I found repugnant.

Now, as I joked to Mariah, I was five thousand miles away and royalty was bossing me around in my own household. But the girl was so play-deprived that I felt duty-bound to indulge her. I dragged myself off the bed, went to her room and sat on the floor. I gave her words of encouragement and fashion suggestions that she shot down on principle as she dressed up her stuffed animals in doll clothes. Then Mariah rallied herself and the royal ball took place. We didn't get dressed up, but we made grandiloquent speeches, air-nibbled toy foods at the banquet, and took turns waltzing around the bedroom with a delighted Isobel.

———

The next morning we began teaching her about her surroundings, with a focus on safety. The swimming pool was the main worry, because she couldn't swim, but there were also thorned plants that could impale her to the bone and potentially dangerous insects and reptiles. Arizona has more poisonous creatures than any other state, including thirteen species of rattlesnake and more than forty different scorpions. Isobel was quick to learn the basics of desert safety, and for once she didn't argue and try to prove us wrong, because she understood that bad, painful things could happen to her.

Don't touch cactus, even if it looks cute and fuzzy. Careful picking up rocks because there might be a scorpion underneath. Always watch where you're walking in case of rattlesnakes, and back away if you see one. Careful reaching under bushes because a snake might be there. Gila monsters could be dangerous too, but these burly venomous lizards, weighing up to five pounds, with mottled pink and black coloring, were rarely seen and easy to avoid. So were coral snakes, poisonous centipedes, black widows, brown spiders, and relatively benign tarantulas.

Itchy welts appeared on my torso that morning. At first I thought they were bedbug bites. Then I started looking at skin rashes on my phone. Could it be chiggers? Scabies? Contact dermatitis? I tried ignoring them and hoping they would go away—my go-to strategy with medical ailments— but they spread and became painful. Two days later my oldest, softest T-shirt felt like wire wool and needle points. Finally I went to a doctor, who took one look and said, "You have shingles. There's not much we can do. You should have come here earlier." She explained that it was caused by a virus that had entered my body when I had chicken pox as a child. Then it had lain dormant in my spinal fluid for half a century until it had an opportunity to reactivate itself. The doctor said, "Have you been under a lot of stress lately? That often triggers it."

We had packed up and sold a house during a flood with last-minute inspection nightmares. We had moved across the country and been swindled by the moving company. We had nowhere permanent to live. We were trying to buy a house in a market with extremely tight inventory and soaring prices. We needed a job for Mariah, a school for Isobel, and family health insurance, which would be extortionate even for crappy coverage. I needed to come up with some story ideas and persuade magazine editors to commission them, because we had no current source of income. My insomnia was worse than ever and I was drinking too much to knock myself out at night. I was worried about money-money-money, and the worsening pain from the arthritis and degenerated discs in my spine, and my complete lack of retirement plan. Underneath all this and the ordinary stresses of parenthood was a deeper level of twenty-first-century anxiety.

Unlike our parents and grandparents or any other generation in human history, we were raising our child at a time when the health of the entire planet was threatened and mass extinctions were already underway. Simultaneously we were living through an era of super-charged technological change that amounted to a vast unregulated experiment on human consciousness. America's social fabric was ripping apart, mass shootings had become normal everyday events, deranged conspiracy theories rocketed around the internet, and there was a pervasive sense that all the old norms were unraveling and collapsing.

Here in the Arizona desert the population was soaring even though the rains were failing, the rivers drying up, and the aquifers plummeting. We were twenty years into the worst drought in 1,200 years, and a large segment of the population was heavily armed with weapons of war. I found it all too easy to envisage a dystopian near-future, but these visions had to be kept in check, because you have to bring up a child with hope. As Chuck Bowden used to say, "It's going to be a bloody mess, but we have to believe in the future. Every goddamn bird on Earth is going to mate and build a nest next spring."

The doctor advised me to lower my stress levels, gave me a prescription for lidocaine cream, and said the symptoms would go away in three to five weeks. The lidocaine, I discovered, had almost no effect, but a gin martini or an iced bourbon effected a marked improvement in my levels of discomfort and general morale.

———

It was a time of limbo, with neither parent working, no school for Isobel, and no physical affection between me and my family members because the shingles virus is transmissible through contact. This was tough for all of us, but especially Isobel who was a highly affectionate child. She had no friends to play with, she missed Gray and Birdie and Cora in Mississippi, and she was understandably bored when we visited our friends, none of whom had children in her age bracket. She liked the big white house in the foothills, but she wanted a permanent room of her own and the rest of her stuff out of storage, and she didn't understand why it wasn't happening. "Maybe Tucson doesn't want us to live here," she said, and I knew the feeling.

Every day we spent hours searching the real estate websites, and we had asked all of our Tucson friends if they knew of anything coming on the market. Our Danish real estate agent Anne, who was wonderful with Isobel and starting to feel like a friend, showed us what there was in our price range. One featured overzealous tile work on the walls and an apartment under the house in a death-trap basement. Another offered the opportunity of socializing with meth and fentanyl addicts on a street corner just a block away. A third had a ferociously organized cactus garden that looked like an artist's interpretation of a neurotic brain. A fourth was a lovely old fixer-upper with a guesthouse, but it had a slumping foundation that looked like a money pit.

The impossible housing market, high stress levels and the sharp, aggravating pain of shingles dominated the experience of being back in Tucson, but there were joys and pleasures as well. It was glorious to sit on the balcony and get reacquainted with the Arizona sky, not just the famous sunsets, but the breathtakingly beautiful cloud formations that drifted across during the day, the ladders of light that broke through occasional early spring rainstorms, the rainbows and double rainbows, and the desert stars at night. It was wonderful to go on family hikes and introduce our daughter to the birds, animals and plants of the Sonoran Desert, until she decided that she hated hiking and refused to go anymore. Nor did she enjoy our frequent visits to restaurants.

I had been enthusiastically omnivorous as a child, but Isobel was a fussy eater. This was partly because she was cautious, with a highly sensitive palate and an overactive sense of disgust. And it was partly because refusing to eat something was a way of exercising power and autonomy. Even though she loved steak and enjoyed flour tortillas, she folded her arms and scowled when her mother suggested that she try an ungarnished carne asada taco. "Sweetie, it's just cut-up steak and a small flour tortilla," said Mariah. "Those are literally the only ingredients." Isobel shouted, "NO! You know I don't like mixed foods."

It was acceptable to have more than one food type on the plate. Her usual dinner was salami, cheese, bread, grapes and nuts, but they had to stay in separate areas of the plate or they could become cross-contaminated, and they had be eaten separately. Putting cheese on a cracker, for example, was disgusting. Mariah then suggested carne asada without a tortilla, which Isobel rejected because the meat was cut up into little cubes instead of little strips like the steak she normally had at home. So she dined on tortilla chips and nothing else as we loaded up our tacos with pickled red onion, finely shredded cabbage, guacamole salsa, a squirt of fresh lime juice, and a fat stripe of hot red salsa made with roasted chiles. We ate them with grunts and moans of pleasure and wondered how on earth we'd survived without them for so long in New York and Mississippi.

There are more than a hundred Mexican restaurants in Tucson and its overwhelmingly Hispanic "sister city" of South Tucson. Most of them serve the cuisine of the Sonoran Desert, which encompasses Southern Arizona and Sonora. Its hallmarks are flour tortillas, pinto beans, an emphasis on beef dishes reflecting the region's ranching heritage, the use of a wild chile called the chiltepin, and the Sonoran dog. This is a grilled, bacon-wrapped hot dog served in a slightly sweet bun with mustard, mayo, pinto beans, salsa verde, onions, tomatoes and a grilled güerito chile on top. It's the signature dish of Tucson street food and our homecoming wasn't complete until we disgusted our daughter by eating a few of them.

It was also imperative to feast on carne seca, which is shredded sun-dried beef sautéed with green chiles, onions, and tomatoes, preferably served with a paper-thin flour tortilla the size of a bicycle wheel. The Little Poca Cosa restaurant downtown was now calling itself The Little One, and it was still a great spot for soul-nourishing huevos rancheros (fried eggs and refried beans on a crispy corn tortilla with a tomato chili sauce), and lunch combos including chicken *en mole negro,* a sauce made with bitter chocolate, pumpkin seeds, peanuts, mild red chiles and a dozen other ingredients. And for me at least, there was no point living in Tucson without regular infusions of birria, a rich, earthy, spicy stew of beef or sometimes goat.

Rocco's Little Chicago was still a great spot for spicy chicken wings and meatball subs with marinara sauce; breadsticks were the only thing Isobel would eat on the extensive menu of pizzas, pastas, sandwiches and salads. And we had to drag her to Time Market on University Boulevard, not just because it has killer sandwiches and the best wine selection in town, but because it was where her parents first met.

I was forty-one years old, getting over a fairly recent divorce and renting a small house not far from the University of Arizona. I would walk the eight blocks to Time Market in the morning to drink an espresso or two and read the newspaper. I was starting to develop a taste for wine at that time, which the owner of Time Market, Peter Wilke, encouraged by giving me recommendations, pours of wine to taste, and the occasional free bottle to take home. He had a young barista working for him in the mornings. She was petite, graceful, kind and beautiful, and I found it difficult to take my eyes off her, even though she was obviously far too young for me. I upped my morning espresso intake so I could interact with her more often at the counter, which she didn't seem to mind.

One day I saw her sitting by the front window reading William Vollmann's *The Atlas,* which I thought was a very interesting choice of book. Dark, haunting, wounded and hypnotic, it consists of fifty-three interconnected pieces of reportage and invention from fifty-three locations around the world, starting with Mount Aetna and ending with Zagreb. We talked about Vollmann and other writers. Mariah said she loved to read, but had no ambitions to write. She had dropped out of college and given up on a nursing career. She didn't know what she wanted to do with her life. She was into cycling, yoga, rock climbing, food and wine. I had no interest in the first three pursuits, but real enthusiasm for the last two.

I engineered a small dinner party, inviting Mariah along with her boss Peter and his girlfriend Bree. I cooked Indian food, which was one of the only things I really missed about London, and Peter brought some wines to taste. It was a fun, convivial evening, and Peter and Bree left first, as I had hoped. Then I was alone with Mariah in my small walled backyard in the moonlight. She was wearing a white shift dress with spaghetti straps and delicate embroidery at the neckline, a beautiful dress that fit her perfectly. Instead of trying to avert my gaze out of politeness, as I normally did, I allowed myself to look at her with all the pleasure that looking at her brought me.

We stood there looking and smiling at each other. We kissed briefly and held each other. Neither of us was ready for anything more. As

I walked her home through the hot summer night, I finally asked the question I had been putting off: "How old are you?" She replied, "Twenty-six," a shocking number. I told her I was forty-one and we walked in silence for a while. There were other obstacles. She had sworn off men, following a number of bad experiences, and I was dating one of her best friends—casually dating, but dating nonetheless.

About a week after the dinner party, I took in a shaggy dog who needed a home and named him Roscoe. I asked Mariah if she wanted to drive down to Ruby near the Mexican border, with me and Roscoe, to see 100,000 bats fly out of an abandoned mineshaft at sunset. She said, "I would love to." On the way down there, in my little bench-seat Toyota pickup truck on a winding road through the desert hills, Roscoe got carsick and vomited on Mariah's jeans. I was impressed that she took it in her stride. It seemed like a sign of good character.

Ruby was a ghost town with a population of one, an old hippie named Sundog who walked us over to the mineshaft and asked us for a small donation. I knew about him and the bats because in the early 2000s I had lived just a few miles away on the Ruby Road. I gave him ten dollars and we waited for the sun to go all the way down. Then the first Mexican free-tailed bats came flying out of the rocks, darting and chittering. Five minutes later there was a river of bats pouring over our heads into the sky. Both of us found this equally beautiful and unforgettable, and romance prospered soon afterwards.

I broke up with Mariah's friend, who was understandably furious and hurt. Then I broke up with Mariah because of the age difference— we had little in common because we were at different stages of our lives. After about two weeks of being apart, Mariah came over to my house, told me that she loved me and persuaded me to give it another go. It never occurred to either of us that we would still be together fifteen years later, let alone married and telling this story to our daughter in Time Market.

"That's so cool," she said. "You really met here?"

"Yup," I said. "And if we hadn't met here, you wouldn't exist."

"Yes I would," she said huffily, even she knew where babies come from. I tried to explain that she was mistaken, but she refused to back down from her position.

Days later, she explained why: "You guys are always right because you're grown-ups and it's not fair. Sometimes I want to be right about everything, and that means you have to be wrong."

F or generations Arizona's schoolchildren were taught that the state's name derived from the Spanish term for arid zone—árida zona—even though this wasn't true and couldn't be true, because the adjective follows the noun in Spanish. Even today, very few residents of the state know the true story of its nomenclature.

Arizona was named after a place in Sonora, Mexico, that inspired overhyped fantasies of extravagant wealth and might have been a scam. In 1736 a Yaqui Indian prospector named Antonio Siraumea found large chunks of silver on the ground in a remote valley about ten miles south of the present-day international border. A settler of Basque origin lived twelve miles away on a ranch he had named Arizona, a Basque word meaning "the good oak tree." Hundreds of prospectors from all over Sonora rushed in a frenzy to the silver strike. One found an enormous slab weighing over a ton.

Captain Juan Bautista de Anza, the chief justice of Sonora, rode in with soldiers to stop the illegal mining and investigate the origins of the silver, which was so pure that it looked already refined. De Anza suspected that it had been stolen, perhaps from the royal treasury, and hidden in the valley to be "found" later. He placed guards around the site, impounded the silver and took statements. Then the matter went to Mexico City, where it was debated for ten years without a satisfactory conclusion.

Arizona, meanwhile, had become a talismanic word in Mexico, conjuring up a place where pure silver was so plentiful that you could pick up a fortune with your bare hands. More than a century later, the promoters of a new U.S. territory in the Southwest were looking for a name that embodied fantastic mineral wealth and they remembered the story of the Arizona silver. Congress established the Arizona Territory in December 1858.

Chapter Four

BIG EMPTY

In the early 1990s, Chuck Bowden's house on Ninth Street was the lair of a bachelor who worked and drank and smoked and never cleaned. It was a ramshackle arrangement of books, magazines, newspapers, files and notebooks, ashtrays and wine jugs, beetles and spiders and other insects that he regarded as housemates, fornicating figurines made by Indigenous artists in Mexico, a black-and-white poster of Janis Joplin, and his desk and early model Apple computer at the nexus of it all.

The entire house had a patina of dirt, the windows were coated with dust, and the bathtub was blackened with a thick layer of hardened grime. Once, staying at the house while Chuck was away, I ventured naked into the bathroom to take a shower and then backed away, unpersuaded by the logic of going in there to get clean. The small grease-and-filth-encrusted kitchen faced out on to the front yard and the street. Chuck, who had a lively and varied romantic life, complained about jealous women peering in the window. Instead of putting up blinds or curtains, he smeared the window glass with pork fat to foil their prying eyes.

Unless he was working, sleeping or cooking, he was usually out in the backyard, which was partially shaded by a big Chilean mesquite tree he had planted as a seedling and watered assiduously to speed up its growth. Chuck loved plants and botany as he loved every aspect of nature, including the gory and cruel, including slime molds, which he insisted were of equal value to the world as human beings. In rock-studded beds all over the backyard he had planted succulents, shrubs and trees, including Madagascar palms, a tall columnar San Pedro cactus from Peru with psychedelic properties, a bearded cactus from Mexico, and night-blooming cereus or *Harrisia* from South America. There were chuparosas and other flowering bushes to attract hummingbirds and a hackberry tree to bring in finches, cardinals and mockingbirds. To increase the avian population, Chuck showered the ground with birdseed every day. He was between dogs at that time, but he had a desert tortoise named Lightning who would lumber around the backyard and feed aggressively on lettuce leaves.

When I was in Tucson, which amounted to about half of the year, I would go over there two or three times a week, arriving in midafternoon when Chuck wanted a drinking companion and someone to regale with his latest thoughts and theories. I would usually show up with a cold six-pack and Chuck would invariably drink red wine from an old scarred and water-stained tumbler, even when it was 107 degrees in the backyard shade and the wine was as superheated as the air. One roasting hot day I brought chilled white wine, which he denounced as a pale and insipid beverage. In his writing and his life, he was a champion of boldness, vibrancy, passion, intensity. "Why would I drink wine that looks like watery piss when I could drink wine the color of rubies and blood?" he asked rhetorically.

Unless a check from a magazine had just arrived, in which case he would treat himself to a good bottle of California Cabernet, his wine came from a jug or a box, and he subsisted on cheap Mexican food and homemade stews that he referred to as "slop." He was a cult figure among the small minority of people in the Southwest who cared about books—"the dark prince of Arizona letters," as his fellow writer Tom Zoellner described him—and Chuck accepted the low income of this position without complaint. "Ya hungry?" he would say after a few hours of drinking and one-sided conversation. "Want some slop?"

He was always deeply tanned. He would lie out in the sun for hours, smoking those untipped Lucky Strikes, drinking big plastic beakers of water, reading academic and nonfiction books and a very occasional novel. He devoured big biographies, read everything published about the Southwest, and Mexico too if it was in English, and kept up with the latest scientific research on climate change, species extinctions, desert-ification and other forms of environmental destruction taking place. In addition, he would take deep plunges into the literature of his latest obsessions, which ranged from medieval trade routes to rattlesnakes, the history of Australian penal colonies to the future of agriculture. He would even lie out there reading and tanning at the height of summer, when most living things in Southern Arizona cower and hide from the sun. It was a way of decompressing after writing, feeding his voracious intellect and drinking in heat and light through his skin. Chuck had no fear of skin cancer, lung cancer, cirrhosis of the liver, or any other way of dying. "What's the difference?" he would growl. "No one gets out alive."

He seemed to be powered by an engine of unusual capacity, and he had an aggressive disregard for his health and safety. He thought nothing of driving a thousand miles in a day and refused to wear a seat belt. He took himself on 150-mile backpacking marches through the harshest deserts in Arizona. He usually wore shorts on these treks and he had a peculiar habit of walking through vegetation, rather than deviating around it, so his legs would get covered with scratches and lacerations. One of his book editors, my friend Greg McNamee, was convinced that no other writer was capable of working so effectively while drinking so much, not even Hunter S. Thompson in his prime. Unlike Thompson, however, Chuck didn't write under the influence, and it had been many years since he took drugs or drank hard liquor—"I was drinking whiskey with my cornflakes one morning and I said, 'Fuck this.'"

I found it hard to tell if he was disciplined and hardworking as a writer, or in the grips of a compulsion that he couldn't control. He usually went to bed early after copious amounts of wine, got up around three in the morning, and went straight to his keyboard with a pack of Luckies and strong black coffee—Nescafé instant when I first met him, although he later became a serious convert to espresso after an assignment in Italy. He wrote for seven or eight hours on a normal day, fifteen or sixteen hours if the crunch was on, and hardly ever took a day off. Sometimes he'd produce 20,000 words in a few days, sitting there at the computer in a kind of trance, not really looking at the screen as the words flowed out of his brain through his fingertips. Then he would print it out, mark it up, and sometimes rewrite it six or seven times.

By this method he would produce more than thirty books of utterly distinctive nonfiction and well over a hundred magazine articles. At his best, in books like *Killing the Hidden Waters, Blue Desert, Desierto,* and *Down by the River,* he was searing, incandescent, a hard-nosed investigative reporter who wrote like a poet or a prophet and seemed wired into the deepest currents of his time. At his worst, he was overblown, macho, teetering on self-parody—too many perfumed whores and fierce dark hungers in the midnight streets. Too many portents of dark conspiracies and impending apocalypse.

I was one of at least fifteen people—writers, broadcasters, photographers, filmmakers, artists—that Chuck befriended, helped and supported. The word *mentor* never passed between us, but he took that role in our friendship. Seeing what he could do on the page with language and nonfiction, listening to him talk with so much verve and passion about books and writing, I began to take my own work more seriously. I had started writing for magazines as a way to keep traveling and avoid getting a real job. I had always tried my hardest to do it well, but I wasn't sure I was going to stick with it. Chuck convinced me that writing matters. Almost invariably I left his house with important books to read, an idea for a story that he'd gifted to me, a useful contact, and pieces of his latest wine-fueled monologue churning through my head.

"Fear is what will destroy us, not climate change. I talk to people in their twenties and they want to know about their fucking pension plan. What the hell has happened to this country? Fear has taken over. I've watched it happen in my lifetime. It's destroying our ability to look squarely at the goddamn facts and do what we need to do to save ourselves. We can't deal with overpopulation. We can't even say the fucking word. We can't deal with the fact that resources are finite. We can't deal with race in any meaningful way. We're terrified of death. Fear is paralyzing us and a lot of it comes from materialism, mistaking objects for security, when all you need is 2,000 calories a day and a place to sleep . . ."

————

My house on Speedway, a thirty-minute walk from Chuck's place, functioned more like a base camp than a home. Women often made the same comment when they came through the front door: "It doesn't look like anyone lives here." This was partly because of freelancer's poverty. I was living on rice and five-pound sacks of pinto beans, plus beer and cigarettes, with occasional street tacos and nights out at the bars. I had no budget for home decor and only a slight interest, because I never spent more than three consecutive weeks in the house. I was either away working on magazine assignments or traveling on my own account. I was in fact psychologically incapable of spending more than three weeks in my house or anywhere else without becoming unbearably restless, irritable and out of sorts. All the usual metaphors—itchy feet, climbing the walls, white line fever—applied to me. My nomadism felt like a character trait, something encoded in my genes. In order to feel stable again, I had to experience velocity and change location.

But it always felt good to return to Tucson, to unpack my bag and put away my things, to reconnect with my friends and the city. In the summer, partly as a way to acclimate my body, I liked to walk from my house to Hotel Congress in the full heat and glare of midafternoon. It took about twenty minutes and the reward was a gloriously refreshing cold beer in the Tap Room and a chat with Tiger the bartender, who had been pouring drinks there since the 1950s. He was a small, slightly built gay man with glasses. He wore bolo ties and vests, and sometimes Hawaiian shirts. It was easy to picture him in a 1970s TV detective show like *Columbo* or *The Rockford Files*. Despite his elfin stature, he was a gallant defender of women in his bar. If he saw a woman getting pestered, harassed or made uncomfortable, he would become enraged and order the offender out the door with absolute conviction.

The Tap Room felt cool and dark after walking through the afternoon heat, but it didn't have air conditioning. Neither did my house, or the house of anyone I knew in Tucson. In my social circle, air conditioning was frowned upon as an expensive indulgence for weak rich people who should be living somewhere else. What we all had were boxy metal units known as swamp coolers. A noisy fan blew the hot dry outside air through pads saturated with water. The water vapor cooled as it evaporated, and the fan blew that cool air into the room. Swamp coolers were cheap and fairly effective in June when the humidity was low, but almost useless during the monsoon season of July, August and September, when the humidity climbed and thunderstorms deluged the city.

Cold showers were not an option, because the water coming out of the cold tap in summer was the temperature of warm bathwater. I learned to pour gallon jugs of water from the fridge over my head and clothes, to store wet sheets in the fridge and sleep under them with a fan blowing, to drink at least a gallon of water a day and two or three gallons if I was outside and exerting myself. There was nothing pleasant about the heat, but it had an all-consuming intensity that was impressive and demanded respect. Some people went completely nocturnal in summer, which made good sense if you could pull it off. Others spent the afternoons in air-conditioned movie theaters like the Catalina on Campbell Avenue. I would go there myself sometimes, although the air conditioning seemed aggressively cold once you were acclimated to the heat, and I had to bring a sweatshirt.

No one detested air conditioning more than Chuck Bowden, the consummate desert rat and the only person I knew who actually relished the summer inferno. One evening in his backyard, around 8:30 p.m., which was normally his bedtime, the thermometer on the outside wall of his house read 99 degrees. "It's the perfect temperature," he said. "The air is the same temperature as my body and it feels like velvet. Don't fight the heat. You have to become one with it."

I had never met anyone whose senses were so hungry and alive. Even when he was interviewing a Mexican cartel enforcer about the horrific atrocities he had committed, Chuck's fingertips would be registering the texture of the tabletop that lay between them, because he was incapable of ignoring such things. When the *Harrisia* cacti in his backyard unfurled their heavily scented white flowers on summer nights, he would plunge his face into the blooms with pure ecstasy. He rhapsodized about intense heat, bitter cold, violent thunderstorms and reeking bat caves, because they amplified the feeling of being physically alive in the moment. He loved wine but had no interest in analyzing its characteristics. If it was big and red, sluicing across his tongue and palate and buzzing in his brain, he was delighted by it.

He lusted mightily after women, slept with as many of them as he felt like, and much preferred their company and conversation. "Men are a dull predictable bunch on the whole," he told me. "Women are far more interesting." Music was a great passion—Bob Dylan, Jimi Hendrix, Miles Davis and Beethoven were probably his favorites—and he often listened to music while he wrote, which is detectable in the rhythms of his prose. Television didn't pack the same sensory wallop and with a few exceptions—he loved *The Sopranos* and *The Wire*—it bored him. He never went to a movie theater for as long as I knew him. It was as unthinkable as going to the dentist.

For me, a generation younger and far more colonized by technology, media and marketing, Chuck's heightened sensory awareness and closeness to nature offered a last-ditch hope of an honest, unmediated connection to a real living world. I felt so bombarded with advertising and consumerist lifestyle propaganda. How could I even trust my own thoughts and desires when they had been exposed to such a vast mechanism of manipulation? I decided not to have a television in my house so I could at least sit in my own personal living space without someone trying to grab my attention and sell me something. I had no desire to withdraw completely from consumer society, but I didn't want to be owned by it.

As modern life became ever more processed, mediated and monetized, I tried to open up another realm of consciousness by cultivating my senses. I'd always listened very closely to music. Now I started listening in the same way to birdsong, insect noise, the different sound combinations that wind and traffic make, the rhythms that form and dissolve in the urban grind and clatter. When people came to my wooden-floored house, I paid close attention to the weight and rhythm of their footsteps. I tried to learn the sound of their gaits so I could recognize them as they walked up the stone path to the front door. When I heard a bird, I made a point of stopping and looking for it, but I often failed to see it in the foliage. I tried using a softer, less direct gaze as I scanned the area, and that was more effective.

At Chuck's suggestion, I drove out into the desert one day in the late afternoon, parked my truck, and walked away from the road until I found a dry streambed—a wash, or arroyo, as they're called in the Southwest. I sat down on one of its banks partially concealed by jojoba and creosote bushes. I stayed still without making a sound for twenty minutes or so, just focused my eyes and ears on my surroundings and tried to taste the air with my nostrils and upper palate. As Chuck predicted, the animals that had gone into hiding when they heard me approach had now forgotten I was there. It was like being invisible. Washes function as travel corridors in the desert, and within a few minutes I saw a kit fox, a jackrabbit, a doe and her fawn, and then a coyote that caught my scent, gave me a disparaging look, and took off through the saguaros and palo verdes.

I started spending more and more time in the desert, mainly because I loved the feeling of being out there and I wanted to understand how it functioned and fit together. But on another level, it was an attempt to deprogram myself. I wanted to strip away my background and cultural influences, as much as possible, and see what was underneath. If I walked far enough in the desert, I no longer felt like a well-educated white misfit Englishman whose tastes and sensibilities were largely shaped by London music and youth culture in the late 1970s and 1980s. I felt like a human being moving across a wild landscape and absorbing it through my senses. Temporarily at least, I was free.

———

The part of Arizona that Chuck talked about with the most awe and reverence was the far southwest. As you travel west from Tucson, the Sonoran Desert gets progressively lower, drier, hotter and more remote, culminating in an area of 6,000 square miles without a human settlement and only one paved road near its eastern edge. All of this land is owned by the federal government and divided up into Organ Pipe Cactus National Monument, the Cabeza Prieta National Wildlife Refuge, and the Barry M. Goldwater Air Force Range. Chuck advised me to skip Organ Pipe—"too many goddamn rules, signs, parking lots, water fountains, rest areas"—and go on foot into the Cabeza Prieta, where none of that clutter existed and the Sonoran Desert was at its most pristine.

He would risk his life by tramping across it in full summer, but I went the first time in early spring. I drove through a hundred miles of the sparsely populated Tohono O'Odham reservation, then passed through the small towns of Why and Ajo (the Spanish word for garlic) and parked my truck near the edge of the refuge. I shouldered a backpack loaded with three gallons of water and started walking west on a dirt road known as El Camino del Diablo, or the Devil's Highway. The thousand-year-old trail acquired this name in the nineteenth century when hundreds of people died on it from thirst and heatstroke, many of them trying to reach the goldfields in California. Their horses, cattle, and sheep died too and a macabre tradition developed. People would stand the stiffened animals on all fours again. A traveler in 1861 described the trail as "a long avenue between rows of mummified cattle, horses, and sheep." People were still dying out there of thirst and heatstroke every summer as they crossed the Mexican border and walked north in hopes of a better life.

I had about eighty miles of walking ahead of me and I was not without trepidation, even though the killing heat was months away. I had a weak right ankle. A sprain might be a death sentence, or a forty-mile hobble and crawl to Interstate 8. There were no rangers or emergency services, and no way to call for help without a satellite phone, a device that had just been invented and was far beyond my price range. Rattlesnakes were probably starting to get active. I would be sleeping on the ground without a tent, and I was concerned they would be attracted to the warmth of my body in the cool nights. I didn't have enough water to complete the trip, but it was all I could reasonably carry along with my food, coffee, camp stove, flashlight, sleeping bag, maps, sunscreen and a few other items.

There are no rivers or springs in the Cabeza Prieta and all the streams are ephemeral. They come to life after heavy rains, flow for a day or two, and then die in the sand. But there is usually a water source if you know where to look for it. Rainwater collects in natural rock cisterns called *tinajas,* the Spanish word for tanks, or earthenware jars of water. Chuck would often cross these deserts by bringing a small water pump with a filter and refilling his canteens at tinajas. But they weren't always easy to find, and sometimes you got there and all the water had evaporated. Sometimes years would pass with no rain at all. I didn't feel courageous or experienced enough to take that risk, so I had arranged for a friend to drive in from the west, cache water at two points along the way, and pick me on the other side of the refuge.

As I walked that first day, I passed an old abandoned well and some nineteenth-century graves. Then I saw no sign of human presence for many hours, except for the dirt road and the occasional plane high in the sky. I became gently hypnotized by the steady crunching rhythm of my boots on the sandy ground, mile after mile, and my apprehension faded into calm alertness and humility. I felt so puny and insignificant, like a flea crawling across the hide of a dinosaur. The sky was enormous and the land was unfathomably ancient, a procession of jagged volcanic mountain ranges and wide flat sandy valleys. The desert is often described as a hostile place, but what I sensed was vast indifference. This was a place that could kill you without expending any effort or knowing you were there. The same, of course, was true of the world, but you got the message loud and clear in the desert.

I walked north away from the dirt road, so I didn't have to look at its linear intrusion, and made my own way west through smooth, untrammeled desert space. The creatures avoided me. I startled a sidewinder rattlesnake, which whisked itself away at astonishing speed, leaving J-shaped tracks in the sand and my heart hammering in my ribcage. Sitting motionless on a rock at the end of the day, I watched a badger chasing off a coyote. Then they both noticed me. The badger went down into its den and the coyote vanished like a ghost into the creosote flats. It was too dry for the usual mule deer and javelinas, but desert bighorn sheep manage to survive and I saw a ram silhouetted on a ridge, gazing south into Mexico.

I was tired and young enough to fall asleep easily on the ground. No heat-seeking reptiles slithered up to my sleeping bag. When I woke up after midnight with a dry mouth, the Milky Way was bigger and brighter than I had ever imagined it could be. I lay stunned underneath it, feeling flattened by its beauty. I listened carefully but could hear nothing at all except a faint ringing in my ears. This was the residual sound of the city, which would soon fade away and usher in the true desert silence.

Drinking black coffee as the dawn spread apricot light across the desert, I thought about the Hia Ced O'Odham, or Sand People, who had raised their families here for thousands of years and endured a summer heat that was often lethal to outsiders. They hunted elusive bighorns with bows and arrows, chased down jackrabbits, grabbed lizards, burned pack rats out of their nests, and gathered a wide variety of roots, seeds, cactus fruits and nutritious flower stalks known as camotes that grew under the sand. Dressed in rabbit-hide skirts and sandals, the women would grind up the ripened seedpods of mesquite trees, mix the floury powder with water from the tinajas, and lay out the paste to dry on the rocks. It made a kind of bread, sweet to the taste, and might be accompanied by toasted caterpillars and moth larvae. In a few locations, they used the summer rains to raise crops. When Europeans told them they lived a poor and miserable life in a godforsaken wasteland, they scorned the idea and said they lived well.

They made hundred-mile treks to the Gulf of California to spear fish with the tailbones of the barbed stingray and collect shellfish, salt and colored seashells for trade. They hunted sea lions and made sandals from their hides, and went back into the desert to harvest the plants coming into season and hunt the animals that came to drink at the tinajas. As they slept in the desert, sometimes in "sleeping circles" of rocks stacked up to keep the wind out, stories, visions and songs arrived in their dreams, and these had economic value. The songs and dances of the Sand People were renowned for their spiritual power and could be traded for food and pottery at the Cocopa villages on the Colorado River. Their descendants, numbering approximately one thousand, were mostly living with related tribes on reservations in Arizona and trying to get federally recognized as a separate people.

Walking through their former homeland, I noticed a dramatic improvement in my sensory capabilities on the third day. The ringing in my ears was gone, the air had more taste to it, my vision was keener. Walking across a stony flat, I noticed a small inconspicuous grayish plant about the circumference of a quarter. Looking around, I saw that there were hundreds of them. I hadn't noticed them before. Now I couldn't fail to see them. The same thing happened with other visual details in the landscape. I became better at seeing insect tracks, spider holes, desiccated droppings, bird nests. The camouflage of stationary lizards became less effective. What first appeared to be a tan-colored desert plain revealed shades of pink, purple, brown, gray, ocher and tan. As my peripheral vision started to engage, my eyes became more sensitive to movement and I started seeing more birds and wildlife. The danger of treading on a rattlesnake also helped to focus and concentrate the eyesight, and my ears were always listening for that sinister husky buzzing sound.

It was this blossoming of the senses, and the attendant feeling of being fully alive in the present moment, that kept me coming back to the Cabeza Prieta and exploring the other big desert wilderness areas in Arizona. These sojourns became an essential part of my life, and I wonder now if it was a form of spiritual activity. Especially after a few days in the desert, I felt a connection with something ancient, inscrutable, mysterious and much larger and more powerful than I was—the life force in nature as I thought of it. That the connection was probably an illusion only made it more like religion.

*I*n August 1905, a professor named W. J. McGee was camped with a Tohono O'Odham assistant on the Camino del Diablo by the Tinajas Altas Mountains, collecting meteorological and other scientific data. They were wakened one morning by a hoarse, rasping, moaning sound and rushed down the trail towards it. Under an ironwood tree in the sand lay the wreck of a man they knew, a Mexican prospector named Pablo Valencia. He had gone six and a half days without water. Had he not been so robust and acclimated to desert heat, and the weather so unusually cool and overcast, with high temperatures of 103°F instead of the usual 110°F or above, he would have been dead.

Dr. McGee later described his condition in a paper called "Desert Thirst as Disease." Like most people in the final stage of dehydration, Valencia was delirious and stark naked, having taken off his clothes because they felt unbearable on his skin. His face had turned black and the rest of his skin was "ghastly purplish yet ashen gray." He was shrunken, emaciated, deaf and blind, his eyes set in a "winkless stare." His tongue had shriveled to a black stump, "his lips had disappeared as if amputated, leaving low edges of blackened tissue; his teeth and gums projected like those of a skinned animal." His legs, feet, hands, and arms were scratched and torn from rock and cactus, but they looked like cuts in leather because his body was too parched to bleed. He had no discernible pulse, his extremities were cold, and his breathing was "slow, spasmodic, and accompanied by a deep guttural moaning or roaring—the sound that had awakened us a quarter of a mile away."

McGee managed to nurse him back to partial health, but the ordeal turned Valencia's hair gray and he never fully recovered. From 2001 to 2020, 3,378 border crossers were found dead in the Arizona desert, mostly from dehydration and heat-related illness.

Chapter Five

BRICK HOUSE

It was the middle of March in the year 2020 as we packed up to leave the big white house in the foothills. The World Health Organization had classified the novel coronavirus outbreak as a pandemic and the first cases were showing up in Arizona. The Navajo Nation was under a state of emergency and in Tucson we were seeing more and more people wearing surgical masks—against the advice of public health experts, who were telling people not to wear masks because they were needed by essential healthcare workers. Then Arizona's Republican governor Doug Ducey temporarily closed down the schools and day-care centers, but decreed that "essential services" should remain open. To our astonishment, these included golf courses, hair salons, nail salons, massage parlors, pawnshops, gun shops, and tattoo parlors. Apparently the governor thought they were indispensable parts of the Arizona lifestyle, in a way that education and child care were not.

After many days of arduous searching, Mariah had found us a fairly inexpensive casita to rent at a former dude ranch called El Mesquital.

It was on Tucson's far east side, not far from Paul McCartney's 151-acre ranch, which he bought with Linda in 1979; she was a University of Arizona graduate who loved Tucson and the Sonoran Desert. Driving out there through cactus patches and mesquite thickets, then seeing the old rustic casitas come into view among big trees, I felt myself unwind a little, as if I was going on a camping trip. It looked like a good place to ride out the pandemic, which was widely expected to be under control in a few weeks.

Casita means "little house" in Spanish and Isobel was disappointed that it wasn't big and fancy. Mariah found it pleasant enough, if a bit cramped and basic, and it sat very well with me. The tiled floors and wooden beams brought back memories of a similar casita in Sonora where I had spent a magical summer in my mid-thirties. There was a fenced-in yard for our dogs, a firepit with chairs and a barbecue grill that was crying out for steaks. Exploring the rest of El Mesquital, we found a swimming pool, a corral full of horses and the Tanque Verde wash just a short stroll away. Dry and sandy for most of the year, it was flowing eighteen inches deep with snowmelt from the mountains. "Let's just live here for the rest of our lives," I said to Mariah, who gave me an unimpressed look. She was determined to crack the riddle of the Tucson real estate market and our borrowing capabilities. I was starting to give up and think about other options.

Toward the end of March, Tucson's Democratic mayor Regina Romero angered many local Republicans by imposing a stricter lockdown and mask mandate than Governor Ducey's looser directives for the state. Then Ducey—a transplant from Toledo, Ohio, who had prospered in the ice cream business before entering politics—issued a statewide stay-at-home order and closed down the schools for the rest of the year. Mariah stopped applying for jobs, because she would have to look after Isobel while I was away researching magazine stories, assuming I could drum up some assignments. The five pitches I had submitted to editors since moving to Tucson had all been rejected. My torso was still covered with hideous welts, but the pain of shingles had lessened considerably, and moving to El Mesquital had a therapeutic effect. Finally I started to relax.

In the mornings I took the dogs on a long splashy walk up the Tanque Verde wash, which was lined with cottonwood trees and full of birdlife. I kept the dogs on a leash because we often saw coyotes, which regard dogs as a possible food source, and because I didn't trust Savanna, even at the age of twelve, not to run off and take herself on an adventure. As a young dog, she was a determined escapee. She placed almost no value on the food, affection, companionship, and shelter that we provided, because she didn't want to be our dog. She wanted to run wild and loose as she had in East Texas until a friend of ours brought her to Tucson as a stray needing a home.

In the Mississippi Delta she tore off through the cotton fields and swamps one day and didn't come back. We put a reward sign in the window of the local store. We asked the tractor drivers and crop duster pilots to look out for a big German shepherd/Lab/hound mix with outsized ears and a collar. After three days, we started to mourn her. Then the phone rang. A woman with a deep Delta drawl said, "Hi, this is Bessie Outlaw over by Silver City. I think I've got your dog. She came to our family wedding and we all thought she belonged to one of the guests."

To get to the Outlaw house, Savanna had swum across the Yazoo River, which flowed with a powerful current and was full of alligators and water moccasins. Quite possibly she was chasing a deer. Then she kept going for a few miles and presumably her nose detected the aromas of the Outlaw family wedding feast. "She was very well behaved," said Bessie. "People were feeding her meatballs and chicken wings. After three days all the wedding guests left and the dog was still here. That's when I checked her collar and found your number."

When we arrived to pick her up, Savanna looked chagrined and pleased to see us. She behaved perfectly for weeks afterwards. Then she took off again and disappeared for two days. This time she came home with a sucking puncture wound in her chest and a gash that exposed the bones of her ribcage. The vet had no doubt that she had been gored by a wild hog. That incident and the advancing years had slowed her down considerably, but like Cool Hand Luke she had rabbit in her blood and I wasn't going to risk taking off the leash in the Tanque Verde wash.

The owner of El Mesquital was kind enough to let me use an unoccupied casita, without payment, to work on the proofs of a book I had written about Mississippi. I would put in a few hours in the late morning or early afternoon, and then take Isobel to the corral to feed carrots and apples to the horses. I wanted to be outside all the time, soaking up the warm sunshine, breathing in the clean desert air, taking two or three long walks a day if possible. I tried to get Isobel to join me. "Come on, it'll be fun," I said. "We'll collect bird feathers and look for animal tracks."

"Walking is boring and it's tiring," she said. "I'm staying in the casita." Sometimes we would force her to take some exercise in the fresh air, and she would usually enjoy herself, but it was always a battle. She wanted to be inside at all times, where things were soft, cozy and familiar, and she could FaceTime with her Nonna in Mississippi, watch cartoons and play with her dolls and stuffed animals, and whenever possible with her parents, who were the only playmates the poor girl had.

With Mariah, she played Teenagers, which required both of them to talk in affected Valley Girl accents, and a bath game in which Isobel would become a sea monster. She invented a number of games to play with me. One was Clamber. I was required to lie on my back, make an obstacle with my arms and legs, and then try to stop her climbing over it, but not really. Barricade entailed building a pillow fort on the bed and then hiding inside it, squealing with excitement, from imaginary bears, wolves and lions prowling around outside. But her favorite game was Moley.

She would wriggle under a couple of pillows, scrunch herself into a little ball, and pretend to be a sad and abandoned baby mole. I would find her, take pity on her, befriend her, and build her a mole house out of pillows with a blanket for a roof. Then I fed her imaginary worms and became her teacher at mole school, giving lessons and testing her knowledge on digging, tunneling, claw maintenance, foraging and predator evasion. She came up with a variant called Zoo Moley, which required an initial rescue from a zoo enclosure and a pretend car ride back to my house. She could play Moley for hours, day after day, week after week, but it became increasingly problematic for me. I was always tired from lack of sleep, and lying under a blanket with my head on a pillow, going through the familiar lessons at mole school, I found it almost impossible to stay awake. "Wake up, Dada!" She would get frustrated because it spoiled the game, and I would get frustrated because she never let me take a nap in peace.

In the evenings, after Mariah and Isobel had gone to bed, I sat outside with a glass of tequila or whiskey, fed mesquite branches into a fire, listened to the owls and coyotes, picked out star constellations, and felt extremely contented to be back in Arizona. At first light I rekindled the embers with twigs, drank black coffee, watched the first sunlight filter through the mesquite trees, listened to the dawn chorus of birds and watched them as they became visible. By far the most interesting birds to observe were a family of Harris's hawks. These large reddish-brown birds are the only raptors that hunt cooperatively and they were like a pack of airborne wolves as they went after rabbits and ground squirrels.

They would converge on the prey animal from all directions, or take turns harrying a luckless rabbit, swooping in, one after another, making it run in circles. Once I saw two hawks flush a rabbit from cover into the waiting talons of another two. Harris's hawks also practice a highly unusual behavior known as backstanding. On top of a saguaro cactus or an electricity pole, two or three birds will stand on each other's backs to form a kind of tower. Occasionally a fourth hawk will alight on top. Sometimes they opened their wings as if deliberately shading the bird underneath. Was that the point? Or did the bird on top use its elevated position to scan the area for prey? I consulted an ornithologist friend. He said, "They probably do it for both those reasons, but we don't really know."

———

As the number of COVID infections and deaths soared in Tucson, our main worry was transmitting the virus to our friend Clark, one of our favorite people in the world. I met him soon after moving to Tucson with Rebecca in 1991. He was working as a doorman at the Cushing Street Bar & Restaurant, where Rebecca was selling baked goods and I loved to go carousing. It was housed in a beautiful 1860s adobe building with live blues and rock bands in the courtyard and a lively, diverse, hedonistic crowd. Clark was smaller than the average bouncer, but strong, quick and fearless. He had a rugged handsome face and could make it look extremely intimidating, which defused a lot of potential confrontations. When ejecting belligerent drunks, he had a trick of yanking down their jackets to immobilize their arms, and if someone was puffing up their chest to fight, he punched them hard in the solar plexus. As they doubled over in pain and struggled for air, he would say, "Now what are you going to do?"

Clark knew about fighting because he was a professional stuntman who had worked on Western movies; he also knew how to fall off a galloping horse without hurting himself. In addition to that, he was an actor who had appeared in *Tombstone* and other films and TV shows, a master carpenter who could frame a house or make high-end custom furniture, an arborist who could take down a big tree between two buildings with a chainsaw and a rope, a visual artist, and a handyman extraordinaire who could build or fix almost anything. He studied quantum physics as a hobby, read good books, smoked a lot of weed and enjoyed his drink. He could do Western gunfighter tricks for a paying audience of tourists. He knew how to hunt, fish, tan a deer hide, cook a tough stringy desert jackrabbit so that it became tender and succulent. If you were on a plane that went down in a remote wilderness, Clark would be the guy that kept you alive in the days and weeks to come.

Now he was in his early sixties. He had lost some muscle mass, but his face was still handsome, although deeply lined and weathered from the Arizona sun. From decades of doing stunts and being accident-prone in his normal everyday life, he had broken nearly every bone in his body, including his spine, and he was now in chronic pain, although still active and vigorous. He had lived with type 1 diabetes since he was twenty-four, which had taken a heavy toll on his kidneys. He was a heart attack survivor with chronic obstructive pulmonary disease from a lifetime of smoking cigarettes, which he had finally quit, and weed, which he still smoked in very small quantities, mainly for medicinal purposes.

"I basically have all the preexisting conditions that you don't want to have with this COVID virus, and I can't take antibiotics because I have a terrible reaction to them," he said, sitting in the backyard of the casita with an N95 mask on his face and Savanna laying at his feet. It was Clark who found her in East Texas and brought her to us in Tucson. She had adored him ever since. "If I get infected, I'll almost certainly die a horrible suffocating death, so I'm doing what it takes to not get infected. I won't go inside a building if people are in it. And this might be the last time I leave my house for a while."

———

Under Tucson lockdown rules, we could get tacos to go and continue house-hunting in person by employing masks, hand sanitizer and social distancing. The real estate market was cooling slightly as the surging global pandemic threatened the financial markets and normal life as we all knew it. Investors were spooked. On a bright, sunny, unseasonably hot afternoon in late March, Anne took us to see a house in the historic midtown neighborhood where Clark lived with his girlfriend Jill and her two teenage children. It was more affordable than our preferred neighborhoods near downtown, and Clark had been urging us to consider it. "You're in the middle of town so everything is close, but it's quiet and you see a lot of birds and wildlife," he said. "And the crime isn't bad by Tucson standards, just a few meth heads and lowlifes coming through looking for stuff to steal."

The house was a small 1940s brick bungalow with a pleasing array of cactus and other desert plants and trees growing in the recently landscaped front yard. "Do you like the bricks?" asked Mariah. "Not really, I wish they were adobe or stucco, but I can live with them," I replied. "Same here," she said. Anne opened the front door and we all put on masks and gloves. The walls of the kitchen, dining room and living room had been knocked through by the sellers to form one harmonious space. There were wooden floors throughout, a working fireplace, and a refurbished kitchen with subway tiles and stout farmhouse shelves. Both bedrooms were small, with small closets; Mariah would have to downsize her wardrobe considerably. There was a big crack in the bathroom floor but I didn't care.

"Yes," I said after being in the house for two or three minutes. "I can live here for sure. Let's buy it." Mariah made a more thorough inspection before reaching the same conclusion. Isobel was excited by the prospect of having her own room again, but unimpressed by the house. "It's different," she said. She was comparing it to our 1960s ranch house in Jackson, which was nearly 2,000 square feet, with big rooms, long picture windows, and almost an acre of lush green lawns, azaleas, flower beds and oak trees.

This house was 1,100 square feet and it cost a lot more money. You walked out of a sliding glass door into a large backyard with a free-standing brick garage that matched the house. The yard was surfaced with gravel, surrounded by an old wooden fence, and it didn't have much vegetation—a fifteen-foot saguaro working on its first arms, two large Indian fig prickly pears, a pair of smallish mesquites, a dying palo verde, an incongruous boxwood bush, and some scraggly oleanders. The overall impression was of a flat, rectangular gravel parking lot.

The sellers were a married couple who had moved to Tucson from somewhere else and were now moving on to Boise, Idaho. He was a doctor who had served with the military in the Middle East, and he had turned the brick garage into a man cave dedicated to Teddy Roosevelt. A banner reading "Bull Moose Club" hung from the ceiling and maybe a hundred empty liquor bottles were lined up on an old wooden shelf. Books, pictures and memorabilia related to his hero decorated the rest of the space. The garage had a nice old Douglas fir ceiling with crossbeams, a sliding metal door that hinged upward so you could drive your car inside, a cracked concrete floor, and no windows, heating, cooling or electrical outlets. Anne the real estate agent thought it would make a great writing office if we sunk enough money into it, and I was inclined to agree.

We called our mortgage guy that afternoon. The house was priced above our borrowing limit, but he managed to juggle the numbers somehow and convince his software program to be upwardly flexible. We made an offer the following day, and at Anne's insistence I wrote the sellers a letter introducing ourselves. I explained that we had moved back to Tucson and hoped to raise our daughter in the house. We wanted to preserve its character and plant more trees and vegetation in the backyard. I pictured myself writing books in the former Bull Moose Club. I stressed that we wanted to live the rest of our lives and grow old in the house. A letter came back promptly from the doctor. He appreciated our sentiments and loved the idea of a British writer in the house. Our offer was accepted pending the inspection.

The inspector found major plumbing and electrical problems, and said the only hope for the bathroom was to demolish it and build a new one. The roofs were old and failing on the house and the garage. The air conditioner was at the end of its natural lifespan, and there were a dozen other minor issues. The sellers cordially agreed to drop the price by a reasonable amount and the deal was done. Anne said it was one of the smoothest, sweetest house sales she had ever been involved in.

Signing the papers, I felt relieved that the house hunting was finally over and we had a place to live. But I didn't feel elated, and I realized to my disappointment that I was still a vagabond at heart. My spirits sank at the thought of shackling myself once again to mortgage payments, insurance payments, property taxes, maintenance and repair bills, but I lacked a convincing alternative and I didn't want to let my wife down. I kept my mouth shut and told myself that I would make the best of it, that it was the right thing to do for Isobel, that maybe shallow, transient, sunblasted Tucson, Arizona, wasn't the best place to raise a child, but hopefully it was good enough.

*T*he thirteenth session of the Arizona Territorial Legislature took place in the mining town of Prescott in January 1885. As the members decided which towns and cities would reap the financial benefits of housing the state's first university, prison, insane asylum and teacher training school, they drank heavily and indulged in so much fraud that the session became known as the Thieving Thirteenth.

The legal limit for operating expenses was $4,000. They exceeded it by $46,745, and much of that went into their pockets. They grotesquely inflated their traveling expenses, paid clerks that did no work, and authorized $19,967 in dubious printing expenses.

The session was also known as the Fighting Thirteenth and the Bloody Thirteenth because of fistfights that broke out in the legislature and the nearby saloons on Whiskey Row. Following an insult, council member W. C. Bridwell bloodied the nose and broke the glasses of a copper company lobbyist, who then challenged him to a duel. The men were separated before they could decide on weapons. Another question of honor was reportedly settled with a bullwhip and a monkey wrench.

Chapter Six

RISK

Looking back at my younger self—slim, handsome, energetic, full head of hair—the only thing I really miss is the ability to sleep like a normal person. That went away in my late thirties while I was writing my first book and has never returned. More recently, since Isobel was born, I have lost the urge to risk my life in dangerous parts of the world, and I'm left wondering where it came from. Was it youthful testosterone and delusions of invulnerability? Was it a death wish, as some people suggested, or an unconscious strategy to keep depression at bay? I don't know. As Joseph Conrad wrote, "No man ever understands quite his own artful dodges to escape from the grim shadow of self-knowledge." My intentions were to travel widely and learn about the world, to live life intensely and have some adventures along the way.

Some of this can be traced back to London. In my early twenties I was living on the dole in a damp, cold, moldy flat on a rain-lashed council estate between a gasworks and a motorway in Bromley-by-Bow. Weaselly adolescent thieves smirked and cupped their cigarettes in the urine-scented stairwells. A drunken wife-beater lived in the flat below. My daily existence was ruled by lack of money, boredom, and a sense that I was surrounded by an immovable force of dull, grim mediocrity. I hated England, and most of my friends felt the same way. The pleasures of life seemed underpowered and inadequate. "I like reality, but it's not strong enough," as someone put it. The remedy was drugs, alcohol and Black American dance music, which supplied the joy and soulful uplift that was so sorely lacking in Britain in the mid-1980s.

On Saturday nights, if we could scrape up the funds, we put on our best thrift-store clothes, took the Tube into Central London, got wired on espressos at the Bar Italia in Soho, and walked over to a nightclub called RAW. Housed in the cavernous basement of a tower block, it had a great sound system, a diverse crowd of music-loving people, and none of the hipper-than-thou fashion snootiness that prevailed in London clubs at that time. We threw down shots at the tequila bar and danced for hours to hip-hop, disco and "rare groove," as it was known—old obscure James Brown cuts and other little-known funk gems from the 1970s, such as "Funky Like a Train" by the Equals, "I Believe in Miracles" by the Jackson Sisters, and "Cross the Track (We Better Go Back)" by Maceo and the Macks, which brought the dance floor to a climax.

I was a music head and record collector, digging in secondhand stores for soul, funk, jazz, blues, hip-hop, Latin, Afrobeat, singer-songwriters like Tim Buckley and Tom Waits, and very occasional rock albums. I DJed on a semiregular basis at parties and club nights and went to live music shows as often as I could afford. I remember being filled with joy and happiness by Maze with Frankie Beverly at the Hammersmith Odeon, hypnotized by Nina Simone at Ronnie Scott's, astounded by Fela Kuti at the Brixton Academy, with a dozen of his twenty-seven wives singing backup. It was music more than anything that kept alive my sense of wonder, and getting blasted was the nearest thing I had to adventure.

I wasn't a heavy drinker by British standards, but those standards were outrageous. When I started going to pubs as a teenager, my father sat me down and gave me some drinking advice. "Eight pints is enough," he said, and bear in mind that a British pint is twenty ounces. "Don't go one over the eight, or you'll get too drunk." Five or six pints of lager was all I needed to get happily sloshed, and once or twice a week was the usual frequency. Drug-wise, I stuck mainly to hashish, weed, mushrooms and LSD, which was the greatest adventure of all, unless you had a bad trip, in which case it was a horrifying ordeal that seemed to last forever.

We bought our drugs from a wild Scotsman named Steve who lived across the motorway from our block of flats. I remember him marching across the forecourt in a leather biker jacket and boots, Iggy Pop haircut, gaunt chapped face, aggressive Glaswegian body language. Children were playing soccer and when their ball rolled up to him, he booted it over the back fence into the filthy canal, an enormous punt of fifty or sixty yards. "I could have played for Hibs," he bellowed, referring to the Scottish soccer team Hibernian. "But I chose drugs." He had an antic sense of humor. Once in Central London I saw him walk up to a police officer, show him a lump of hashish, and then accuse a random passerby of trying to sell it to him. In the ensuing confusion Steve sprinted away laughing maniacally and disappeared into the Tottenham Court Road tube station. He sold us MDMA, or ecstasy, when it reached Britain in the late 1980s and transformed the youth culture. I didn't mind it, but I preferred the wilder, edgier, more unpredictable ride of an acid trip.

Once I got to Arizona, there was no need for psychedelic drugs.

Reality was mind-blowing enough. All I had to do was go out into the desert, especially in the spring, when it was carpeted with wildflowers, or up in the sky island mountain ranges where occasional jaguars were coming up from Mexico and trying to reclaim their ancestral range, or into one of the phantasmagoric red and purple sandstone canyons. Not only were these places overpoweringly beautiful to my eyes, but alive with plants and birds and creatures, and older than humanity. The ecosystem that we call the Sonoran Desert is a relatively new development in Arizona, having evolved into something close to its current form about 8 million years ago. The first *Homo sapiens* in East Africa evolved about 300,000 years ago.

Perhaps the last place on earth where drugs are needed to have a peak experience is at the bottom of the Grand Canyon on a raft, smashing through Class V rapids on the Colorado River, then floating serenely between the multicolored mile-high walls and battlements. I loved rafting the Grand so much that I kept pitching it as a story idea to different travel magazines in different countries, without telling them I had already written it. By this small subterfuge, I was able to go again and again on two- and three-week rafting trips without paying the thousands of dollars they normally cost.

I was also doing a lot of backpacking and car camping between magazine assignments, and I liked to stay out for at least three nights to experience that blossoming of the senses. My friend Clark the actor/ bouncer/stuntman and I would make regular excursions into the western deserts to look for animal skulls to add to his collection. He had a pet tarantula named Jack that lived in a javelina skull in an aquarium, and his other skulls were displayed as totemic art objects. We took a minimalist old-school approach to camping. We slept on the ground under the stars and used rolled-up jackets for pillows. We ate steaks cooked on the coals the first night, and cans of beans and beef jerky after that. Apart from eating utensils, the only camping equipment we had were flashlights, Clark's revolver and a large, bone-handled knife that he named Mike. Our supplies were completed by whiskey, cigarettes, marijuana and gallon plastic jugs of water.

On a hot day in summer, I was on the return leg of a two-day solo backpacking trip in the red rock canyon country near the Utah border. My last gallon jug of water split open in my backpack and dumped its contents down the backs of my legs. In that moment, everything changed. What had looked majestically beautiful now looked brutally unforgiving and charged with primordial menace. It was over 100 degrees and I had nine or ten miles back to my truck, including a long section of uphill.

After walking for two hours, I felt dangerously overheated and more thirsty than I had ever been in my life. I sat down in the lee of a rock. Should I wait here in the shade for the sun to set and the air to cool down? That would mean another six hours without water. So I walked on through the heat of the afternoon in order to get to water sooner. As the miles wore on, I started to feel weak and dizzy. It took more and more willpower to stop my feet from stumbling. My mouth and throat were too dry to swallow. The parched desert air was drinking the moisture from my body. My mind swam with awful visions of what would happen as dehydration and hyperthermia (dangerously elevated body temperature) became more advanced.

In the final stages, clothes become painful on the scalding skin, and people stagger around naked. In their delirium, they often try to eat cactus for moisture, and their faces and bodies get impaled and covered in detachable spines. Vultures don't always wait until you're dead. They begin feeding on the part of the dying body that's easiest to access and contains the most moisture, so the last thing you see is a red wrinkled face and a big sharp curved beak plunging into your eyeball.

By the time I made it back to my truck, I was having muscle cramps and it was hard to think straight. My lips were badly cracked, and my tongue felt like a piece of beef jerky. On the passenger seat was the plastic gallon jug of water that had dominated my thoughts ever since the other one split and betrayed me. The water was the temperature of hot coffee. I gulped it down greedily. Then I vomited. It seemed cruelly ironic that my body was rejecting the substance it desperately needed. I took a small sip and it stayed down. Then another. And another. I drove twenty miles to a gas station and bought cold water and cold Gatorade. I sat in my truck with the windows open, wishing it had air conditioning, taking sips of Gatorade. I poured the cold water over my head and shirt to bring down my body temperature. Slowly I began to improve, although it took weeks to fully recover. I have never taken a store-bought plastic jug of water into the desert again. Stout canteens only. And since that day, I have endangered my life in many different ways, in many different countries, but I've never run out of water in the desert again.

———

In 1995, I drove to Los Angeles to cover Snoop Dogg's murder trial for British *Esquire*, but it was afflicted with delays so I went down to East-side Long Beach to get a sense of where Snoop grew up. In the V.I.P. record store, where he used to hang out and get high in the back room, I got talking to some aspiring rappers trying to break into the music industry. They were finding out that the rap game was nearly as treach-erous and dangerous as the drug game, but they were still half-crazed with ambition and determination to achieve hip-hop stardom. This, I decided, was the story I wanted to write, and my editor agreed. On a shoestring budget, I was able to stay for two weeks in Long Beach and Compton, hanging around with rappers and producers. I tried using my knowledge of funk and R&B as a point of common reference, but they didn't care about that. It was smoking weed with them that broke the ice.

I met Snoop briefly in a recording studio. He and his entourage were so stoned that they could barely mumble, let alone rap. But I was able to watch and listen as other rappers wrote, rehearsed and performed, and the producers worked up the backing tracks, sometimes looping samples from old records, sometimes adding funky synth basslines of their own. And because they wanted the exposure of being in *Esquire,* a couple of the rappers talked very candidly about their life experiences, their feelings and worldviews, and the beatings, threats and feuds that were taking place in the music industry. None of them would name the perpetrators on the record, or the alleged perpetrator in chief, who was Marion "Suge" Knight, head of Death Row Records, currently serving twenty-eight years for a fatal hit-and-run. I met him briefly at the trial, requested an interview, and received an extraordinarily cold and menacing stare in return.

While I was trying and failing to keep up with the blunts and forty-ounces circulating at an impromptu party in a mini-mall parking lot in Long Beach, a tall muscle-bound Crip just out of prison pistol-whipped a woman right in front of me, felling her with one hard blow to the side of the head. As she lay bleeding, he pointed the gun at me. "You get the fuck out of here now," he instructed, and I complied. A few days later I was smoking a blunt in a Jamaican restaurant that I used as my daytime headquarters, because I had become friendly with the owner. In walked the Jheri-curled barber from the shop next door, blasted out of his mind on PCP, or sherm, as it was called. He got right up in my face and told me I had come to the Eastside to get raped by a Black man. "You ready?" he said. "Because I'm man enough to do it. You ready, motherfucker?" I was grievously stoned and I started physically trembling with fear, which made the barber feel even more emboldened. "Yeah you scared, you better be scared." Other people managed to talk him down and steer him away and the next day the barber was all apologies: "I'm sorry, man, that sherm got my head all fucked up. No hard feelings, right?"

I went on to write about the Chicano ganglands of East LA and the murderous Mexican American prison mafia known as La Eme. I rode freight trains across Montana and Washington State in order to write about a violent hobo gang called the Freight Train Riders of America, or FTRA. I drove down to Chiapas, Mexico, to cover the Zapatista uprising. People were always warning me about danger, but I kept emerging unscathed and concluded that most places aren't as dangerous as people say. My acceptable level of risk continued to rise, and I began to crave that edgy, hyperintense feeling that comes with pushing your luck in a volatile environment where you don't belong, living on your wits and instincts, and trying to make sense of it all at the same time.

To stay up half the night taking notes in a crumbling Port-au-Prince mansion full of flowering tropical plants, as big green lizards prowled the floors and a Haitian intellectual expounded brilliantly on his country's history and political situation—that was exactly the sort of thing I was after and it kept me coming back to Haiti, even after a riot took place outside my hotel and a dead body lay in the street for three days afterwards.

I became increasingly disinterested in what most people called normal life. I had already jettisoned television, and I stopped paying attention to sports, celebrities, movies, the chatter of the culture, the zeitgeist. I avoided shopping as much as possible, didn't own any electronic gadgets except a computer and a flip phone, and I still had no desire to settle down or start a family. I wanted to keep traveling and see the world, to have peak experiences and push toward extremes.

———

Like most people who knew him, I was worried that Chuck Bowden was going to get himself killed. His acceptable levels of risk were now far in excess of mine. He had become seduced and fascinated by Ciudad Juárez, the Mexican border city across the Rio Grande from El Paso, Texas. It began by chance. In 1995, while investigating a murder in El Paso, he went to the office of one of the Juárez city newspapers. He was looking for a photograph. He started talking with the reporters and photographers, who told him they were documenting an unprecedented wave of violence and lawlessness in the city. They described warring drug cartels, hundreds of violent street gangs, rampant kidnappings and executions, an epidemic of women being abducted, raped, tortured and killed, and municipal, state and federal police officers not just turning a blind eye because of corruption but actively working for the cartels as bodyguards, assassins, kidnappers and torturers.

None of this was being reported in the U.S. media, not even in El Paso right across the river. Nor was it being discussed by U.S. politicians, academics or activists. The conventional wisdom at the time was that Mexico was an "emerging democracy" on track to becoming a First World nation, and Juárez was being hailed as a poster child for the new free trade agreements. Hundreds of foreign-owned factories had opened in the city and they were employing thousands of people who needed jobs. But, as Chuck learned on that first visit, the wages were so low that it was almost impossible to live on them. The maquiladoras, as the foreign-owned factories were called, paid only $20 to $35 for a six-day week, in a city where prices were at 90 percent of U.S. prices. And displaced poverty-stricken people were pouring into Juárez by the tens of thousands because free trade policies had wiped out their agricultural livelihoods in rural Mexico.

When Chuck got back to Tucson, I went over to his house with a good bottle of wine. I'd just got paid for a magazine story and that was our tradition. After needling me for swirling the wine and sniffing it—"I like to drink the goddamn stuff," he growled—he began talking about Juárez: "The violence is stunning. The impunity is stunning. In the last year and a half there have been hundreds of murders and hardly any arrests, let alone convictions. The poverty is stunning. People making our refrigerators are living in shacks without running water or electricity. Gangs are preying on them. The city is absolutely feral. I'm going back there as soon as I can. I may never leave. It's a laboratory of the future."

"Why is it the future?" I asked.

"The rich get richer, the poor get poorer, industrial growth generates poverty faster than it distributes wealth. Then the wheels come off and you get Juárez."

"Aren't you worried about getting killed?" I asked.

He shot me a look of absolute disgust and his voice descended to its deepest register. "I'm not going to turn away from what's happening there because I might get killed," he said. "I'm a fucking reporter."

In time, with his usual generosity, Chuck started offering me contacts and story ideas in Juárez, and I went there because I wanted to be a fucking reporter too. I met up with a Mexican journalist named Carlos who showed me around. He said I had just missed an open gun battle in the streets between municipal police officers and federal police officers, each working for rival cartels. It was a Friday afternoon—payday at the maquiladoras. We waited outside one of the factories in his car. "Why are we here?" I asked. "You will see," he said.

When the factory gates opened, the workers, who were nearly all young women, formed a kind of phalanx to break through the gang members who had showed up to rob them of their meager wages. The factory provided no security. The police were nowhere to be seen, because they were paid off by the gang. Scuffles broke out on the edges of the phalanx. A woman was dragged screaming to the ground and robbed by tattooed thugs. Then another and another and two more as the main body of women battled through the swarming, cursing men and boarded a bus. When it was over, I said, "Jesus fucking Christ." Carlos said, "Now we go to Anapra."

Colonia Anapra was a shantytown in the scrubby desert on the edge of the city, pressed up against the U.S. border. A cold winter wind was blowing up the dust. Carlos knew people there and he translated as I interviewed them. One woman was living in a shack made from wooden pallets; she had jammed plastic bags between the slats to block the wind. She was working full-time at a factory owned by a U.S. corporation, and she was in debt to the local gang for the pallets. "And the plastic bags?" asked Carlos. "No," she said. "I didn't have to pay for them. I collected them myself."

The gang members of Colonia Anapra had gained international notoriety by robbing freight trains on the U.S. side of the border. We could see the holes they had cut in the fence. They would pile up rocks or other obstacles on the tracks to bring the trains to a halt and then

swarm the freight cars, stealing anything of value and carrying it off into
Anapra, where U.S. law enforcement had no jurisdiction and Mexican
law enforcement was only interested in its cut of the profits. Carlos
asked if I wanted to interview some train thieves. He said it would be
difficult and possibly dangerous, but he could ask around and try. "No,"
I said, "it's getting dark. We need to leave." I couldn't wait to get out of
Juárez and back across the U.S. border into El Paso.

I went to Juárez one more time, at Chuck's suggestion, to write a
story about a journalist named Rafael Cora who was nicknamed La
Pantera, the Panther. He worked for a local television station and he
had a popular morning news segment called *While You Were Sleeping*.
It featured his handheld footage of bloody crime scenes from the night
before. It looked like cheap sensationalism, especially when he included
footage of a road-killed goat on a slow murder night, but La Pantera
was an idealist. "Only by showing people the true reality of the violence
in the city will they rise up to stop it," he told me. He had filmed more
than eight hundred murdered bodies.

In his small rattletrap car, we spent a few nights in Juárez listening to
a police scanner and driving at high speed toward crime scenes, trying
to get there before the police and ambulances. It was easier to film that
way and the blood was still fresh and shiny. I forget how many murdered
bodies we saw. Six or seven maybe. I remember a woman slumped on a
couch with her brains splattered over a velvet painting of a tiger on the
wall behind her. I remember arriving at a body with multiple bullet holes
in the middle of a street in the central part of the city. La Pantera noted
that there were no police around, no ambulances and no bystanders. "It
is not safe to film here, cartel men are watching," he said. "They want
people to see this body tomorrow. This is a message murder."

After researching and writing two books and a slew of articles about Juárez, Chuck talked about the toll it was taking on him. He was sometimes accused of relishing violence, but that wasn't true at all. He detested violence. He thrust it in your face in his writing because he wanted you to acknowledge the pain and suffering it caused. "They killed fifteen in Juárez today," he said one day when I showed up at his house. "Someone has to bear witness to this endless fucking carnage. Why does it have to be me? Why is no one else showing up to do this work?" Chuck was attacked by the political and business elites in Juárez and El Paso for his dark, dystopian vision and razor-cutting criticism of free trade. Leftists attacked him for ignoring grassroots resistance movements and employing white male literary tropes. "If both of those groups are attacking me, I must be doing something right," he quipped.

For the sake of his mental health, he knew he had to get away from Juárez, but the city kept pulling him back. In the mid-1990s when he first arrived, it was averaging 25 murders a month, which had been "stunning." By 2008, the rate had quadrupled, to 100 murders a month. In 2009, the murder rate tripled again, to 300 a month. In 2010, Ciudad Juárez, with an official population of 1.3 million but probably closer to 2 million, had more than 3,500 homicides. It was the murder capital of the world.

Chuck was incapable of turning away from these developments. For the sake of the people living and dying and grieving in Juárez, he felt morally compelled to record what was happening there and use his gifts as a writer to make the wider world care about it. And he was psychologically compelled, as always, to go toward the darkness and report back from it. Another factor was his contacts. One source would lead to a better one, enabling him to go deeper into the labyrinth of violence and corruption. The culmination of this process was a Chihuahua state police officer who had been a paid assassin (*sicario*), kidnapper and torture specialist for the Juárez cartel. He had killed hundreds of people and I can't bring myself to describe his torture methods. Then he found God and made a narrow escape from the drug world with a $250,000 bounty on his head. He was the subject of Chuck's fifth book about the city, *El Sicario,* and a harrowing documentary of the same name.

Chuck didn't like to talk, at least not to me, about the risks he was taking and the danger he was in. But I knew he was going into rough barrios asking questions, and drinking in bars and clubs where he was the only gringo. And I think I'm correct in saying that he was the first journalist to name Amado Carrillo Fuentes—aka El Señor de los Cielos, the Lord of the Skies—as the head of the Juárez cartel, and to present evidence that cocaine was being flown into Juárez on commercial airplanes and unloaded by the Mexican military. Chuck wrote about some of his other methods. When a load of cocaine was intercepted by law enforcement, for example, Carrillo would have everyone connected with it killed, on the assumption that one of them must have snitched.

Chuck exposed corruption and criminal activity within Mexican law enforcement agencies. He described the Mexican army on the front page of a Juárez newspaper as a "criminal organization." The main reason for the hyperviolence, he stated, was that the cartels, the army and the government were all fighting for control of the illegal drug business and its multibillion-dollar profits. "If I was a Mexican reporter, they'd have killed me a long time ago," Chuck said to me. "But it makes more trouble when you kill an American." Nonetheless, there were multiple contracts out on his life. If Charles Bowden ever wanted to commit suicide, people said, all he'd have to do was stand on a street corner in Juárez and wait for half an hour.

His house on Ninth Steet was no longer a squalid bachelor's nest. It had been transformed by the arrival of Mary Martha Miles, an elegant and charming Louisianan who enjoyed describing herself as "Chuck's concubine," but also managed his affairs and edited his manuscripts. Before moving into the house, she undertook the herculean task of cleaning it, scrubbing away the accumulated grime of several decades. Empty wine jugs and overflowing ashtrays were replaced by cloth table napkins, antique silverware and vases of flowers. Dust and smeared pork fat disappeared from the windowpanes and the insects were evicted. Chuck decamped with his ashtrays into the shed, which he converted into an office.

His house had become genteel and civilized, and it felt like a sanctuary from the outside world, unless you knew that the Juárez cartel had persuaded a Mexican newspaper to print its address on the front page. Chuck had handguns stashed in every room. In the bathroom linen closet, Mary Martha became accustomed to moving a pistol out of the way to get a bath towel or her face cream. Twice she was with Chuck in Mexico as he made narrow, high-speed escapes in his truck from men with their guns drawn. It seemed like only a matter of time before he was riddled with bullets, or kidnapped and tortured to death.

*A*rizona is too cheap to provide its governors with a mansion, and the state capitol complex in Phoenix has been widely deplored as an architectural disgrace. It's an ungainly cluster of mismatched buildings that are each equally unimpressive in different ways. The original 1901 capitol, now a museum, looks like a small-town Mississippi courthouse with a copper dome stuck on top. The flanking house and senate buildings, added in 1960 in the modernist block style, resemble a provincial government electricity department in apartheid-era South Africa. Rising above them is a nine-story beige brutalist "Executive Tower" built in 1973.

It didn't have to be this way. In 1957 Frank Lloyd Wright, widely recognized as the greatest American architect of all time, came up with a spectacular modernist design for a new Arizona capitol complex among the red rocks of Papago Park just south of Phoenix. Wright named it Oasis and said it was inspired by the Alhambra palace complex in Granada, Spain. He offered it as a pro bono gift to his adopted home state and lobbied energetically on its behalf.

Arizona state legislators aggressively rejected his design, now regarded as one of Wright's unbuilt masterpieces, saying it was "too expensive" and "too ornate." One enraged lawmaker compared it to an "oriental whorehouse." They voted instead to approve a version of the current design, which Wright dismissed as "a telephone pole with a derby hat and two wastebaskets for the legislature."

Chapter Seven

HOME AT LAST

W e took possession of our brick house during an ominous April heat wave in that plague year of 2020. Temperatures were running 9 or 10 degrees hotter than normal, and toward the end of the month, we had our first 100-degree day of the year—an event known in Tucson as "the breaking of the ice on the Santa Cruz River," or Icebreak Day.

The Santa Cruz, just west of downtown, was the main reason for Tucson's existence. Native American farmers diverted water from the river into canal networks that irrigated fields of corn, squash, beans, melons and other crops. The Tohono O'Odham called this place Ts-iuk-shan, or Black Base, referring to a nearby mountain whose base was darker than its top (now called Sentinel Peak, or A Mountain). When the Spanish arrived in the 1770s they wrote down the name as Tucson, introduced new crops like figs and wine grapes, and continued farming in the riverside fields.

Now the idea of ice breaking on the Santa Cruz was doubly sarcastic. Not only was it far too hot, but there was no longer any water in the river. So much groundwater was pumped out during the nineteenth and twentieth centuries for agriculture, and then golf courses, faucets, showerheads, toilets, washing machines, garden hoses and sprinklers in rapidly expanding Tucson, that the water table sank too low to sustain the river's existence. The Santa Cruz, like many other rivers in Arizona, had succumbed to the thing we call progress. It was now a river of sand, scrubby plants, trash and shopping carts that only flowed with water after heavy rains. There was a welcome new project to restore some riparian areas with treated wastewater, but the Santa Cruz would never be the lifeblood of the city again.

Most of Tucson's water now came hundreds of miles across the desert in canals from the Colorado River, which also supplies Phoenix, Las Vegas, Los Angeles and an empire of irrigated farmlands in western and central Arizona and Southern California. And the Colorado River was in crisis with record low water levels because of overuse by agriculture and fast-growing cities, and because the Southwest was going through its worst drought in 1,200 years, an event almost certainly exacerbated by climate change. There was a phrase that I had omitted from my letter to the sellers of our new house. We hoped to grow old in the house *unless the water started to run out,* in which case the value of the house would plummet and we would have to move somewhere else.

The unseasonably hot weather continued as plumbers, electricians, roofers and handymen worked on the house. It was Tucson's hottest May on record, an average of 5 degrees hotter than normal, with high temperatures reaching 108 degrees. We were living in the casita and driving across the sprawling city twice a day to let the workmen in and out—a new phase of living in limbo. It was a time of marital strain and flare-ups, because we had so many important decisions to make about the house and didn't always see eye to eye. We needed to pick out bathroom tiles and fixtures, without being able to go into stores and look at them because lockdown orders were in place. I had limited patience for scrolling through the websites and became increasingly bored and annoyed by the whole subject of bathroom fixtures.

The vanity became a battleground. I was fine with something standard and inexpensive in which to spit out toothpaste and store bathroom gear, but Mariah scorned my choices as better suited to a rental apartment or a cheap hotel room. She wanted something stylish and beautiful that would give her pleasure every time she looked at it, and as usual she ground down my resistance until she got her way. With my reluctant agreement and the proviso that I would be exempted from any and all future discussions on the subject of bathroom fixtures, she asked Clark to design and build something elegant, timeless and lovely out of box elder wood.

The punishing heat added another layer of strain. I started getting up at 5:00 a.m., when it was still cool and fresh, to take the long walks that I found so satisfying and therapeutic. I started parking like a Tucsonan again, always looking for a spot in the shade, even if it meant a longer walk across the parking lot. I never ventured outside without a hat and sunglasses, because I felt like a naked mole rat exposed to the sun without them. One 107-degree afternoon, after parking my black vehicle in the sun for several hours because no shade was available, I was putting Isobel in her car seat and I accidentally touched her bare thigh with the metal seat buckle. She screamed and howled in pain, an ugly red welt appeared on her skin, and I stood there transfixed in mortified horror, feeling like the worst parent in the world.

We were constantly imploring her to drink more water, because dehydration and heatstroke can happen so fast in the dry heat of Arizona. You can walk around in 95 degrees without sweating, but you're still losing water from your body at a rapid rate. It evaporates right out of the pores of your skin before it can form as sweat droplets. It was incredible to us that our house, which had been there since the 1940s, had no shade in the backyard. Nothing was more important than shade in a Tucson backyard, in our opinion, so we started planting trees—a desert willow, a chitalpa, a Texas ebony—and we asked Clark to design a ramada, a rectangular open-walled shade structure. Attached at roof level to the south-facing kitchen wall, it would also keep the sun off the bricks and reduce our air conditioning bills.

We moved into the house as soon as we had a working toilet and shower. Clark was still working on the vanity, installing self-closing drawer glides and applying ten coats of spar urethane so it would be fully waterproof. It was undeniably a thing of beauty and exquisite craftsmanship, and my objections faded away.

As we got to know the property and the neighborhood, we were surprised by the abundance of birds and wildlife right in the middle of the city. We watched a bobcat walking down our street, and just a few doors down, a pack of javelinas was living under an old lady's house. These tusked, bristly, pig-like animals could be dangerous, but did their best to avoid humans. At night we heard coyotes and great horned owls. A family of Gambel's quail—plump, charming, ground-dwelling birds with gray and chestnut coloring and black plumes on their heads—were regular visitors to our front yard. Isobel was entranced by their babies, which she described as "puffballs on roller skates," because they were tiny round balls of fluff and seemed to glide across the ground after their parents.

I had forgotten how soothing the mourning doves sounded on a quiet Tucson morning—a gentle dreamy cooing—and how suddenly it could change to panicked whirring wingbeats when a Cooper's hawk came arrowing toward them. We saw cardinals, mockingbirds, woodpeckers, curve-billed thrashers, goldfinches, pretty little verdins and gnatcatchers, a male vermilion flycatcher as bright as a flame, three species of hummingbirds, and other birds we didn't know. Abert's towhees hopped around, looking like they were up to no good. A male roadrunner lived on our block, the first we had ever seen in the city, and for the other birds and the omnipresent lizards, it was like having a marauding velociraptor in the neighborhood. Roadrunners are fast and ferocious, capable of killing and eating a rattlesnake or catching a hummingbird in midair. Whenever this one showed himself, there was a cascade of alarm calls and flurried departures from the other birds. One day he caught a lizard in his beak, flew up on top of Mariah's car, and performed a wild stomping dance with his crest rising and falling and his feet drumming loudly on the metal roof, presumably trying to attract a mate.

The only problem animals were mice, rats and an extended family of cottontail rabbits who lived under the same bush as the quail and decimated the penstemons, globe mallows, woolly butterflybushes, and nearly everything else Mariah planted in the front yard. We snap-trapped the mice and rats, and after much discussion over possible extermination strategies, we decided to live with the rabbits. Riley and Savanna managed to kill one in the backyard and that plus the coyotes and bobcats seemed the best way to keep their numbers down.

By the end of May the house was coming together. The vanity was installed and fitted with a porcelain sink. Isobel had a hanging princess canopy over her bed—she called it her "bed castle." Her illustrated storybooks were lined up neatly on white bookshelves, and the full collection of sixty-odd stuffed animals liberated from storage. An electrician named John Wayne and a multitalented Italian carpenter and handyman named Michele were transforming the old brick garage once known as the Bull Moose Club into my new office.

He installed French doors where the old sliding garage door had been. He built a new window high in the eaves and hung another glass door to get more light into the room. He left one wall in the original weathered brick and drywalled the other three. Then he made floor-to-ceiling bookshelves for one of the walls. After many delays and aggravations, an HVAC company put in a mini-split for heating and cooling, and John Wayne came back to install track lighting on the roof beams. Once my desk and rugs and furniture were in place, I had the greatest writing office I could possibly imagine, but it came with an unexpected side effect. When the writing didn't go well in such an ideal environment, it produced even more frustration and self-loathing than normal.

I have writer friends who banish their family members from their writing rooms, because interruptions are so ruinous to the fragile, elusive state of concentration that you have to reach and maintain in order to work effectively. The policy made a lot of sense to me, but I was too softhearted to impose it on Isobel. She loved to bust through the door and seize her father's attention, to clamber on the big leather armchair, practice her cartwheels on the long rug that ran down the center of the room, and pester me to play Dictionary, a new game we had come up with. We would get out the two big volumes of my dictionary, set them on the floor, and leaf through them looking for funny words like *igloo, nincompoop, catawampus, pandiculation* (morning stretching), and *erinaceous* (resembling a hedgehog).

Sometimes I would play the guitar and she would sing improvised lyrics. She was still going through her princess phase, but the girl had rock 'n' roll in her too. One day I was playing "La Grange" by ZZ Top, just starting to get the hang of the blues boogie riff they borrowed from John Lee Hooker, and Isobel came out with this:

Lady Prison
I choose mean
In my soul
I pull my hair
I stomp my feet
I'm Lady Prison
I'm bad to meet

I've been in prison for a hundred years
They put me in prison for no reason
So I choose mean
With a magic guitar
My fairy godmother busted me right out of there
I choose mean

———

After much discussion and disagreement, Mariah and I reached a consensus about the backyard. It needed to feel like a refuge or a sanctuary and be a little wild and overgrown, with separate distinctive areas linked by flagstone pathways. In the southwest quadrant, to honor our saguaro cactus, we would grow only native Sonoran Desert plants, starting with a small palo verde tree, a creosote bush, some agaves and three brittlebushes, a favorite shrub of mine with silver-gray leaves and bright yellow flowers. Between my office and the house, we cleared off the gravel and dug out a large bed. Mariah planted tecomas, chuparosas, firecracker bushes, milkweed and other plants that attract hummingbirds and butterflies.

By the side of the house was a narrow rectangular area filled with junk and debris. She cleared it out, planted some more tecomas and a flowering vine over an arched trellis doorway, and put in children's outdoor furniture. This was Isobel's private garden, which she named her "paradise." We took out the boxwood, the scraggly oleanders and the dying palo verde. The backyard still looked like a parking lot, because the square footage under gravel was still far greater than the square footage containing plants, but we were off to a good start.

All the plants and trees we put in were adapted to heat and aridity, but Mariah was still watering them every day to help them get established in the unseasonably hot weather and grow faster. She bought most of the plants from a militant leftist eco-crusader named Jared who had a plant nursery with his partner and was fantastically knowledgeable about botany and horticulture. He encouraged us to not feel guilty about watering, as so many Tucsonans did.

"You're making habitat, you're helping other species to live," he said. "If your plants are not getting eaten by bugs and caterpillars, they don't belong here and they're essentially useless. If you want to save water, which we all must, quit flushing your toilet so much. But the real problem is that we're growing cotton and alfalfa in the desert, on a massive scale, and these are super water-intensive crops. It's insane! It drives me nuts! Agriculture uses up nearly 80 percent of Arizona's water supply."

Once Michele had finished building the ramada from Clark's design, which was rustic, elegant and faintly Japanese, we could sit in the shade, watch hummingbirds and butterflies on the plants we had put in, and start to wonder what home might actually feel like here. In my mind it was still a project, dominated by never-ending lists of things to do and buy, except at night sometimes when the air conditioner clicked off and I sat out under the moon and the stars in the quiet city, feeling an aching rush of gratitude that we were here and this was ours.

———

It turned into the hottest summer in Southern Arizona since records began. In Tucson, we had 108 days at or above 100 degrees, and a high temperature of 113 degrees. In Phoenix, which is at a lower elevation, they had 53 days at or above 110 degrees and a high of 118 degrees. It was even hotter than that in the western Arizona deserts. I started thinking of the sun as a monstrous tyrant who had declared war on all living things. It rose like an implacable curse, climbed up into its throne, and then assaulted the world below with merciless heat and a glaring, bleached-out light that made the mountains look like bones. The sun stung and burned the skin, even when you were walking from the house to the oven-like car. It struck people down and killed them. Two hundred and twenty-seven migrants died in the Arizona desert that year—a new record—and 323 heat deaths were reported in Phoenix, most of them homeless people. At the end of the day, when the sun sank down to the horizon, it looked fat, malevolent and orange, or sometimes bloodred and quavering. Bird and mammal populations were crashing in the desert. Even the prickly pears were shriveling and dying.

At the beginning of June, a dry lightning strike ignited a wildfire in the Santa Catalinas. It spread to 115,000 acres—that's nearly 180 square miles—and covered the city in a pall of smoke and drifting ash particles, amplifying the apocalyptic feel of that summer. Driving north on a magazine assignment, I saw nine different wildfires before reaching the Utah border. The high country pine forests were parched from twenty years of drought and in many areas the weakened trees had been invaded by bark beetles, leaving stands of dead timber ready to burn. When I got back to Tucson, the Catalinas were still ablaze and everyone was waiting for the monsoons to arrive and put out the flames. June 15 is the official start of Tucson's monsoon season, when we get most of our precious rains. The heat has to be extreme, with winds from the south bringing in moisture. Then cumulonimbus clouds build up in the sky and climb higher and higher until they turn into dramatic thunderstorms that flood the streets and flashflood the canyons and gulches.

We had told Isobel how children in Tucson jump around and dance in the monsoon rains and make tinfoil boats to float through the streets. "Fun!" she said. But even as the heat was breaking records, the moisture didn't arrive, the monsoons failed, and the fire burned in the mountains above the city for weeks and weeks. A few times we witnessed the arid land weather phenomenon known in the borderlands as virga. Rain falls from a cloud, but it evaporates in the hot dry air before it reaches the ground. Visually it resembles a hanging veil. Finally in late July, the sun was blotted out by a massive advancing, climbing wall of dark clouds. The wind started raging, the temperature cooled slightly, and the three of us went outside in the backyard, ready to dance and whoop in rain at long last. But it turned out to be a vicious dust storm that ripped down two large sections of fence in our backyard.

The next morning Clark came to the rescue, with digging tools, two-by-fours, four-by-fours, bags of Quikrete, a big framing hammer and a box of nails. We worked on the fence most of the morning in the heat, me with a surgical mask and Clark with a KN95. COVID-19 at that time was spreading more rapidly in Arizona than any other state in the U.S. and any other country in the world. We had the same number of new infections as the entire European Union, with one-sixtieth of its population.

One important factor was Governor Ducey's leadership, which was vacillating and easily swayed by the unscientific winds of Republican political opinion. He issued stay-at-home orders in the spring and then removed them in May, right before Donald Trump came to Arizona. That initiated the surge that turned us into the world's number one hot spot. Arizona was also consumed by conspiracy theories about the virus: it was a fake disease that the government was exploiting to control the people; it was part of Bill Gates's evil plan to vaccinate the entire world; it was a Chinese biowarfare weapon, a plot by the Deep State to overthrow Trump, a self-enrichment scheme by Dr. Anthony Fauci. These fantasies were by no means limited to the Republican right. You heard them also from libertarians, contrarians, and the naturopathic left.

Tucson had a mask mandate, but Clark couldn't go into a supermarket or a hardware store because so many people were unmasked. It wasn't just the risk of getting infected with all his comorbidities that kept him away. He and Jill both knew that he was liable to start a physical altercation, because his blood was boiling about the unmasked and he had a long history of starting and winning fights with strangers whose behavior he deemed obnoxious. Despite his liberal politics and artistic talents, Clark was Scotch-Irish to the bone. He lived by a code of honor, and it included the use of violence.

"The idea of wearing a mask to prevent other people—like me—from getting sick and maybe dying just doesn't compute in their selfish, arrogant, all-American brains," he said while pounding in nails with his framing hammer. "Why should they give a shit about someone else they don't even know? Why should they listen to scientists or experts? We're number one for COVID because we've got more assholes than anywhere else."

As usual, Clark refused payment for fixing our fence, even though he needed the money. I forget how we got onto the subject of Leonardo da Vinci, but Clark talked about him at length as he put away his tools and stood around afterwards in the shade of his battered old cowboy hat. He regarded Leonardo as the greatest genius who had ever lived, which I hadn't realized. A couple of years earlier I had attended a dinner in Mississippi with the great biographer Walter Isaacson, who at that time was working on a book about Leonardo da Vinci. As soon as Clark drove away, I checked the internet, saw that the book was now published, and ordered an illustrated hardback copy. I gave it to Clark, who found it utterly fascinating and then began reading Walter Isaacson's other books. "It was a good trade," he said. "I fixed your fence, you enriched my reading life, no money passed between us."

*I*n 1540 the conquistador Francisco Vázquez de Coronado and an army of Spanish soldiers, wives, African slaves, Moors and Indigenous soldiers marched north out of Mexico with more than a thousand horses and mules, and hundreds of cattle, sheep and pigs. They were looking for the Seven Cities of Cíbola, which were rumored to be laden with gold and located somewhere in present-day Arizona or New Mexico. After an arduous four-month journey, they discovered that Cíbola was a collection of Zuni villages with no gold and nothing worth stealing.

An army captain named García López de Cárdenas was dispatched with Hopi guides and a small party of soldiers to investigate reports of a navigable river to the west. After traveling through high red deserts and mesas for twenty days, they reached the south rim of the Grand Canyon. Cárdenas and his men were the first Europeans to see it, but they were unable to perceive its true dimensions because they had never seen another landform on such a gigantic scale. Looking down at the Colorado River, a vertical mile below them, they saw a small stream no more than six feet across. Cárdenas ordered three men to climb down to it and bring back water. The men spent three days trying, but could get only a third of the way down. The stream, they reported, was a big turbulent river and the rock formations on the cliffs were taller than the great tower of Seville.

By showing them the river at its most inaccessible point, the Hopi guides were almost certainly misleading the Spaniards, who dismissed the region as an impenetrable wasteland and withdrew from all further exploration in what is now Northern Arizona. Coronado became convinced that the seven golden cities lay to the east and marched his army all the way to Kansas before giving up on this fantasy. The Grand Canyon was left unexplored by Europeans and Anglo-Americans for the next 235 years.

Chapter Eight

TO PLEASE THE TRIGGER FINGER

As Chuck Bowden went deeper and deeper into Ciudad Juárez, I became seduced and fascinated by another dangerous part of Mexico. If you drive down to the border town of Douglas, Arizona, and look south, you will see mountains climbing out of the desert on bony outlying fingers and knuckled ridges, rising up into high cliffs, peaks and battlements, with more mountains stacked up behind them as far as the eye can see. This is the northern end of the Sierra Madre Occidental, the Mother Mountain range of northwestern Mexico. It extends for 700 or 1,000 miles, depending which cartographer you believe, and in the early years of the twenty-first century it was crossed by only two paved roads and one railroad.

The Sierra Madre reaches 11,000 feet at its highest point and its volcanic rock is dramatically eroded by gorges, ravines and gigantic canyons known as barrancas. The mountains have long provided refuge for bandits and outlaws. Indigenous tribes—Tarahumaras, Guarijios, Huicholes, Tepehuanes—have managed to hang on to most of their culture in its remote folds, and in the late twentieth century the Sierra Madre became one of the world's biggest production zones for heroin, marijuana and billionaire drug lords. The Mexican government has never managed to impose the rule of law on the Sierra Madre, mainly because its topography is so rugged, and it persists as a kind of Wild West on America's back doorstep, with a sky-high homicide rate and an economy dominated by drug production and trafficking. It was my bright idea to travel the length of the range and write a book about it.

But first I needed a month in a Spanish immersion language school in Mexico, and I was very much hoping to get some travel advice and culture lessons from a remarkable Arizonan named J. P. S. Brown. He was a fifth-generation cowboy and rancher who had won literature prizes for his Hemingwayesque novels about the cattle culture of Arizona and Sonora. He was bilingual and bicultural, equally at home in Arizona or Sonora, and he knew the northern Sierra Madre intimately, having spent a good part of forty years there gathering cattle on horseback and prospecting for gold. Chuck Bowden, who preferred Joe Brown's writing to Hemingway's, gave me the introduction and in 2005 I drove down to the small town of Patagonia, Arizona, to meet him for the first time.

He was a big, broad-shouldered, powerful-looking man in his early seventies, with a white mustache and smoky green eyes, standing in his front yard in a cowboy hat and boots with a pack of dogs at his feet. We exchanged some pleasantries and then I told him about the journey I had in mind. "I don't see how you can do this without getting killed," he said.

"I was hoping you might have some advice for me about that," I said. "I was thinking about posing as an academic of some kind, a historian maybe, and trying to steer clear of the really dangerous places."

"Look," he said, those smoky green eyes boring into mine, "if you go up in those mountains, what you're going to find is murder. Lots of murder. The last place you want to find is the heart of the Sierra Madre, because that's where you'll get shot on sight, no questions asked, and the guy who shoots you will probably still have a smile on his face from saying hello."

It started to rain and he said, "I guess you better come inside."

Sitting in the front room of the small house that he shared with his fourth wife Patsy, Joe poured me a shot of lechuguilla—bootleg Sonoran mezcal that had been distilled by a nephew of his former business partner at a remote ranch in the Sierra Madre. It had a green, spiny, fiery taste and it sent my brain skidding around inside my skull. He poured a little into a glass ashtray and set fire to it with a cigarette lighter, to show that it was pure alcohol. "If you're offered lechuguilla straight from the still, take only a little sip or your throat might get permanently damaged."

As I cautiously sipped the lechuguilla, Joe drank black coffee, having given up alcohol twelve years previously. "I was drinking four bottles of whiskey a day and that's too many," he said. The more we talked about the Sierra Madre, the more nostalgic he grew for the mountains and the more stories he told about them. His voice was dry, husky and authoritative, and it slipped in and out of norteño-accented Mexican Spanish. "Sometimes I would fly down there in a little Cessna I had. I liked to come in low over the main street and throw out cans of beer for people to catch. Once in Navojoa I was flying drunk with a beautiful whore next to me and I knocked the TV aerial off the whorehouse so the madam couldn't watch her telenovelas [Spanish-language soap operas] anymore. I didn't want to listen to that shit while I was making love to a beautiful woman."

When he ran out of money, he would put up posters that said in Spanish: "Joe Brown fights anybody for $100." Nobody in Sonora knew that he'd been the heavyweight boxing champion of the University of Notre Dame and had sparred with Rocky Marciano for a few weeks in the early 1950s. "I made good money winning fights in Mexico. And I made better money by losing fights on purpose and collecting my share from the guys that bet against me. I'd pretend that I'd been knocked down or knocked out and the audience would go wild. They just loved to see a big gringo get beaten down by one of their own."

I bought a four-wheel-drive Toyota pickup with outsize wheels for the Sierra Madre journey. I hoped that it was old and scarred enough to deter thieves, and strong enough to handle some of the roughest, steepest roads in the world. Joe Brown doubted that a truck would be of much use, because in the Sierra Madre he remembered everyone rode a horse or a mule or went on foot. "How are you horseback?" he asked. "Not good at all," I said. He insisted that I needed to learn how to ride and he started giving me lessons for $20 an hour.

After showing me how to saddle and cinch, he put me on a twenty-four-year-old roan named Mike and we walked the horses out of Joe's corral and onto a trail that led up into the Patagonia Mountains. Once we gained some elevation, we could see for eighty or ninety miles in the cool crisp November air. Joe talked in great detail about the nature and character of horses and the way they think, but when it came to riding instruction he had only this to say: "Ride with your feet and don't let your ass hit the saddle in an undignified manner."

We walked the horses most of the time because the trails were steep and rocky, and when they flattened out I tried to get the hang of the trot. Joe rode in front of me in Wrangler jeans, handmade Mexican boots and an old faded black cowboy hat, telling stories over his shoulder and answering my questions about his life. He had been a U.S. Marine, a rodeo cowboy, a ranch hand, a ranch owner, and a cattle trader. He had worked alpine search-and-rescue in the Sierra Nevada of California. He had smuggled guns and whiskey into Mexico and prospected for gold. He had been a friend and drinking partner of the legendary tough-guy actor Lee Marvin. They met during the filming of *Pocket Money,* a movie adapted from Joe Brown's autobiographical novel *Jim Kane* and filmed in Tucson and Álamos, Sonora, in 1971.

"How did you like the movie?" I asked.

"It made me want to puke and hurt somebody."

Paul Newman played the lead character Jim Kane, who in the book was Joe Brown as honestly and accurately as he could portray himself. "He followed me around for two weeks, studying the way I walked, the way I spoke, asking me all these questions about myself. I guess I got to feeling a little flattered by the attention and my hat size might have gone up a couple of notches. Then I saw the movie and that son of a bitch played me as this dumb, stupid cowboy jackass, just as dumb as he could possibly be and still move the plot along and not walk into a fence post."

"Did you make good money off it?"

"Yeah."

"What happened to the money?"

"I just kept buying and selling cattle until it was all gone."

I became hugely excited when Joe said he was going back into the Sierra Madre and invited me to tag along. He wanted to research a sequel to *The Forests of the Night,* which was set high in the Sierra Madre and in my opinion his best novel. But on our next riding lesson, he informed me that drug mafiosos had just killed six Mexican army soldiers where he was planning to take me, and all his friends had come downhill to avoid the bloodletting and brutalities that would follow. He said it was a good time to stay away from the Sierra Madre, and he started up again with the warnings.

If you go by yourself, you become prey . . . People are getting killed up there for no reason now, because some mafioso is drunk off his ass and wants to test out his new automatic weapon . . . It's the kind of anarchy that gives anarchy a bad name.

———

Mariah liked older men (I wasn't the first). She liked tall men (I'm six-two) and she liked Englishmen, although she knew them mostly from movies and television. I don't know what she made of my restlessness, which forced me to leave town every three weeks or so, but she clearly enjoyed my company when I was around. I liked the way she looked, her kindness and intelligence, her taste in books, clothes and friends, the way her cheeks dimpled when she cracked up laughing, and I was infatuated with the way she smelled. Part of me was falling in love with her, and part of me was putting up barriers and pulling away, mainly because I was about to embark on a long dangerous journey through the Sierra Madre. We had been dating about four months when I packed my bags and said goodbye.

"I don't know when I'll be back. Three or four months maybe. There's no cell service up there and I don't have a satellite phone, so there'll be no way to get in touch with me. I think they have an internet café now in Creel, and I'll email you when I get there. Hopefully in a month or so. Maybe six weeks."

"Well then," she said. "I guess I'll see you when I see you." She had no real idea what I was getting into. I had told her that the Sierra Madre could be dangerous, but I hadn't gone into any details, and she had decided not to worry because there was absolutely nothing she could do about it. As soon as I drove away, she put our relationship in a box, stored it at the back of a high shelf in her mental pantry, and got on with the rest of her life. She had decided to go back to school, study library science and become a librarian.

What in the goat-fornicating hell was I thinking? Now it seems almost inconceivable that I sallied forth so blithely into a place where the growing and trafficking of illegal drugs was the foundation of the economy, where homicide was the number one cause of death for men (followed by cirrhosis of the liver), where cocaine and AK-47s were arriving in stick-and-mud villages before electricity and running water. I kept telling myself that I would be fine because I had my wits about me and good instincts and I had come through other dangerous places unscathed and I was going to be *careful*.

That was the watchword and what it meant in the Sierra was this: never arrive in a place without someone to vouch for you. Where the rule of law didn't exist and people murdered with impunity, everything was personal and depended on trust. "You need someone from there to take you in there under their protection," said Joe Brown. "Whatever you do, don't mention drugs. If they mention drugs, don't show any interest. And if you can't make friends with the people there in twenty minutes, get out immediately."

As my journey got under way, these safety guidelines proved reliable. Through Joe's contacts and my own, I found people to take me into different parts of the mountains. One was a musician-filmmaker in Tucson with a family ranch in the Sierra. Another was my former landlord in Álamos, Sonora, who took me into a drug village himself and introduced me to a schoolteacher who took me into an Indigenous

Guarijio region of the mountains. One guide would lead to another, and they joked that it was like a game of "pass the gringo" through the mountains, even though they were vouching for me with their lives.

I learned other ways to be careful on the journey, and sometimes they had a surreal aspect because this was Mexico, where surrealism is as natural as rain. Beware of cross-dressing cowboys, I was repeatedly advised. If you see a man riding a horse and wearing a dress with a cowboy hat, look out, because many of them are killers. I was also warned about a murderous gay drug lord who wore pink cowboy gear and was nicknamed El Guante, the Glove.

Never refuse a snort of cocaine when it's offered by the police; otherwise they will think you are disrespecting them or working for the U.S. Drug Enforcement Administration. I learned this lesson in a rough-hewn cantina in Álamos, Sonora. On the wall behind the bar was a taxidermied mountain lion with its mouth clamped on the throat of a deer. Next to it, a stuffed ocelot was biting the throat of a squirrel. Prostitutes fed the jukebox and the music was all *narcocorridos*, which are accordion-driven story songs about drug traffickers: *I'm one of the players in the Sierra where the opium poppy grows . . . I like risky action, I like to do cocaine . . . I've got an AK-47 for anyone who wants to try me.*

I was drinking at the bar when I was summoned to the table of a large-bellied cop with a magnificent Roman nose. His nickname was El Pelícano, the Pelican. He was drinking beer with another police officer and some other men. As soon as I sat down, the Pelican thumped his empty quart bottle of Tecate beer on the table, the bartender scurried over with a fresh one, and everyone looked at me to pay. They were all ripped on cocaine. Their lips were twitching and writhing, and they were chewing at their tongues. I kept buying quart bottles of beer and they kept emptying them in a few minutes. The younger cop asked me if I liked *perico,* the slang term for cocaine (literally, parakeet), and I prevaricated, "Sometimes, but not now, thank you." He looked insulted and suspicious. The Pelican growled disapprovingly. Then he casually vomited on the floor, slammed down another empty bottle on the table, and called for more beer.

When I went to the bathroom, the two police officers followed me in there. After we had all zipped up, the Pelican raised his forefinger to stop me leaving. He scooped up a small mound of cocaine on the end of a knife and offered it to me, with a very challenging look in his eyes. This was clearly a test. I snorted it up—it was decent coke, but by no means pure. I turned to leave and the two police officers said, "No, no, no! You must do the other nostril. It is very important."

We kept on drinking. Every twenty minutes or so we would do another *pericazo*—literally a parakeet-blast. Then the cocaine ran out and there was no cash left in my wallet. I thanked them for a great evening and got up to leave. The Pelican said, "No, we need more *perico*. We need more beer. You can get more money from the bank. Or are you too proud to drink with Mexicans?" To leave a Mexican drinking session before it reaches its natural conclusion, which is complete drunkenness, is often considered rude and disrespectful, and in the Sierra it was dangerous.

I told them I was getting more money from the bank, so we could finish what we had started, but instead I staggered off to my rented room and passed out, hoping the Pelican and his partner wouldn't remember too much about the night before when they woke up in the morning. "To refuse a drink," wrote a Mexican professor studying the hyperviolence in the Sierra Madre, "is almost a declaration of war, a very serious discourtesy and many times an insult that ends in tragedy. . . . Wounded masculine dignity is the most important motivation to explain the great numbers of killings in the Sierra."

This was true, from what I heard and saw on my journey. People were getting killed over drugs, but far more people were getting killed over slights and perceived slights, and there were also murderous psychopaths on the loose and a widespread idea that you weren't a real man until you had killed a man. Joe Brown and others had warned me not to describe myself as a journalist. Mexico is the most dangerous country in the world in which to practice journalism, and a journalist in the Sierra Madre would immediately be suspected of reporting on the illegal drug trade and official corruption. Nor was it safe to say that I was a traveler who wanted to see the country, because travelers didn't go into the Sierra Madre except for a few sanctioned tourism areas. I tried posing as a scholar, asking questions about the history of the area, but that aroused suspicions, so in the end I simply described myself as a "friend" of whoever had agreed to vouch for me. Most people assumed I was in the Sierra to buy drugs, and that seemed like the most plausible cover story of all.

The terror I experienced in the Sierra dominates my memory of the journey, but it wasn't all darkness, drugs, violence and danger. I made deeply bonded cross-cultural friendships. I heard amazing norteño musicians wailing away in cantinas on accordions and guitars, singing the ballads of the mountains. I stood on the rim of a canyon in snowy pine forest and looked down at birds flying through tropical jungle at the bottom of the canyon. People in the Sierra, I learned, could be incredibly hostile and violent, and they could also be incredibly generous and hospitable. I spent a few days with a woman called Nelda Villa and her husband, Efrén, who gathered me into their ranch family on the Gavilán River, even though I was a complete stranger to them, with only one semi-local Mormon to introduce me. I wanted to meet Nelda because she was an authority on the last free Apaches in the Sierra Madre, a fascination of mine.

Most history books will tell you that all the Apaches were pacified and confined to reservations after Geronimo's final surrender at Skeleton Canyon in southeast Arizona in 1886. But in the early twentieth century there were about a hundred Chiricahua Apaches—men, women and children—who had never surrendered and were living in the northern Sierra Madre. The warriors continued to raid and plunder farms and ranches on both sides of the border well into the 1920s. They snatched female captives from Apache reservations in Arizona, killed a cowboy while stealing horses and mules in New Mexico in 1924, and murdered men, women and children in Sonora. After their raids they would vanish into the Sierra Madre's tortuously steep and rugged topography. The last of them were hunted down by Mexican ranchers in the late 1930s.

Nelda Villa had spent most of her life gathering information from the old people in remote villages about these *bronco* or wild Apaches as they were known in Mexico. With extraordinary generosity she passed nearly all of her knowledge over to me and gave me directions to one of Geronimo's old strongholds that the last free Apaches had used. Alone and hiking on foot, I discovered that it was now a drug camp, used for the clandestine cultivation of marijuana. Thankfully there were no people around and I was able to make a speedy exit.

The hardest lesson I learned in the Sierra was this: nothing happens until it happens. There is no escalation in danger that points toward life-threatening peril. I had been badly scared a couple of times, but my journey was going quite smoothly until I ran out of personal connections in the state of Durango. I heard about a Centro Turístico high in the mountains that offered cabins, horseback rides and fishing, and I decided that I would go there as a tourist, make some friends, and establish a new chain of connections to get me through the next stretch of mountains.

When I arrived in the Toyota, after a bone-rattling drive of three and half hours, I knew immediately that I was in bad trouble. Standing by a battered old Chevrolet truck were two drunk men in cowboy hats who looked at me like a great big pork chop that had just landed on their plate. They were obviously predators, no one else was around, my instincts were screaming at me to get out of there, but the sun was going down and I had been warned about bandits on the road at night.

I tried to make friends with them. They asked if I had a gun. When I said no, the man named Abel said, "You're up here alone and unarmed?" He gave a sinister chuckle, whistled and shook his head. The other man, Lupe, said, "Aren't you afraid someone will kill you?"

"Why would anyone want to kill me?" I said.

Abel said, "To please the trigger finger," and my blood ran cold.

He pointed to the silver scorpion decal on his straw cowboy hat and thumped his chest. "We are scorpions here," he said. "We are one hundred percent killers."

He poured out a small pile of cocaine on the palm of his hand and did the same for Lupe. Then they gulped the cocaine down their throats with a swig of beer. They toyed with me for a while. They named an exorbitant price for sleeping in an unfinished cabin, and then said I could sleep under the trees for free.

I drove over there in my truck and got out my sleeping bag. I knew they would come for me, so I went off and hid in the woods. I watched them walk over to my truck and look around for me. Then they got in their truck, turned the high beams on and roared through the woods looking for me. I ran and hid, ran and hid, heart hammering in pure terror, feeling like a hunted animal. Finally they gave up and drove away, and I went back to my truck and got into my sleeping bag, badly shaken.

Then I heard the Chevrolet engine again and immediately sprinted off into the woods. I crossed a broad shallow stream, climbed up a rocky slope and hid in a thicket. They had come back with flashlights and two other men. I didn't know if they wanted to rob me or kill me, but my guess was both, and it was easy to imagine Abel making it as painful and humiliating as possible. With two men driving around in the truck and two on foot with flashlights, they spent two hours combing the woods for me.

Then they went to where my truck was parked and lit a fire near it. As I shivered in the thicket, wearing only a T-shirt, they sat around the fire drinking. After several hours they lay down on the ground under blankets, but occasionally one would get up and put more wood on the fire. I slipped out of the thicket and went back across the stream. Creeping slowly and quietly on all fours, heart pounding, absolutely terrified but highly focused, I reached my sleeping bag, put on the warm shirt I had rolled up as a pillow, and got inside the bag.

Once I had stopped shivering, I crept over to my truck, unlocked the door, eased into the driver's seat and turned the ignition key. There was a sickening hiccup before the engine caught, and then I was roaring past them as they rose out of their blankets, looking bleary and confused. I gunned it up the hill that led out of there, expecting to see that big Chevy truck in my rearview mirror at any second. But I never did.

———

I drove for fifteen hours, stopping only for gas, and cursed myself repeatedly for being so stupid and reckless. I relived the experience many times over and realized that it would make good material in the book I was going to write, which didn't make me feel any less shaken and traumatized. Finally, exhausted, I pulled into a motel a few hours south of the U.S. border. I slept for a few hours and then drove home to Tucson, desperate for sanctuary and safety, tenderness and kindness. Mariah and I spent that night at my small rented house not far from Time Market, holding on to each other.

The next day as I was unpacking she walked back to her house and found that someone had broken in, masturbated into multiple condoms, and then hung the condoms from light switches all over the house. He had stabbed her mattress repeatedly and left a kitchen knife in the bed. He had masturbated all over the sheets. So much for safety and sanctuary. Two nights ago I had been hunted through the woods at night by Mexican hillbillies. Now a criminal pervert had defiled Mariah's house. It was a gruesome reminder that some parts of the world are more dangerous than others, but nowhere are women safe from men. I moved in with Mariah soon afterwards, but she never lost her fear of being in that house, and a break-in robbery didn't help. We moved to another rented house in Tucson, then another.

After my bad night in the Sierra Madre, I swore off risky assignments and travel in dangerous places. Gradually I became less jumpy and I was able to go camping again without jolts of fear and panicky hallucinations in the night. Then a year passed and a magazine in Britain asked me if I wanted to go down the Zambezi River in dug-out canoes with Sir Ranulph Fiennes, the English adventurer, and a small group. The river was well supplied with hippos and crocodiles, warned the editor, and I would be camping on its banks among lions, leopards, elephants, hyenas and other potentially dangerous creatures. I had never been to Africa before, because I had always found it too intimidating, but I said yes to the assignment, and that was the start of a long series of perilous and disease-ridden journeys in East and Central Africa.

Looking back on the compulsion to keep pushing my luck in

dangerous places, I can remember the feeling and how strong it was, but it no longer makes any sense to me. Not because I'm older and wiser and less robust, but because of Isobel. If I went off courting danger again and got myself killed, where would that leave her? Not only would she lose her father. She would be entirely justified in thinking that he threw his life away like an idiot.

*L*ike most buildings in Tucson in the 1870s, George Hand's saloon on the corner of Meyer Street and Mesilla was a one-story adobe with a flat earthen roof prone to leaking. He served rotgut whiskey and beer on a plain countertop bar and slept alone in a room in the back. Born in upstate New York, he had gone west with gold fever in 1849 and enlisted with the Union Army in California. After the war he drifted into the rough frontier town of Tucson, which one traveler described as "a city of mud-boxes, dingy and dilapidated . . . littered about with broken corrals, sheds, bake-ovens, carcasses of dead animals." He added, "Murderers, thieves, cut-throats, and gamblers formed the mass of the population."

Hand was a hard drinker in a hard-drinking town, and a friend and client of the local prostitutes. He was a good-hearted man with a long unkempt beard and hardly any meanness. He is remembered today because he kept a daily diary. In terse, blunt, laconic prose, he recorded bar brawls, cockfights, murders, fiestas, Apache raids, political elections, loneliness, tedium and debauchery. One historian regards the diaries as "sacred documents," which might be a stretch, but they do provide a candid view of Tucson's past, from which one central theme emerges.

> Aug. 18. Everybody got drunk.
>
> Aug. 19. Everybody still drunk.
>
> Nov. 16. John Dawson (drunk) made a demand (in fun) with a pistol on full cock for the purses of some loafers in Cockney Jack's saloon. He was knocked down and beaten unmercifully. I closed at 11 and went to bed very much intoxicated.
>
> June 25. The church was busy today. All the whores in town went to get Holy Water and pray off the sins of yesterday. No one killed today.
>
> Aug. 30. I was drunk early and late. Drunk all day. Very drunk. Disgustingly drunk. Everyone is drunk.

Chapter Nine

THE CHIRICAHUAS

On a scorching hot morning, we packed up my vehicle with gear and supplies and left the dogs in the care of Clark and Jill and her teenage daughter Tessa. This was Isobel's first camping trip and she was excited about it, although apprehensive about bears, mountain lions, jaguars, rattlesnakes and scorpions, and terribly disappointed by the ban on campfires. The Santa Catalinas were still ablaze above Tucson and the Forest Service was rightfully worried that a campfire might ignite a catastrophic wildfire in one of the other sky island mountain ranges. Isobel understood the logic of the ban when we explained it to her, but it meant she wouldn't be able to toast marshmallows and melt chocolate for s'mores, which was the part of camping she had been most excited about. So she groaned and wailed and worked herself up into a self-pitying tantrum that was partially faked and so defused fairly easily.

With the air conditioner on full blast and struggling to cool down the vehicle, we drove out of the city and gradually emerged from the enormous pall of hazy wildfire smoke that surrounded it. Heading southeast, we gained some elevation, left the cactus desert behind, threaded through some hills and came out into a region of arid grasslands and thornscrub that reminded me strongly of Kenya and Tanzania. Instead of umbrella thorn acacias, there were mesquite trees. Instead of giraffes and elephants, there were mule deer and pronghorn antelope. Both places were overgrazed by cattle under an enormous high-vaulted sky.

With Isobel watching cartoons on her pink tablet and oblivious to her surroundings, and her parents feeling slightly guilty about letting her watch but enjoying the peace and quiet, we drove on between mountain ranges into the Sulphur Springs Valley. It's a large flat expanse of degraded grasslands, dry lake beds, rural properties, and big corporate farms pumping out massive amounts of groundwater—most notably a mega-dairy operation with more than 200,000 cows and irrigated fields of alfalfa to feed them. Having mined out most of the copper, gold, silver and other precious metals from its bedrock, Arizona was now mining its aquifers, even though they had taken millions of years of rainfall to accumulate and could never be replaced, even though it threatened human survival in places like the Sulphur Springs Valley, where the aquifer was the only source of water.

The future was arriving early here. Wells were going dry in rural communities, deep fissures were opening up in the ground, and there was a rush of incoming corporate farms trying to make a quick profit while there was still some water left in the aquifer. Under Arizona law, groundwater is completely unregulated in rural areas, and many Arizonans and their state representatives were determined to keep it that way, because of hostility to government regulations, a quasi-religious belief in the sanctity of free market capitalism, and an ingrained Wild West attitude toward natural resources. Net result: industrial-scale farms owned by foreign and out-of-state corporations were able to pump out as much groundwater as they wanted without paying for it or even measuring how much they were pumping.

In the 1940s there was enough water in this aquifer to keep Tucson, the nearest city, supplied for more than 900 years. Now it was so depleted that only capital-rich corporations could afford to drill wells deep enough to reach what was left. It was a race to the bottom of the aquifer, and a race to the bottom of crazy. Some local people were now advocating for state management of the diminishing groundwater, but it was proving a hard sell to many of their neighbors. Even as their wells were going dry and they were trucking in water to take showers and flush their toilets, the idea of government oversight and regulation was still anathema to their politics and their self-image as rugged individualists.

———

Our destination was visible on the far side of the Sulphur Springs Valley. Rising out of the scrubby flatlands to nearly 10,000 feet, the Chiricahua Mountains are the largest of the sky island ranges, and they had been a favorite haunt of the Chiricahua Apaches. The most famous Apache chiefs and war leaders—Cochise, Geronimo, Mangas Coloradas, Victorio—all belonged to the loosely connected nomadic bands that the Spanish named Chiricahuas after the mountains in the heart of their territory. The Chiricahua Apaches ranged across southeast Arizona, southwest New Mexico, and northern Sonora and Chihuahua in Mexico. As Geronimo later recollected, they once moved like the wind. Like the other main Apache groups (Jicarilla, Lipan, Mescalero, Western Apaches), the Chiricahuas lived primarily by hunting, gathering and raiding, and they earned a reputation as fierce and formidable fighters who could disappear into a landscape, spring a devastating ambush, and travel long distances on foot at extraordinary speed.

In the floor-to-ceiling bookshelves in my new office, I had a collection of books about the Apaches—histories, biographies, ethnographies, firsthand accounts by Apache fighters and U.S. soldiers. I read them twenty years ago while researching my first book, which was about nomads in North America. Now, as I drove toward the mountains and saw the crags and rock spires they had used as a stronghold, what I remembered about the Apaches came back to me in a long loose train of thought.

They were relative newcomers here. We don't know when they arrived—sometime after AD 1000, perhaps as late as 1550—but their language, which is Athapaskan, tells us that they were originally from Canada. By invasion, conquest and military strength, they established a vast new homeland in the mountains and deserts of the Southwest, extending from West Texas to eastern Arizona and south into northern Mexico. They made enemies of nearly all their neighbors—the Tohono O'Odham to the west, the Navajo to the north, the Pueblo tribes and the Spanish in New Mexico, the Comanche further east, and both Indigenous tribes and Hispanic settlers in Mexico.

Maybe because I'm from Europe and take a long view of history, it doesn't seem that long ago that Apaches were the dominant people in this part of the world. In 1932, when he was interviewed by the ethnologist Grenville Goodwin, an Apache man in his nineties named Palmer Valor could remember when there were no white people in Arizona. In the same interview, he underscored the vital importance of raiding, which is essentially long-distance armed robbery, to the Apache economy and lifeway: "Our people used to go on raids down into Mexico to bring back horses, mules, burros and cattle. This is the way we used to take the property of the Mexicans and make a living off them. There were no White people to take things from in those days."

When white American miners and settlers started moving into Apache territory in the mid-1800s, they too were targeted for raids. The aim was to make off with the livestock and anything else worth stealing, including women and children, without getting into a fight, but it didn't always work out that way and an Apache raid could easily turn into a bloodbath. Warfare, however, was a completely different activity.

The purpose of war was to avenge the murder of a kinsman, or some other injustice. War parties were much larger than raiding parties, and the preparations required dancing, chanting, medicine making and bragging rituals that could go on for three or four nights. The warriors wore small hide war caps tied under the chin, often decorated with a knot of eagle or turkey feathers, and they routinely covered seventy or eighty miles a day on foot in rough terrain, running at a steady trot in moccasins with rawhide soles and high buckskin uppers.

It was a cruel, lawless, extraordinarily violent era in the Southwest, with whites and Mexicans routinely killing and scalping Apaches, making souvenirs from their body parts and slaughtering their women and children, and the Apaches murdering and mutilating with equal viciousness. All three groups were taking captives and the Apaches were notoriously inventive torturers. A chief named Eskiminzin described burying an American in an anthill and allowing the ants to eat his head off. Other methods included flaying the skin in strips from neck to heel, cutting off the limbs one by one until the victim bled to death, slicing off the penis and smashing the testicles with a rock, and lashing naked bodies to cactus plants with wet rawhide that contracted as it dried. The worst fate of all was to be turned over to the Apache women, who had crueler, more extended methods, although no worse than those employed by the ancient Romans, the medieval Catholic Church, the Spanish Inquisition, and many other civilizations in human history.

"Are we there yet?" came a small high voice from the back seat, snapping me out of my reverie. "We'll be there soon," I said. We were entering the foothills of the mountains on a bumpy dirt road. As we climbed higher, we saw mule deer moving through the trees, brightly colored birds that we didn't recognize, and I thought about how terrified I would have been here in the mid-nineteenth century.

What I envied most about the Apaches was their unsurpassed sensory awareness and encyclopedic knowledge of nature. They were renowned for their stealth, which they practiced by stalking wild animals, their ability to find and follow tracks on rocky ground, and their superb physical condition. The boys trained by running up and down mountains and they took predawn plunges in ice-covered lakes and rivers to toughen themselves. They learned to ride a horse down a steep slope while hanging off the animal's side and grabbing objects from the ground. As a kind of graduation ceremony into warriorhood, adolescent males had to run for two days without food or sleep.

Females could become warriors too and a notable example was Lozen, Victorio's beautiful sister, who rejected her numerous suitors to ride with the male warriors and sit on the war council. The Apache universe was a magical web of interconnected spiritual forces and natural phenomena, and Lozen had a supernatural power for locating the enemy. She would turn slowly in a circle with her arms outstretched while chanting a prayer to Ussen the Creator and Life-Giver. When her palms tingled and changed color, she knew she was facing the enemy.

———

High in the mountains we found a level piece of ground by a small flowing creek in a glade of oaks, pines, and junipers. It was such an obvious place to camp that I felt certain that countless generations of Chiricahuas must have camped here before us. It took the women about four hours to construct their wickiups—dome-shaped structures of brush and sticks laid on a framework of poles, with an animal hide or a blanket for a low door. It took us twenty minutes to put up our polyester tent with aluminum poles. As I hammered in the stakes with a rock, I wondered if Apache children had splashed around in the stream that Isobel thought was too cold to put her toes in, if their mothers had gathered acorns and juniper berries from these same trees or their forebears.

Isobel was scampering about in high spirits, invigorated by the cool fresh mountain air after months of being cooped up in the air-conditioned house or assaulted by the heat. As soon as the tent was up, she dived inside and squealed. "It's like a playhouse we get to sleep in!" We inflated the sleeping pads and unrolled the sleeping bags. Since we were car camping, we had brought pillows and blankets too. Mariah made the interior of the tent soft, comfortable and welcoming, and arranged Isobel's stuffed animals neatly on her pillow. By the time she finished, the sun was an orange globe on a ridgeline through the trees. I got two beers out of the cooler and set out the chips and salsa.

"This is why we came back to Arizona," said Mariah, sitting in her camp chair and letting out a long soulful sigh. "Do you remember talking in Mississippi about how much we missed this?"

"I do," I said. "And one of the main reasons we left Arizona is that we had stopped doing this." For some foolish reason, we had allowed our previous lives in Tucson to slide into a rut of work and chores and going out to restaurants and bars, and we had fallen out of the habit of going hiking and camping, even though these were our favorite things to do. As a result, we grew bored of Tucson and talked about moving somewhere else. Another factor was that Chuck Bowden had split up with Mary Martha and moved to Las Cruces, New Mexico. Tucson was a much duller place without him, and I realized how much I had relied on him for intellectual stimulation, social entertainment and general inspiration for writing and living.

Occasionally I would visit him in Las Cruces, where he was living with a woman named Molly Molloy, a librarian who was documenting the astronomical murder rate in Ciudad Juárez. He seemed calmer and less angry. He was drinking far less and had given up smoking. Yet he was still taking enormous risks by reporting and writing about the drug trade, and corruption and violence in Juárez, and after each visit I wondered if it would be the last time I would see him.

Around the same time, in 2010 and 2011, I wrote and hosted a TV documentary for the BBC based on my *American Nomads* book. When it was finished, I had a five-figure balance in my bank account for the first time in my life. Mariah and I decided to blow that money by moving to New York City for a year, never expecting that we would buy an old farmhouse in the Mississippi Delta before that year was up, and never dreaming that we would have a child together. I was dead set against the idea, because I didn't want to be tied down, and Mariah didn't want children either, or was at least leaning strongly against it. Then, at the age of fifty, in that Mississippi farmhouse, I came to the decision that parenthood was too big a thing to miss out on and I talked Mariah into it.

There were raw, sleep-deprived, tantrum-ravaged moments during

Isobel's first three years when we both regretted having her, but now we were in full agreement that she was the best thing that had ever happened to us. We watched her running about the campsite, collecting leaves, going down to the stream and trailing her fingers in it, exclaiming at butterflies. This was exactly what we hoped for during the long stressful process of leaving Mississippi and establishing ourselves once again in Arizona.

On a small single-burner stove, I warmed up some roasted green chile stew with pork and hominy that I had made the day before. Mariah prepared Isobel's "usual" as she called it: bread, salami, cheese, grapes, nuts. Our five-year-old daughter basically subsisted on charcuterie. We ate the hot spicy stew with flour tortillas, a garnish of thinly sliced cabbage and radishes, and a squirt of fresh lime juice. Then I washed the dishes and packed them away in the vehicle with all the food, not wanting to attract bears, while Mariah made Isobel her first s'mores with uncooked marshmallow and unmelted chocolate. She eagerly devoured it and declared, "I love s'mores! I love camping! This is so much fun!"

Isobel was delighted by the coziness of the tent, but found it difficult to fall asleep in such unfamiliar circumstances, and she needed lots of reassurance about bears and mountain lions. Mariah's lullabies didn't work, so I was called into the tent to sing my ballads. I know only three songs by heart and I had been singing them to Isobel since she was two, even though they weren't exactly age appropriate.

I started with "Gun Street Girl" by Tom Waits, a strange, haunting, off-kilter song about a guy who's having trouble with the law and blaming it all on a woman. Isobel loved it because the lyrics never clarified what was going on, which made it mysterious and always slightly out of reach, no matter how many times she heard it. Then I sang "Tennessee Stud," which features a murder, a love affair and a horse the color of the sun. Isobel finally fell asleep to "Blackjack Davey," a traditional ballad about a teenage mother who abandons her husband and baby to run off with a roving ladies' man. Mariah fell asleep soon afterwards and I stayed up late as usual, reading about Apaches by headlamp in a camp chair, missing a campfire but savoring the cool fragrant air, the trickling of the creek, the moonlight shining down through the trees and the glass of whiskey in my hand.

————

The speed and mobility of the Chiricahuas presented a unique problem to the U.S. Army during the Apache Wars, which were essentially a conflict over land and freedom. The government wanted to confine the Chiricahuas to a reservation like the other Apache groups and allow white Americans to take their lands. The Chiricahuas fought to avoid this fate and preserve their traditional life as nomadic raiders. Even though they were vastly outnumbered and outgunned, the Chiricahuas had the upper hand in the conflict, because the army found it almost impossible to find them or keep up with them. Apache warriors could travel for five consecutive days and nights without food or sleep. "My legs were like automobiles," Palmer Valor told Grenville Goodwin. On foot or on horses, the Chiricahuas could move faster than the cavalry through rough terrain, even when they were traveling with the elderly and women and children, who slept with pouches of food tied to their bodies in case they had to flee in the night. Boys and girls were both trained to shoot weapons and stay in peak physical condition, so they could fight or run as the circumstances required.

The warriors would raid white settlements for fresh horses, food supplies and ammunition, and then foil their pursuers by scattering into small groups with a plan to meet up again at some far distant place. They had no compunction against riding their horses to death and then eating them, which gave them another advantage over the cavalry, and they sometimes poisoned water sources with coyote intestines. During the day, they kept to the mountains where they were invisible, and they crossed the wide desert plains under cover of darkness. They were so expert at concealing themselves that it seemed as though every bush and rock suddenly turned into an Apache when they sprang an ambush.

In the summer of 1881 a Chiricahua chief named Nana launched the most astounding military campaign ever performed by his people. In two months, Nana with probably fifteen warriors rode three thousand miles—an average of fifty miles a day. They fought and won seven battles with the U.S. cavalry, raided more than a dozen ranches and towns, killed at least thirty-five people, and captured more than two hundred horses and mules. They were pursued by a thousand soldiers and hundreds of mounted civilians, and yet they made it safely back to their refuge in the Sierra Madre. Here's the kicker: Nana was at least seventy-five years old at the time, half-blind with a lame foot and hunched over with arthritis.

Geronimo, whose name we yelled as schoolboys in England, led the last Native war of resistance on the American continent, in the 1880s, and there was only one reason why the U.S. Army was eventually able to demand his surrender. A decade earlier General George Crook, a keen student of Apache ways, had come to the wise conclusion that the only way to catch Apaches was to use other Apaches. Crook understood that they had no sense of being one people or one nation. The different groups and bands were united only by language and cultural traits, and each pursued its own interests. He convinced Coyotero and White Mountain Apache men to work as scouts for the U.S. Army, and they proved so effective that the army continued to rely on them. It was Apache and Navajo scouts who tracked down Geronimo and his band and forced their final surrender at Skeleton Canyon, Arizona, in 1886.

True to form, the U.S. government did not provide Geronimo's people with their promised reservation. They were shipped off to Florida as prisoners on a train and they never saw their homelands again. Disgracefully, the Apache scouts who helped the U.S. Army find Geronimo were also put on the train. After a hellish confinement in Fort Marion, Florida, they were moved to Alabama and then Oklahoma. Geronimo became a minor celebrity, appearing in Wild West shows, shooting a buffalo in a staged hunt, riding in the first Cadillac, getting baptized into the Dutch Reformed Church, selling autographs and handicrafts, and publishing an evasive memoir.

In 1909, approximately eighty-five years old, he fell off his horse, drunk, lay on the cold ground all night, and contracted a fatal case of pneumonia.

———

In the morning Isobel saw wild turkeys for the first time. A group of seven traversed the steep slope behind our campsite, the males with blue naked heads and long red wattles, making their gobbling sounds. I asked her what she thought of them. She said, "They look kind of mean, but mainly they look weird." Then two mule deer descended the same slope to drink from the creek. We told Isobel to be still and quiet and watch them without staring because it would make them afraid. After breakfast, which was coffee and oatmeal for the grown-ups, hot chocolate and cereal for Isobel, I made the mistake of asking my daughter if she wanted to go on a hike. I had overlooked the fact that *hike* was a trigger word, eliciting an automatic scowl and a crossed-arms refusal. I let some time elapse and said brightly, "Let's go exploring! Let's see what we can find!"

This went well until the exploring turned into steady forward walking. With every fiber of my being, I yearned for a long vigorous hike in the fresh mountain air, but parenthood requires sacrifice. So I put my own desires aside and went exploring with Isobel in the way that she wanted to explore, which was slowly on a micro level in a small area close to the tent. She was attracted to small shiny rocks, animal tracks, a tuft of moss on a fallen piece of tree bark, a spider's web, leaves on the ground with interesting colors and shapes. A tiny feather was a thrilling treasure, and so was a minuscule white flower by the creek.

She wanted me to take photographs of her, but Mariah and I had turned our phones off and packed them away. At first this felt strange and unsettling, but then it became calming, relaxing and ultimately luxurious. We were in a beautiful, fascinating, wild place, and for once we were completely undistracted by texts, emails, news, social media, scams, lies, glitches and sales pitches, service renewal notices, spam, trash, phishing, and the latest political outrages. For once we were fully inhabiting the present moment and absorbing information through our senses, not our screens. The birds flitted through the trees, clouds passed across the sun, water trickled in the creek. No one was trying to sell us anything. No one knew where we were. It felt like the last honest place.

Having secured Geronimo's final surrender with false promises, General Nelson Miles implemented a plan to remove the Chiricahua warriors living peacefully on the Fort Apache reservation in East Central Arizona. They were invited to Washington, D.C., to meet the president and discuss their future. Four hundred and thirty-four men accepted the invitation. After several days on the train, they realized they had been tricked. The train was bound for Florida, where they would join Geronimo's people as prisoners of war.

The windows were barred and locked shut to prevent escape, and they were given no access to toilets. In the September heat, the stench became overpowering. A young warrior named Massai spent three days surreptitiously loosening the bars on a window. Somewhere in eastern Missouri, as the train slowed to climb a hill, he and a man named Gray Lizard pulled up the window, jumped out, rolled down the bank, and hid in the brush until dark.

Then, in their breechclouts and moccasins, they started walking southwest. The landscape was thick with houses, but they slipped through it without being seen. They continued to hide by day and travel at night, navigating by the stars. They ate roots and killed quail and rabbits with rocks. After four or five days, they came to a mining camp in the Ozarks. When the miners left for the day, they took meat, bread, knives, guns and ammunition. Now they could hunt deer.

They kept going southwest, living off the land. They crossed long stretches of desert, using a deer's stomach as a water bag, and finally reached familiar mountains in southern New Mexico. Having traveled some 1,200 miles, the two men split up. Gray Lizard went to the San Carlos Apache reservation in Arizona. Massai became a lone raider, stealing cattle and robbing travelers and traders along the Arizona–New Mexico border. Yearning for a wife, he kidnapped a young woman from the Mescalero Apache reservation, and they had several children together. Some accounts say Massai was killed in a shootout in 1911. Others say he joined the last free Apaches in the Sierra Madre.

Chapter Ten

VIOLENCE AND DELUSION

I had driven that stretch of East Golf Links Road several times since we returned, and I had noticed the corner property with carefully stenciled messages on its exterior block walls. The messages were slightly cryptic but appeared to be tributes to dead family members who had served in the U.S. military, with a denunciation of President Trump underneath: "I am ashamed at who this country is allowing to call himself com. in chief."

On the afternoon of Election Day 2020, the owner of this property, Robert Norwood, an ex-soldier aged sixty-three, was using a can of spray paint to deliver a more urgent message. "I have not watched 1 sec of this cluster fuck election. But if you can't c u should put this country before your party u are part of the problem not the solution," he wrote on one side of his corner wall. On the other: "My family has (5) gen. in this. So far (6) lives lost in service to it. So don't drive by waving your Trump flags."

As Norwood was finishing up with his spray can, a convoy of Trump supporters drove along East Golf Links Road with flags flying from their vehicles. One of them, a scrappy fifty-three-year-old named John Hodson, saw Norwood and pulled over in his Jeep Cherokee. Hodson didn't understand that Norwood was spray-painting messages on his own property and accused him of vandalism. The ensuing argument turned physical. As they wrestled on the ground, Hodson got the older man in a choke hold.

Two bystanders called the police and tried to break it up. Hodson continued to choke Norwood's throat. "This is the most American thing I can be doing," he told the horrified bystanders, repeating that extraordinary sentence over and over again, like an incantation, until Norwood's face went purple and he stopped breathing. Hodson was arrested for manslaughter, and to my astonishment a judge set him free on bond until his trial.

It was a horrible, stupid, chilling crime, but I didn't find it that surprising because Arizona's homicide rate was soaring, people were angry and divided over politics and the pandemic, and the state felt primed for political violence. The George Floyd protest marches in Phoenix had turned ugly that summer, with protestors vandalizing property and firing shots in the air, and the police responding aggressively with tear gas, pepper spray, physical assaults, and hundreds of arrests.

At the Republican Party headquarters in Bullhead City, a meeting was disrupted by a gunshot shattering the window by the door. Fortunately no one was hurt. When the Democratic Party headquarters in Phoenix was burned down by an arsonist, it seemed emblematic of the volatile political climate, although the arsonist turned out to be a mentally unstable Democratic activist and former volunteer.

Large swaths of the population were heavily armed and gripped by paranoid delusions about communists, child sex traffickers, Jewish bankers, the federal government, and other evil conspirators against conservative Christian America. The state was home to half a dozen militias and a slew of ultra-far-right political groups, and it had emerged as an epicenter of QAnon activity, which was not surprising in the least. As the author Tom Zoellner has observed, Arizona doesn't reflect national trends. It exaggerates them.

According to polls, nearly 30 percent of Arizona Trump supporters believed the core tenets of the QAnon conspiracy theory: a secretive cabal of Satan-worshipping, blood-drinking Democratic elitists was running a global child sex trafficking network, controlling governments and media around the world, and plotting to destroy Donald Trump, who would single-handedly dismantle the cabal. It was surely one of the wackiest cases of mass hysteria in American history, right up there with the Salem witch trials, or the Satanic panic over false accusations of ritual child abuse in the 1980s.

A man pled guilty to terrorism charges in Arizona after he blocked the Hoover Dam with an armored truck containing two assault rifles, two handguns, and more than 900 rounds of ammunition. He was holding up a sign that read: "Release the OIG report," a prominent QAnon demand related to Hillary Clinton and the FBI. In Sedona, in the gorgeous red rock country northwest of Phoenix, a QAnon believer burst into a Catholic chapel and smashed up the altar with a crowbar while screaming to startled onlookers about the Catholic Church's involvement in child sex trafficking. Arizona had more QAnon-friendly elected officials than any other state (followed by Florida and California) and it was home to some key Q influencers, including a couple in Gilbert who superspread the theory that Wayfair, the online furniture company, was engaged in child sex trafficking.

Then there was Austin Steinbart, a Scottsdale man in his twenties who called himself BabyQ. He and thousands of followers believed that the "Q" who had been dropping messages about the conspiracy on

8Chan and other internet forums was Steinbart's future self, sending messages back through time to Steinbart's present-day self. He was a divisive figure among the 30 million QAnon adherents in the United States. They had no trouble believing that Hollywood actors ate babies, or that Hillary Clinton tortured children to death, drank their blood, harvested their adrenochrome and cut off their faces to wear as masks, but many of them found Austin Steinbart's time-travel claims too far-fetched and dismissed him as a kook.

In April of that election year, Steinbart was arrested for leading a harassment and extortion campaign against a file-sharing company. In September he was arrested for smoking weed in violation of his court release agreement, and for being in possession of an artificial penis called a Whizzinator, designed to smuggle clean urine into a drug test. After serving 225 days in jail on his extortion charges, Steinbart was then hired as a political campaign manager by a Republican candidate running for U.S. Congress, which made my brain hurt and plead for mercy. But that was often the way of things in Arizona. Just when you thought you'd reached the bottom of crazy, another level opened up.

Guess which state has the highest reported levels of road rage and is second for road rage shootings? Correct on both counts! We have plenty of friendly, decent people in our beautiful state, but a broad streak of belligerence and hostility runs through it too. After nine years in Mississippi, where we never saw profanity on a bumper sticker, a T-shirt, or a hat, we were shocked to see the "Fuck You" and "Fuck Gun Control" bumper stickers in Arizona. Another sticker featured the word *Arizona* with an angry snorting bull and two raised middle fingers, which really got the point across.

Gunfights were breaking out at convenience stores, strip malls and outlet malls. A woman hiking was stabbed to death by a random stranger on the trail. A group of affluent teenagers in suburban Gilbert were carrying out vicious attacks with brass knuckles, culminating in the murder of sixteen-year-old Preston Lord. A twenty-year-old incel opened up with an assault rifle at the Westgate shopping mall in the Phoenix suburb of Glendale. He managed to film the attack with his cellphone while blasting away with his AR-15 in the other hand, and posted the video to Snapchat while he was still shooting. He wounded three people and said it was "society's fault." Fentanyl overdose was the leading cause of death for teenagers here in Pima County, with gun violence and suicide close behind. In Tucson, two teenagers beat a disabled man to death with a baseball bat.

Sitting in my backyard under the stars and the moon could be so quiet and peaceful, except on those nights when gunshots rang out, or police helicopters combed the neighborhood. Sometimes the violence came closer. A thirty-year-old math tutor who was teaching Jill's son and one of our real estate agent Anne's daughters was shot and killed in a random drive-by attack as he took a Saturday-afternoon fitness walk about a mile from our house. I kept telling myself that the risk of violence was still very low. I kept telling myself that I had spent many years traveling in far more dangerous places. But I became extremely wary and watchful in public, especially at night, and hypervigilant on the roads where drivers were blasting through red lights and driving at insane speeds. Arizona's traffic fatalities were soaring right alongside its homicides.

———

On Election Day, as John Hodson was strangling Robert Norwood in the name of American patriotism, conspiracy theories were hatching, multiplying, crossbreeding and proliferating at viral speeds. MAGA Republicans were convinced that voter fraud was taking place in Maricopa County, which contains most of the Greater Phoenix megasprawl and over 60 percent of Arizona's population. That evening hundreds of suspicious Trump supporters gathered outside the county election center in downtown Phoenix. Some were dressed in full tactical gear and carrying AR-15s, and armed county sheriffs barricaded the building. The protestors waved flags and chanted, "Where are the votes? Why aren't you counting? Count the damn ballots!" Inside the building, that's exactly what 4,800 citizen volunteers were doing.

The next day, after Fox News called Arizona for Biden, far-right U.S. congressman and former dentist Paul Gosar showed up with a flag-waving entourage and led the nation's first Stop the Steal rally. They marched from the architectural travesty of the Arizona state capitol to the downtown elections center, where a big crowd of Trump supporters, including Proud Boys, Oath Keepers and members of the Three Percenters militia group, were gathered. Many were armed. A line of Maricopa County sheriff's deputies prevented them from entering the building, and heavily armed deputies in tactical gear were waiting inside. Paul Gosar lifted up his megaphone and yelled, "Patriots! They're not gonna steal this election from us, are they?"

The protests continued night after night, reaching the brink of violence with counterprotestors, but remaining peaceful. The most eye-catching figure at these protests was a muscular, shirtless, tattooed young man with a bison-horned coyote fur headdress and his face painted red, white and blue. Jake Angeli, born in Phoenix as Jacob Chansley, also known as the QAnon Shaman, had been ejected from the navy for refusing to take the anthrax vaccine. He was now trying to establish himself as an actor and voice-over artist while living with his mother and eating a strictly organic diet. He was a familiar figure at rallies and protests in the Phoenix area, and before the election he had harangued shoppers at the Arrowhead Towne Center in Glendale, bellowing that the spiral triangles symbol near the bathroom were "FBI pedophile codes." I thought of him as an only-in-Arizona character, but soon he would be known all over the world as the painted face of the January 6 insurrection at the U.S. Capitol.

It was fitting that the Stop the Steal movement began in Arizona, because no other state would go so long and hard for election conspiracy theories, or cling so fiercely to the fantasy that Donald Trump won the 2020 election. But why was this? Maybe because Arizona is a haphazard improvisation, a random clumping together of people from elsewhere with no hard-and-fast rules. The state was largely built on the idea that you can move here and reinvent yourself in the desert sunshine—be whoever you want to be, and believe whatever you want. There's a high degree of freedom and tolerance—you do your thing and I'll do mine—and a make-believe quality to life, especially in Maricopa County where artificial lakes, fountains, lawns, swimming pools, golf courses and omnipresent air conditioning make it easy to pretend you're not in the Sonoran Desert. The author Tom Zoellner defined the Arizona ethos as follows: "Reality must be defeated, and a more comforting vision set in its place."

Maybe a higher percentage of people in Arizona are at home in the new post-truth world. Maybe they're more gullible or more easily swept up into feverish mass delusions. The most popular election conspiracy theory held that the Maricopa County Board of Supervisors, which runs the county's elections, had thrown the election to Joe Biden, despite the fact that the board was 4–1 Republican. Multiple death threats were leveled at the supervisors and their families. Chanting mobs gathered outside their homes and offices, reminding me of contested election scenes I had witnessed in Africa. Evidence-free accusations flew of ballot-stuffing, machine-hacking, fake ballots, ballots left untended, dead people and illegal immigrants voting by the thousands or the hundreds of thousands, collusion with the Democrats, the Clintons, Chinese communists, South Koreans.

The most outlandish theory targeted Maricopa County supervisor and lifelong Republican Clint Hickman, whose family owns a large-scale egg business. He was accused of stealing paper ballots, feeding them to 162,000 chickens, and then setting fire to two barns to incinerate all the chickens. This accusation went viral after being promoted by the influential right-wing website Gateway Pundit and the far-right Arizona Patriot Party, which conducted its own investigation at the alleged crime scene. It was seriously entertained by at least one Republican lawmaker. What actually happened was an accidental fire that killed 166,000 egg-laying hens, but that was impossible for the conspiracy-minded to believe. They found it far more plausible that Hickman had somehow forced the chickens to eat stolen ballots and then burned down his barns to destroy the evidence in their stomachs.

———

Three days after Election Day, a seventy-three-year-old Trump supporter loaded his 12-gauge shotgun and walked out of his front door, just a few blocks away from our house. He lived across the street from an elementary school that he regarded as an "indoctrination center for youth" run by woke progressives. He marched into the school's parking lot and told an employee, "You need to get out of here. I'm gonna start the next Civil War and I'm gonna shoot up the place."

He blasted away at the vehicles in the school's parking lot, and then took aim at the buildings. Thankfully the students were learning remotely and there were only a few people on campus. A teacher saw him shooting cars right outside her window. She dropped to the floor and crawled to the bathroom, where she and two colleagues waited in terror.

The school was placed on lockdown and people in the neighborhood were told not to leave their homes, but the shooter went back to his house and surrendered to a SWAT team and a hostage negotiator. During the patrol-car ride to the police station, he told the officer driving why he was so angry. The officer reported his remarks as follows: "'Trump won and they are trying to steal' the election from Trump. . . . 'commies' and 'leftists' were stealing the election. He advised that he waited several days after the election for someone to fight against what was happening, and no one was 'forming militias and taking the country back.'"

Journalists later discovered that the shooter was a devoted listener to right-wing radio with fourteen felony convictions and bipolar disorder. He was held in custody on $25,000 bond and three teachers were suing him to pay for the damages to their cars.

We first learned about the shooting in a text message from the school administration, because Isobel was attending kindergarten in person that day at the school's other campus. Even though she hadn't been in danger, I felt a sickening jolt of panic and dread, a desire to move to somewhere else in the world where school shootings didn't happen, and a powerful but short-lived urge to beat the shooter's head into pulp with the stock of his 12-gauge shotgun. When I picked Isobel up from school that afternoon, she didn't know anything about the shooting at the other campus, because the administration had decided not to tell the students about it. I didn't mention it either because I wanted her to feel safe. She could tell that something was slightly off because I hugged her so tightly and had tears in my eyes and found it difficult to let her go.

*P*rospector Ed Schieffelin was a tall, eccentric loner with black hair below his shoulders, a long beard full of knots and mats, and clothing patched together from corduroy, flannel and deerskin. In 1877, when he went looking for gold and silver in Chiricahua Apache country, people said all he would find was his own tombstone. Instead he made the richest silver strike in Arizona history and named it Tombstone.

A settlement of the same name sprang up nearby and rapidly became the biggest boomtown in the West, with a population of 15,000 or 20,000, including famous gunfighters like Wyatt Earp and Doc Holliday, who got into a famous gunfight in an empty lot six doors west of the O.K. Corral's back entrance.

In addition to 110 saloons, 14 gambling halls and innumerable brothels, the town had schools, churches, a bowling alley, an ice cream parlor and a high-toned French restaurant with seafood imported from California. A popular drink, belying Tombstone's straight whiskey reputation, was a frothy, bubbly, sweetened concoction called a gin fizz toddy.

Brothel workers were referred to as good-time girls, soiled doves, ladies of the evening and ceiling experts. One described herself as "horizontally employed." Colorful monikers were in vogue: Crazy Horse Lil, Madam Mustache, Little Gertie the Gold Dollar, Lizette the Flying Nymph. The most formidable woman in Tombstone was Big Minnie Bignon, co-owner with her husband of the Bird Cage Theater, saloon, gambling hall and brothel. Six feet tall and 230 pounds, she once grabbed a pistol-waving drunkard, carried him outside and threw him halfway across the street. She was also a ballet dancer who strolled around town and pirouetted across the stage in pink tights.

Boom went to bust in less than a decade. As the mines deepened, they flooded with groundwater. Pumps were installed, but a fire destroyed them and the denizens of Tombstone moved on. Ed Schieffelin, even though he was rich and married, couldn't stop prospecting. He died alone in a miner's cabin in Oregon and was buried in Tombstone, as he'd requested, wearing miner's clothes with a pick and a canteen.

Chapter Eleven

PATTERNS OF LIFE

After the driest summer on record, the winter rains failed us too. In addition to cold nights and warm afternoon sunshine, December, January and February are supposed to deliver steady soaking rains that last for a couple of days and fall as snow at higher elevations. In the Navajo tradition they're known as female rains, in contrast to the dramatic sky-splitting thunderstorms of summer, which are male rains. Across the border in Sonora, the winter rains are called *las equipatas*, little packages. We received only a few feeble ones, amounting to less than an inch. There was a powerful gloomy temptation to think that this was the new normal in the era of climate change, but it was equally likely that it had just been a particularly dry summer and winter.

Tucson, we learned, was in no immediate danger of running out of water, even though the great majority of our supply came from the dwindling, overtaxed Colorado River via the Central Arizona Project (CAP) canal. Tucson's allocation was 144,000 acre-feet a year, but we had been using only about 100,000 acre-feet. The rest was stored in large excavated basins outside the city and allowed to sink down into the earth and replenish the aquifer. Drastic cuts to our CAP water were expected in the near future, in which case the city would have to go back to pumping groundwater and depleting the aquifer again.

It was impossible to say when Tucson might run out of water because there were too many unknown variables in the future—the rate of population growth, the effects of climate change on rainfall patterns and the Colorado River, how much water would be allotted to agriculture, how much conservation, recycling, and rainfall capture would be implemented in the cities. It was possible that Mexico would agree to a massive desalinization plant on the Sea of Cortez to supply water to Arizona, and some Arizona lawmakers were calling on the federal government to build a 1,000-mile pipeline from the Mississippi River. The worst-case scenario was running out of water in forty years, and the most optimistic was never.

We continued to add plants and trees in the backyard—more tecomas, agaves and milkweeds, Texas rangers, beebrush, a skeleton-leaf goldeneye, a fig tree, a pomegranate tree, a Texas redbud tree. Mariah watered them with hoses and sprinklers until we finally paid the money to have a drip irrigation system installed. A network of pipes and emitters, controlled by a timer, now dribbled water on the roots of the plants—a far more efficient method, although our water usage was still higher than average for Tucson. We justified it by telling ourselves that we were creating cooling shade and a habitat for insects, worms, lizards and birds.

Two feeders filled with sugar water, hanging from the rim of the ramada, persuaded some of the hummingbirds to stay on the property for the winter. The females were shy, but we could get close to the males, and vice versa. One broad-billed hummingbird would hover on his whirring wings just a few inches away from our faces, as if inspecting us. With his vivid red bill and shimmering emerald and sapphire feathers, he was like a bird-shaped piece of jewelry. Isobel named him Mr. Glamourzon. One day, as she was admiring him perched on the fig tree, she said, "Mr. Glamourzon, if you were human, I would marry you." He weighed less than a nickel and his heart beat 1,200 times a minute. On cold mornings, tiny puffs of steam rose from his tongue as he flicked it out.

We also had Anna's hummingbirds. The males were green with rosy-red throats and crowns—one of them was almost crimson. In their courtship displays, they would zoom up high in the air and then plummet down in a near-vertical dive. At the bottom of the arc, they would make an explosive popping sound with their tail feathers and then zoom up again to repeat the performance. They oriented these spectacular dives so that the sun reflected from their iridescent throats and crowns toward the female who was the object of the display. I studied her closely but could discern no sign that she was impressed by any of her suitors.

Taking a cue from one of our neighbors, we set out bowls of water in the unfenced front yard for the urban wildlife and the birds. Despite some predation, there was still a good-sized covey of Gambel's quail on the block, but none of us had seen the roadrunner for a couple of months and he was presumed dead. I missed him as a kind of outrageous neighborhood character. He ran so fast, with such an improbable gait, and I loved to watch him dancing with his kills on top of Mariah's car, with his feet drumming on the roof and his shaggy crest flipping up and down. His departure made life slightly less perilous for the other birds, but they still had to contend with the ever-present Cooper's hawks and a great horned owl, and the ground-nesting quail were particularly vulnerable to coyotes, bobcats and feral cats.

Richard Grant

The human inhabitants of the neighborhood were a varied bunch. You were never far from an antiracist yard sign or a little free library, but we also had some MAGA-hat wearers and two houses festooned with American flags and right-wing signs. Most of the neighbors were white, with a smattering of African Americans and Hispanics, a couple of Chinese Americans, a fairly high proportion of gay and lesbian couples, a German, a Canadian, and a Trinidadian named Kevin and his Zambian wife Rudo, who both worked at the university and were close friends with Clark and Jill.

Professions ranged from electronic music producer to pest exterminator, food truck vendor to radiocarbon dating expert. There were students, professors, university employees and an abundance of retirees. One retired couple had shelves by their front gate, on which they set out plants, seedlings, packets of wildflower seeds, fresh fruit from their citrus trees, books, magazines and sometimes home-baked cookies— all for passersby to take and enjoy for free. Mariah picked up several plants there and greatly admired their front yard, which was shady and attractively overgrown, always bright with flowers and a magnet for birds, butterflies, bees and the neighborhood javelinas, who often came through our front yard at night too.

A just-retired physical therapist named Karen, originally from Wisconsin, kept an eye on our block and a group email for the people who lived on it. We used it to send invitations to Isobel's inaugural lemonade stand, which also featured Mariah's home-baked chocolate chip cookies for 50 cents and free water in bowls for dogs. I was touched that so many neighbors came out to support my daughter's enterprise and I enjoyed talking to them; we had barely met each other before, mainly because of the pandemic. Afterwards I thanked them for coming and suggested a future front porch gathering with wine, beer and snacks.

This was met with polite silence, which seemed on brand for Tucson. It was an accepting, tolerant place with a lot of kind, decent people who guarded themselves quite closely. Compared to New York, it was easygoing and welcoming. Compared to Mississippi, it was reserved and evasive.

Homeless people came through the neighborhood often, checking the alleys and dumpsters, or making their way to a nearby church that looked after them, or just passing through on the way to somewhere else. I was on nodding terms with a few of them. A white guy and a Black guy in their mid-forties were always together, pushing their shopping cart of belongings. They would always call out the same slightly derisive greeting when they saw me: "Hey family man!" And I would think back on my own experiences of homelessness—living on the streets of the French Quarter in New Orleans and sleeping in the Marriott Hotel parking lot, sleeping in the back seat of my dented 1969 Buick station wagon for a few months, riding freight trains and flopping in missions, giving no indications of any sort that I would one day end up as a family man.

Every few days I would see a twitchy, scrawny, rat-faced meth head—sagging pants, wife-beater undershirt, baseball cap with the brim upturned, tattoos everywhere—riding a low-slung bicycle around the neighborhood, casing the front porches, sometimes peering over gates into people's yards. One night I failed to lock my vehicle and I was punished for it by a thief who stole some tools and a good pair of binoculars. I wondered if it was the meth head, but he wasn't the only sketchy character drifting through the neighborhood, and sometimes I felt glad that I had a deer rifle and ammunition in the house.

It was a sadness for Isobel when Coco, the only kid on our street and her first friend in Tucson, moved away with her family. The same thing kept happening with her friends at school. "Where is Cristina moving to?" I asked. "The Bay Area," said Isobel glumly, with no clue where that was or what city it contained. Her friend Brooklyn relocated to Washington State and Yogurt Owen moved to San Diego, having become legend for forcing a mouthful of yogurt out of his nose and then eating it again—"the grossest thing ever," according to Isobel. With the exception of her cute little cousin Asher and a nice, kind classmate named David, she had a very low opinion of boys: "Why are they so gross? Why are they so annoying?" One day she left her diary open and we saw this: "Things that make me happy: sugar. Things that made me sad: boys."

Another friend was moving to Indiana and another to Oregon. "How do you feel about all this moving away?" I asked her. "I wish all the annoying boys in my class would move away like Yogurt Owen did," she retorted.

Tucson could feel like a waystation. There was a constant conversation taking place in the city about where people had come from and where they were thinking of moving next and inevitably it had a weakening effect on human connections. Probably the most active back-and-forth migration corridor was between Tucson and the Pacific Northwest, with an overabundance of sunshine and rain at either end of it, but people were showing up in Tucson from all over the country and the world. Since moving back, I had met people from Ethiopia, Cameroon, South Africa, Iran, Morocco, Russia, Turkey, Tasmania, Chile, China, Japan, France, Italy, England and at least a dozen other countries.

People were leaving Tucson in all directions too. Kevin and Rudo were buying a farm in Zambia. Another couple we knew was moving to Portugal. Clark and Jill were talking about moving to Italy, and so were our friends who owned Time Market. Italy sounded enticing to me too, but I didn't want to uproot the family again and I couldn't stand the thought of another move. Isobel said she liked being a Tucson girl, but she was still telling everyone proudly that she was from Mississippi.

———————

That spring, like a weather system moving into our household, Isobel's Mississippi grandmother came for her first visit. We had never seen our daughter so excited. She was jumping up and down and squealing for days in advance. We were all delighted to see Cathy Thompson again, standing outside the Tucson airport with an enormous suitcase stuffed full of gifts and a thrilled expression on her face. She could be bossy and sometimes she got competitive with Mariah, but she was bighearted, enthusiastic and fun, with a lively sense of humor and a Mama Bear's toughness when she needed it, and we all loved her. Part of Isobel's excitement flowed from the knowledge that she would get deluged with toys, clothes, makeup kits, candy, cookies, ice cream and whatever else she wanted, including long hours of cartoons and snacking on junk food in bed. Cathy had been fairly strict with her own three daughters, but she believed strongly that it was a grandmother's duty to spoil her granddaughter rotten.

To deal with the fact that Cathy was a Trumper and we had voted Democrat, we used the compartmentalization method, which was taught to us by a liberal friend when we arrived in Mississippi. We placed each other's politics in an imaginary compartment and sealed it shut. We focused instead on the qualities that we loved, enjoyed and admired in each other. Sometimes the seal worked its way loose and questions were asked, opinions exchanged. Sometimes Cathy took a provocative pleasure in deliberately breaking the seal and trying to get a reaction. But most of the time politics stayed in the compartment, because we all shared the belief that our political views were just one small part of who we were, and ultimately not that important.

Cathy, who gained her knowledge of current affairs from Fox News, was alarmed to be so near the Mexican border. She was being told repeatedly that it was wide-open and overrun with cartels, rapists, human traffickers, fentanyl smugglers and illegal aliens, all pouring into Southern Arizona like an invading army of brown-skinned deviants. "Doesn't it make you nervous?" she asked. "It really doesn't," said Mariah. Admittedly, we might have loosened the seal a little by driving Cathy deep into South Tucson to eat among Mexicans and Mexican Americans at a scruffy little taqueria with great Sonoran food. While we ate our carne asada tacos, I pointed out some of the similarities between Mexican American culture and Mississippi culture: strong family values, respect for elders, high church attendance, majority opposition to abortion, widespread support for law enforcement, widespread belief in the American dream.

"Now," said Cathy to Isobel, sealing the compartment shut again, "are you ready to go home and open presents and snuggle up in bed and watch cartoons with your Nonna?"

We didn't see much of Isobel for the rest of Cathy's visit. They made an outing to the playground at the park, where Cathy did excellent work helping Isobel get over her fear of climbing. They went on a brief shopping spree and visited the local ice cream parlor. But most of the time they stayed in Isobel's room playing Barbies and make-believe games, chatting away and painting nails, until Cathy emerged around five p.m. calling for margaritas in the backyard. She liked the way I made them—no triple sec or Cointreau, but simple syrup and the oil expressed from a fat twist of fresh orange peel, with blanco tequila and fresh lime juice. After an early dinner, they shut themselves up in Isobel's room again and stayed up way too late eating candy and watching cartoons. That set the pattern for the visit and for future visits. We didn't really understand why Cathy felt it was so important to deprive Isobel of sleep and pack her full of sugar, but we let them get on with it because they were enjoying it so much, and we braced ourselves for the inevitable sobbing meltdown when Cathy had to fly home, and the battles and tantrums that would ensue when Isobel had to follow the rules again.

———

The best thing about the neighborhood was having Clark and Jill a few blocks away; we secretly hoped that their plan to move to Italy wouldn't work out. With his multiple comorbidities, Clark was still very COVID-wary, but we were now meeting up regularly in their backyard or ours for socially distanced wine and snacks and sometimes dinner. Mariah told Clark that he was lucky to have Jill, a smart, beautiful, vibrant and highly capable woman, divorced with two teenage children and working in a high-level administrative position at the university. "I don't think you understand how lucky I am," said Clark. "Jill is the only reason I'm still alive. She literally saved my life."

When we left Tucson, Clark was single and lonely, living by himself and sinking ever deeper into debt from visits to the emergency room with ketoacidosis and diabetic seizures in the world's only industrialized nation without universal health coverage. He was addicted to cigarettes, smoking a lot of weed, debauching himself fairly regularly with whiskey and pills, and more disheartened than I had ever seen him. There was almost no demand for his handcrafted custom furniture. His acting career had stalled out, mainly because he was unable to abandon his aged father and move to New Mexico, where movie and television production was booming. He was in chronic pain from old injuries, and type 1 diabetes was slowly destroying his kidneys and his eyesight. It was all too easy to see him succumbing to an early death in some squalid boar's nest bachelor apartment. Fortunately he was still handsome, charismatic and interesting enough to catch Jill's attention when they met at a party.

It was an outdoor party in a bohemian paradise Tucson backyard with flames emerging from sandpits, rusty metal sculptures, cacti in sawed-off industrial barrels and an outdoor bar with furniture. Clark and Jill sat across the bar from each other and had one of those long, intense conversations that makes everything else fade away into the background. At one point Clark talked about his cowboy side and his western code of honor. Jill told him she wasn't impressed. She had lived in rural Colorado and most of the cowboys she met there were jerks. Clark was wearing a leather biker jacket, clutching a pack of cigarettes, and rolling joint after joint. Jill had an eleven-year-old and a nine-year-old at home. She thought to herself, *No way I'm dating this guy.*

After the party Clark started sending her "good morning" and "good evening" texts every day. Jill told him it was too much and he needed to stop. She also told him that she couldn't seriously date a smoker. Her resistance and aloofness—which was genuine, not a tactic—only increased his ardor. She was enjoying being single, but she did agree to go to dinner with Clark at a BYOB Ethiopian restaurant just south of downtown.

Jill arrived late and sweaty on her bicycle. Clark was dressed well and holding a very good bottle of Sean Thackrey wine that he had been saving for five years, waiting for the right occasion. Jill looked at him and thought, *Who are you?* He seemed far more intriguing and substantial than the grown-up frat boys and flaky artists she had given up dating. And he had a nicotine patch on his arm. That first date continued in various venues for the next sixteen hours.

On the second date, they drove out into the desert and Clark took her on foot to a beautiful spot she had never seen before. They drank some wine and watched the sunset, and then he started behaving strangely. The light went out of his eyes and his speech was slurring. She knew he was diabetic and surmised correctly that he was having a massive blood sugar crash. There was a flask of orange juice in his satchel, but the flask was now empty and he had brought no food. It was dark and she had no idea how to get back to the car. She asked Clark, but he didn't know where he was. His brain had stopped working for lack of fuel.

Relying on her instincts, Jill managed to get them both back to the car. She gave him a bag of peanut butter pretzels that she kept in the car for her children. He ate the pretzels but was still uncommunicative. Unsure what to do, she drove to a restaurant and ordered him chicken marsala. As Clark ate the food, his blood sugar rose back to normal and he apologized. "If you decide not to date me, I totally understand," he said. But Jill didn't want to break up with him.

Three weeks later, Clark had a routine surgery on the meniscus of his knee. It became infected, he woke up vomiting at five a.m., and Jill drove him to the hospital, where he stayed for ten days. Three months later, after three more surgeries, he was able to transition from a walking frame to crutches. Some of Jill's friends implored her to ditch Clark as too much burden, but she was falling in love with him and there was no one else around to take care of him. "We felt robbed of that honeymoon phase in a relationship, when everything is new and exciting," Jill told me. "Instead it was just hospitals and surgeries and walking frames. He told me, 'I will spend the rest of my life making this up to you.'" The orthopedic surgeon thought he would never walk normally again, but Clark harnessed his considerable powers of determination and kept pushing himself until he could walk without limping. This took two years.

He should have been on disability long ago, but he had never got around to the daunting paperwork. Jill assembled a two-inch-thick binder, organized with color tabs, that documented all his medical conditions. Within a matter of weeks, Social Security deposited $15,000 in Clark's bank account, enabling him to bargain down his medical debt, and he started getting a regular monthly disability payment. Then she pulled off another coup by adding him, at no extra cost, to her health insurance as a domestic partner. Now, for the first time in his life, Clark had a first-rate primary care doctor and specialists for his diabetes, his kidneys, his eyes and his cancer-prone skin.

On the night that Clark moved into Jill's house, after a long day of lifting and carrying boxes, his face turned gray and he started vomiting violently. "Every time I lay down I can't breathe," he said. *Oh my god,* Jill thought, *he's having a heart attack.* Over Clark's objections, she rushed him to the emergency room and sure enough, it was a massive heart attack, with 100 percent blockage of the left anterior descending artery, the so-called widow-maker.

This was one of five times that Jill had directly saved Clark's life by taking him to the emergency room, but she had also saved it by getting him on disability and properly insured, by pressuring him to give up smoking and take better care of himself, and by being there and doing the right thing when he had medical emergencies. She had lost track of how many times she had called 911. She had learned how to inject him with glucagon when he was having diabetic seizures, and taught her children how to do it too.

When Clark recovered from his knee surgeries and his heart attack, he set about trying to repay his unpayable debts to Jill. He remodeled her bathroom and was now remodeling her kitchen. He built an elegant wooden building in the backyard that contained his workshop and lots of storage space. He drew up plans for a guesthouse that he planned to build in the far quadrant of the backyard, so he and Jill could live in it when she retired, maybe spending half the year in Italy and renting out the main house for income.

"He's always concerned that he doesn't contribute enough, but he's done at least $50,000 worth of work on my house and it's all beautiful, because he doesn't make anything that isn't beautiful," Jill said. "He's an amazing human being, as you know. He has an enormous capacity to love. His health is so fragile and he's also the strongest person I know. He's done an amazing job at making me feel that I'm the lucky one."

As we got to know Jill better and picked up our friendship with Clark right where we left it, we all started to feel more like family than friends. We were completely relaxed in each other's company, and we knew we could depend on each other. When Clark's aged Land Rover broke down halfway up Mount Lemmon with Jill in the passenger seat, we were the obvious people to call for help. When a crack appeared in our bedroom ceiling or other things went wrong around the house, Clark was happy to come over and fix it. When Jill had to leave for three weeks for a family emergency, Clark's health became partially our responsibility, and he ate most of his dinners at our house.

Taking cues from us, Isobel started to think of them as family too, and she loved going over to their house because it held the possibility of an interaction with Tessa, Jill's teenage daughter. You never knew what color Tessa's hair was going to be and she had pet rats that crawled around on her shoulders. She was an introvert with an extroverted sense of style that drew from the punk/New Wave era, and in Isobel's eyes she was a rock star, queen and goddess all rolled into one. For Isobel, as she approached her sixth birthday, nothing was more fascinating or impressive than teenage girls.

Sometimes Tessa could be persuaded to emerge from her bedroom, which was a forest of plants, and come out into the backyard. We would try not to stare as Tessa and Isobel sat cross-legged on the ground facing each other, asking each other questions like "So what's your favorite color?" with follow-up questions that gently eased into conversation. It was polite and formal, as befitting an audience with royalty, with Isobel on her very best behavior and hanging on Tessa's every word. After a few of these interactions, we received some thrilling news: Tessa, who had told Jill many times that she would never babysit because she didn't like children, agreed to babysit Isobel, and only Isobel. "I can't believe it!" Isobel cried out, jumping up and down on her bed. "I've got the coolest babysitter in the whole world!"

Since Cathy Thompson went back to Mississippi, Isobel had been a little maudlin and out of sorts. She kept telling us that she missed her Nonna and asking us why we had left Mississippi. We tried our best to explain it, but there was no getting around the fact that we had torn our daughter away from her friends and her adoptive grandmother. Isobel had long, regular conversations with Cathy on FaceTime, which helped, but it was still a weak substitute for spending whole days together, getting her every whim indulged and sharing a bed at night. The news that Tessa was going to be her babysitter, however, was so deliriously exciting that Isobel was incapable of feeling maudlin, even though she still missed her Nonna. In preparation for the inaugural babysitting event, Isobel made a list of activities with checkboxes in one of her notebooks: "Introduce Tessa to my stuffies. Do art project. Play spies. Talk about stuff. 7:30 Tessa does night time. Yay!"

*T*he Arizona Strip, a remote region of red rock canyon country in the north-west of the state, contains one of the last strongholds of fundamentalist Mormon polygamy in America. In the small town of Colorado City, it's common to see men with five or six wives riding in minivans or Suburbans to gas stations, churches and grocery stores. The wives typically wear prairie dresses sewn from the same bolts of cloth, with their long hair upswept and flipped. Their daughters dress the same way and are often married off as teenagers to much older polygamist men, and sometimes "reassigned" from one husband to another.

By far the most prominent of the various polygamist sects in Colorado City and neighboring Hildale, Utah, is the Fundamentalist Church of Jesus Christ of Latter-day Saints (FLDS). From 1986 to 2002, the church's president and prophet was Rulon Jeffs, known to his followers as Uncle Rulon. He had at least sixty wives and dozens of children. After his death, his son Warren Jeffs took over as president and prophet, married all of Rulon's widows except two, and subsequently added at least twenty more wives to his harem, including minors. He also appointed twelve "seed bearers" to impregnate other men's wives. He is now serving a life sentence for raping two of his child brides and other sex crimes against children.

Once secretive and wary of the outside world, Colorado City has sought to open itself up in recent years and attract tourists. A brewery has opened and a coffee shop. Accommodations are available in covered wagons and glamping resorts. But patriarchal fundamentalism and plural marriages in defiance of the law are still part of the town's culture. And underage girls are still gifted as wives to religious leaders. In 2022 the FBI arrested Samuel Bateman, a self-proclaimed prophet with more than twenty wives in his compound. Ten of them were under eighteen, and according to the FBI, Bateman's youngest bride started wearing her wedding ring when she was nine years old.

Chapter Twelve

ARIVACA

At the opposite end of the state from Colorado City, eleven miles from the Mexican border, is the scruffy, scrappy, unincorporated community of Arivaca. It's a place where hippies, bikers, ranchers, cowboys, dope farmers, smugglers, outlaws and more or less regular people can all agree on a code of live and let live, and as little governance as possible. It has a dark side too, with plenty of drug abuse, alcoholism and occasional murders. One local man abused a woman for years in a bunker that was so fortified with weaponry that no one dared to try to rescue her.

In the late 1990s and early 2000s, Chuck Bowden would go to a small ranch outside Arivaca to write in solitude. The house was small and rustic, overlooking arid grasslands and a tree-lined creek, with hills and craggy mountain ranges on the skyline. It was off the grid with a solar panel and a well, and to get there you drove on a dirt road that led to the ghost mining town of Ruby—where I later took Mariah on our first date to see the bats fly out of the mine. From the ranch house at night there were no lights visible in any direction. I was always nervous about visiting Chuck there, because he shared his back porch with a diamondback rattlesnake that he had named Beulah.

They had formed a kind of friendship or mutual nonaggression pact. When it was just the two of them on the back porch, as he described it, Beulah would come out of the woodpile toward sunset, glide past his feet as he sat drinking wine and listening to Miles Davis after a long day's work, and then go off to hunt for the night. But when visitors were on the back porch, Beulah would come out of the woodpile, approach the chairs, and then coil and rattle, because she could detect an unfamiliar human scent. That husky buzzing sound normally made me levitate and fly backward through the air, and I struggled to sit there calmly like Chuck as Beulah rattled her warning and then retreated.

In time, Chuck stopped using the ranch house and I moved in there with my first wife Gale. We were still then in the happy phase of our marriage, which would end in divorce in 2004. Our landlords in Tucson had sold the house we were renting, we needed a cheap place to live, the ranch was beautiful, and I had long been attracted to Arivaca. It was essentially an improvised experiment in anarchy and tolerance, with no local law enforcement and none wanted by most of its residents. A friend of mine who grew up there, mostly in a tent, describes Arivaca and the borderland hills around it as "the edge of empire, where no authority will hold." It appealed to my desire to maximize my personal freedom and live outside society's rules.

Beulah didn't think much of the new tenants—who included a dog—and to my great relief she moved out and I never saw her on the back porch again. I thought I saw her many times when I was out walking, but there were a lot of diamondback rattlesnakes on that ranch and I was never sure if I was seeing Beulah or one of the others. It was a tough place to live in the summer. There was no cooling in the house except a fan and the well would go dry in June. This meant no showers and a fifty-five-minute drive to Green Valley to fill up water containers so we could do the dishes, until the monsoon rains arrived and replenished the water table under the well. The one solar panel on the house was old and inefficient, but it gave us enough electricity to run a laptop computer, a stereo, a fan, a small fridge and lights at night. But using a toaster or a hair dryer was completely out of the question. Anything that generates a lot of heat, we learned, eats up a day's worth of electricity in minutes. We cooked on propane and used it to heat water in the shower in the winter.

From the house, I could walk as far as I wanted in any direction without encountering private property fences or barriers. There was barely any phone signal and to access the internet I had to drive eight miles into Arivaca and go to the library. The lack of technology and the peace and quiet made the days feel much longer, and I felt happy and free and close to nature. Gale found it too isolated and boring. She found a house to rent in Tucson and I stayed mostly at the ranch by myself.

For company and entertainment I would drive to the one bar in Arivaca, a hard-bitten establishment called La Gitana (the Gypsy). It had bullet holes in the walls, a bloodstain on the scarred old wooden floor, and an adobe ruin outside where people went to smoke weed. The bar-stools had denim seats and were built of heavy timber so they couldn't be picked up and swung as weapons. On Sundays a biker named Mugger would turn his hand to dentistry, pulling out his clientele's rotten teeth with a pair of pliers, and his toothless wife Cindy was always armed with two Colt .45s.

I became good friends with a sweet, funny hippie cowboy type named Red George, who had a long white beard and a plastic baggie of weed extruding from his shirt pocket—unless he'd smoked it all. Hard drugs were around, and it wasn't uncommon to see someone snort a line off the bar, but the everyday maintenance diet was locally grown weed and cheap American beer, and the basic code was to not ask questions about anybody's life, and especially not about their past or their real name. "I ain't saying what I was in there for," growled a man who had just got out of prison. Then he added, "Everyone in this bar has been deeply hurt."

The bloodstain on the floor recorded an ill-fated moment in the life of a grizzled biker called Chance. I was on good terms with him and would invite him to the occasional parties that I threw at the ranch. The story of the bloodstain had a few variants, but this is the one I was told most often. Chance walked into the bar with a sawed-off shotgun in the inside pocket of a long duster coat. He flung the coat open and said, "Look at me, motherfuckers!" His intention was to show off his badass coat with its badass accessory, but he flung it open with such gusto that the loaded shotgun jumped out, landed butt first on the floor, and discharged into his armpit. Then a grisly thud as the severed bloody tattooed arm fell on the wooden floor.

Another version had Chance holding the shotgun under the coat, with the intention of using it on someone in the bar, when it slipped from his grasp. One of the drinkers at the bar, according to a version that was probably embellished but nonetheless captured something of La Gitana's spirit, heard the shotgun blast, turned around briefly to look at the arm on the floor, and commented, "At least we won't have to look at those goddamn tattoos no more."

———

I wanted to go back to Arivaca and see it again. I hugged Mariah and Isobel goodbye and drove down toward Mexico on Interstate 19. I turned off at Amado, where a saloon is housed in a building shaped like an enormous longhorn skull. Then I drove the winding twenty-three-mile road to Arivaca for the first time in fifteen years. Memories flooded my brain. The feral-looking children in rabbit-skin shoes crouched in the back of a pickup as their families drove into town from the tepee and bus encampment out in California Gulch. Meg the librarian, who would bring me small bags of the light clean sativa she grew, and the shoulders of javelinas she had shot in her vegetable garden. She didn't eat meat, but she didn't want it going to waste either. Tom who owned the coffee shop and was rumored to have made a small fortune selling cocaine in Florida. When the county health official arrived at the coffee shop, with the intention of enforcing the inspection, fee and permit process, Tom kept growling at the man, "Take your hand out of my goddamn pocket. Take your fucking hand out of my pocket." The cowboys passing a joint from saddle to saddle as their dogs rounded up the cattle who grazed twice a year on that lovely little ranch with a stream and a grove of trees at the bottom of the hill. The beautiful gray hawks that lived in those trees. The mule deer that walked toward me and then barked like a dog.

It was early on a Saturday afternoon and I went directly to La Gitana. A sign on the door read: "UNWANTED: Members of any vigilante border militia group, including, but not limited to AZ Border Recon. Do Not Enter our establishment." I wondered what that was about. Then I opened the door and stood there absolutely stunned. People were eating food at tables, the old barstools were gone, the place was clean, the patrons were clean, the decor was different, the raunchy smell and the grizzled bikers and dope fiends were all gone.

I spotted Mary Kasualitis, who came from an old Arivaca ranching family and was a storehouse of local history. "Mary," I said, "I'm flabbergasted. What on earth happened here?"

"After you left we had a lot of problems with meth and pills, and it got pretty rough in here," she said. "Do you remember Maggie and her husband? They went in with two local women and bought the bar, restored the building, cleaned it up, redecorated, opened the restaurant, and made the place more welcoming."

"How rough did it get?" I asked, remembering the time that someone was knifed to death in the bar, which the regulars didn't think was a big deal. "It got pretty rough," she said again. Later I was given a more vivid description by a female bartender in a small town forty miles away: "Partially clothed men trying to ransack your purse while basically living their lives in the same three square feet area of that filthy old bar."

I asked Mary about various people I was hoping to see. They were all dead, including Red George and Meg the librarian, the two people I had wanted to see most of all. One-armed Chance, whose bloodstain was no longer visible on the floor, had committed suicide with a gun. "That seems on-brand for him," I said. "Yeah," she said. "It took him four days to die. He shot himself in the head, but he didn't do it right."

And what about the anti-militia sign taped to the door? When I lived in Arivaca, the nearest anti-immigrant border militias were more than a hundred miles away in Cochise County. The most prominent was the Minuteman Project, led by a media-savvy former kindergarten teacher named Chris Simcox, now serving a nineteen-year prison sentence for sexually molesting a five-year-old girl. "Unfortunately we've become a magnet for right-wing militias and most people don't want them here," Mary said. "You probably heard about the Shawna Forde killings. That really shook the community."

I had heard about the killings. Forde, a native of Washington State with a long criminal record, was one of Chris Simcox's deputies in the Minuteman Project. She formed a splinter group called Minuteman American Defense (MAD) with the same basic idea: dress up in military gear and go on heavily armed patrols of the borderlands, looking for migrants and asylum seekers to confront and intimidate and report to the Border Patrol. In 2009, Forde moved to Arivaca. She had trouble funding the militia's weapons and equipment, so she teamed up with some local drug dealers and hatched a scheme to stick up their rivals and use the stolen cash and drugs to finance the militia.

Her second-in-command was Jason Bush, a former Aryan Nations member who had gone to prison for violent crimes. The drug dealers were Albert Gaxiola—I remembered his aunt Clara as one of the many strong, soulful, impressive Arivaca women—and Oin Oakstar, who ran drugs from Arivaca into Tucson. They singled out twenty-nine-year-old Raul Flores Jr. as a suitable target to rob.

Soon after midnight on May 30, 2009, Shawna Forde, Jason Bush, Albert Gaxiola, and a fourth man who was never identified drove to Flores's mobile home on Mesquite Road. Gaxiola waited in the car. The others, dressed in camo, armed with handguns and a shotgun, knocked at the door and announced themselves as Border Patrol agents. Once inside, Forde ordered Raul Flores to sit on the couch with his wife Gina and nine-year-old daughter Brisenia. Flores asked what was going on. Bush answered, "Don't take this personally, but this bullet has your name on it."

Flores leapt toward him, trying to grab the gun. Bush shot him, and put two rounds into Gina. As the wounded Flores begged them to spare his wife and daughter, Bush shot him multiple times until he was dead. Shawna Forde started rifling the house, looking for drugs and money, but finding only some jewelry that she pocketed. Jason Bush questioned Brisenia as her mother played dead on the floor. "Please don't shoot me," the beautiful young girl pleaded, but he shot her twice in the face and killed her. The murderers left.

Gina, bleeding heavily, with her husband and daughter dead on the floor, called 911. While she was on the phone, the murderers came back to finish her off, but Gina grabbed a gun and managed to wound Bush during a brief gunfight. This time they left for good. Gina survived her physical wounds. Shawna Ford and Jason Bush were both sentenced to death.

The Minuteman movement fell apart after the killings, but in 2017 and 2018, probably emboldened by Trump's anti-immigrant rhetoric from the White House, a new crop of border vigilantes appeared in Southern Arizona. The first was Tim Foley, a right-wing activist and leader of Arizona Border Recon, an armed paramilitary group that tries to intercept migrants and smugglers. Having made himself unpopular in nearby Sasabe, Foley moved to Arivaca, where he received an even more hostile reception and was banned from La Gitana, although he did have some supporters, including Jim and Sue Chilton, thoughtful conservative ranchers who used to graze their cattle on the ranch where I lived.

Next in town was Michael "Lewis Arthur" Meyer, known to his critics and his followers as Screwy Louie. He was a motormouthed hothead with a violent criminal past, like so many militia vigilantes, and he was now obsessed with God and child sex trafficking conspiracy theories. He showed up at La Gitana with his camo-clad Veterans on Patrol group. When the bartender told him he wasn't welcome, he filmed her on a Facebook Live video and told his tens of thousands of followers that people in Arivaca supported open borders and child sex trafficking. Next came the Utah Gun Exchange, rumbling into town in a huge BearCat SWAT vehicle with a machine gun mounted to it.

To combat the militia influx, a group of about seventy Arivacans joined forces in a rare collective action that went against the usual live-and-let-live credo. They placed "No Militia" signs around town, urged local businesses to blackball militia members, tracked militia activity online, explored the possibility of legal action, and made it very clear that the vigilantes were unwanted and unwelcome.

"Most people here think the militias are far more threatening and potentially dangerous than the migrants and smugglers," said Mary Kasualitis. "Militia people were responsible for the most horrific violence this community has ever experienced."

———

For the first two and half years that I lived on the ranch, Mexican migrants, usually lone men, occasionally in twos and threes, would sometimes show up at my door asking for food or water or both. I would always give them water at least. I knew that plenty of other migrants were coming through the area without revealing themselves, and that groups of extremely fit young Mexican men were backpacking loads of marijuana through the hills, but like most people in Arivaca, I became thoroughly accustomed to migrants and drug smugglers moving across the landscape. I didn't feel threatened by them because they had never hurt anyone in the area. I knew of several local women who felt safe living by themselves on isolated properties.

Then came one of the periodic surges in illegal immigration on the Arizona border. I started getting groups of forty or fifty coming through the ranch at night, using the stream and the sheltering trees as a migration route. I started to feel more uneasy and bought myself a gun. Nearly every day I was filling up big black bags with empty water bottles, sardine cans, Maruchan instant noodle containers, plastic tortilla packets, and other garbage. I was dealing with a lot more Border Patrol agents, hearing a lot more trucks and helicopters. I was forced to drive through new checkpoints, where I was questioned about where I was going and what I had seen.

The feeling of ease and freedom ebbed away. The occasional migrants who came to my door still wanted food and water, but now they kept asking to "borrow" the keys to my truck as well. Then my landlords got furious with me because I was slow to report a roof leak. I decided it was time to leave Arivaca and close that chapter of my life.

———

Now, under the Biden administration, another big surge in migration was taking place on this stretch of border. As always, it was fueled by poverty, suffering, desperation and hope, but the smugglers were using different routes and methods than the ones I remembered, the migrants were coming from all over the world, and the whole enterprise had reportedly been taken over by the Mexican drug cartels and turned into a multibillion-dollar industry. To better understand these changes, I spent a day riding around the border near Arivaca and Sasabe with a U.S. Border Patrol agent named Jesús Vasavilbaso, a tall, affable, distinguished-looking thirteen-year veteran. He was born in the United States and raised just across the border in Nogales, Sonora, where his father was a customs officer.

"When I was growing up, it was a mom-and-pop operation," he said. "They would charge you a dollar to climb through a hole in the fence. The coyotes [migrant guides] were independents who worked for themselves, and a lot of guys would cross by themselves. All that is gone now. The cartels control every aspect of it. If you try to cross by yourself, they'll kill you. It's become such a big business for them, and such a cruel business."

Two days previously, an eighteen-month-old toddler and a four-month-old infant were abandoned and left to die in the desert near Organ Pipe Cactus National Monument. "Our agents found a group who told them they had seen a toddler just north of the fence. When the agents got there, the toddler was crying and the infant was unresponsive and facedown. They called for EMTs and managed to revive the infant. Guatemalan birth certificates had been left with them."

He asked if I was a father. When I said yes, he said, "Doesn't it just tear at your heart?" Neither of us knew the circumstances, but presumably the smuggler had forced the mother or father, or both parents, to abandon the children in the desert because they were slowing down the group. The children were now in the care of the U.S. Health and Human Services' office of resettlement, and the birth certificates held some hope that they might be reunited with their parents.

I found it hard to think about the border, because you could multiply heartrending stories like this by the hundreds, or the thousands, or the tens of thousands, depending on the time frame you were looking at. Since 1994, when the Clinton administration implemented Operation Gatekeeper, which beefed up the physical barriers and enforcement in Nogales, San Diego and El Paso and pushed the traffic out into the harshest areas of the Sonoran Desert, the Arizona border has been a relentless staging ground of agony, trauma and death, and at best an ordeal to be survived in hopes of a better future.

Well over 8,000 migrants have died in the desert since Operation Gatekeeper began. Its architects expected some people to die, but they assumed that the risk and danger would act as a deterrent. As former commissioner of the U.S. Immigration and Naturalization Service Doris Meissner said in 2000, "We did believe that geography would be an ally to us. It was our sense that the number of people crossing the border through Arizona would go down to a trickle once people realized what it's like."

That didn't happen. Migrants kept risking their lives in the desert, mainly because they had nothing else to lose, so patrols and enforcement increased, which made the journey even more risky and challenging, and consequently far more expensive. Seeing the profits that could be made, the cartels swooped in and took over. They were now charging Mexicans a few thousand dollars on average, $8,000 to $10,000 for Central Americans, and up to $15,000 to people coming from Brazil, Venezuela and Ecuador.

"They're like travel agents, selling you different packages," said Vasavilbaso, driving south from his headquarters in Tucson. "The luxury package includes a day at the beach in Cancún, and every one of them is 'guaranteed' to get you into the U.S. They lie to migrants all the time. They see them as commodities. They call them *pollos*, chickens. They don't care if seventeen die today, because there'll be another hundred tomorrow. They will take your water away if you can't keep up and leave you to die. We see that every day. And they'll squeeze every last penny from you."

In Altar, which is the staging town in Sonora, migrants are required to buy a whole package of goods, including a backpack, clothes, food, water and two phones, one for Mexico and one for the United States. Most of the smuggling was coordinated by phone now. "It's so cruel the way they lie," he continued. "They tell the migrants it's just a short distance to walk, but it's forty-five miles to Three Points, where some get picked up, and sixty miles to Silverbell Mine."

I told him that I had recently walked some of the washes near Silverbell Mine northwest of Tucson, where drivers pick up migrants at the end of their journey. The ground was littered with camouflage clothing and backpacks, carpet-soled shoes, big black water bottles, bottles of Pedialyte, diapers, rattles, dolls, toys, bulbs of garlic, bottles of pain pills, prayer booklets. It was late summer and well over 100 degrees. I tried to imagine walking sixty miles of that ground in the heat with an infant in diapers, trying to keep it alive, trying to give it comfort, but it was impossible for my brain to conceive what that was really like.

"They all wear camo now because it makes them harder to see, the carpet shoes make them harder to track, and the black water bottles don't reflect the sunlight," said Vasavilbaso. "Once they reach the pickup place and call the driver, they dump everything and get into civilian clothes."

I asked about the garlic cloves. "There's a belief that garlic wards off rattlesnakes, but it's not true. I have encountered a few migrants with snakebite over the years, but the heat and dehydration are far more dangerous." In the previous year, Border Patrol recorded 568 deaths on the southwest border, 219 of them heat-related, and 20 sets of skeletal remains in the Tucson sector. Humanitarian groups put out water stations by the main migrant trails, but some border militias, most notably Veterans on Patrol, take pride in stealing or puncturing the plastic barrels of water. In Screwy Louie's mind, the water stations are there to aid child sex traffickers.

"How does it feel to catch someone, knowing everything they've gone through to get that far?" I asked.

"If they're in trouble, it feels great," said Vasavilbaso. "They see you and start crying because they thought they were going to die. If they're not in trouble, you're depriving them of their liberty, which is something to be taken seriously. We know why they want to come here, and most of us would do the same if we were in their shoes, but a nation has to protect its borders and enforce its laws. It also feels good when you catch a bad guy with a criminal record, because you're protecting people from him. They make up about 1 percent of migrants."

Ever since Trump left office and the Biden administration halted construction of the border wall and allowed unaccompanied minors to apply for asylum, Republicans had been repeating the mantra that the border was "wide-open." I wondered if this was insulting to U.S. Customs and Border Protection (CBP), the nation's largest law enforcement agency, with an annual budget of $25 billion and some 60,000 employees, including 20,000 Border Patrol agents. Those agents recorded more than 2 million encounters with migrants in the previous year leading to apprehension or expulsion. "How do you feel when you hear politicians talk about the border being wide-open?" I asked.

"As agents, we could care less about politics. We want to do our job. The immigration system has to change. In the meantime this is what we've got. This is what Congress has authorized."

At Sasabe, he turned on to a dirt road that ran next to Trump's border wall, which Vasavilbaso called "the fence" because it's not a solid object but a see-through construction of heavy steel slats, known as bollards, approximately thirty feet high. He pointed to a large gap where asylum seekers, including many unaccompanied minors, would come through and wait to present themselves to Border Patrol. "We had QAnon and a vigilante group camped out here, giving the children food, water and Bibles, and taking their information, supposedly to save them from sex slavery." In general, he said, the border vigilantes made the job harder. They wore camo like the migrants, it was sometimes hard to tell who was who at a distance, and they added another layer of worry.

What Border Patrol agents found exciting about "the new fence" were the access roads that were bladed through the desert for the work crews, and the new dirt road that runs alongside it. "We're not hiking so much, we can get places much faster." It was helpful to have a more robust physical barrier too, although it was fairly easy to breach. "A lot of times they'll cut through it with an angle grinder, or go over it with ladders and ropes, and as you can see, in this area there are gaps because construction was halted."

West of Sasabe there was a seventy-five-mile gap because the Tohono O'Odham nation had blocked the Trump administration's attempts to extend the barrier across their land. On the other side of the reservation was the Yuma sector in far southwestern Arizona, where the wall resumed. "The way the cartel has arranged it at the moment, it's mostly Mexican and Guatemalan migrants coming through Sasabe into the Tucson sector, and in Yuma it's mostly asylum seekers who surrender to agents, and they come from all over the world—Ukraine, Russia, India, Bangladesh, Venezuela, Haiti, over a hundred countries."

I got out of the vehicle and looked at the tracks coming through the gap in the so-called wall. Sure enough, many of them were made by small children. I looked at the surrounding hilltops and wondered if cartel scouts were up there monitoring us through binoculars. On the drive back to Tucson, I asked about drug smuggling, which used to be the dominant economic activity in the Arivaca/Sasabe borderlands. Marijuana had been the drug most in demand, so it was the most frequently smuggled, although plenty of cocaine and heroin came through too.

"Now it's fentanyl, heroin and liquid meth, but we hardly ever see it out here in the desert," he said. "It comes in through the ports of entry and it's hard to catch because it's in small quantities." Then he grinned and started chuckling. "It doesn't happen often, but sometimes we still catch people with loads of marijuana and we just have to laugh. 'Didn't you hear, amigo? This stuff is legal up here now. You can buy it in the store.'"

I watched the border get farther away in the side mirror of his big government SUV. To the west of us were the rugged Baboquivari Mountains, and to the east the flat arid grasslands of the Buenos Aires National Wildlife Refuge. Both contained well-traveled migrant trails.

"There'll be some groups out there right now," he said. "They've come a long way already, they're tired, they're hot, they're dehydrated, they're scared, and they have a long way to go. Unless we catch them first."

*W*ith the Apache defeated and the arrival of the railroads, the frontier ended and a new era began. Outside capital came into Arizona Territory to extract its natural resources for export. Livestock companies overstocked its grasslands with cattle and sheep until they turned into moonscapes. Logging companies cut down the virgin forests and mining corporations made prodigal fortunes from silver, gold and copper deposits.

The richest copper mine was in Bisbee near the Mexican border; the prospector George Warren had lost his share of it by trying to outrun a horse. In 1917 most of the mine was owned by the Phelps Dodge Corporation, which wielded enormous power in Arizona, controlling newspapers, politicians and law enforcement agencies, even getting church ministers ousted if they spoke in favor of unions. In July, when Bisbee miners went on strike for better pay and working conditions, mining executives told the local sheriff to deputize 2,200 vigilantes into an armed posse, one of the largest ever formed.

At 6:30 a.m. on July 12 they started breaking down doors and pulling striking miners out of bed at gunpoint. Some were beaten and robbed. Wives were thrown to the ground as children screamed. Nearly 2,000 men were rounded up and marched to the ballpark. If they renounced the strike, they were told, they would be released. More than 800 men chose this option. The remaining 1,186 were crammed into twenty-three railroad cattle cars, many of which had a layer of manure on the floor. It was a hot July day and no water had been provided to the men since their early morning arrests.

In cramped, overheated, reeking conditions, they endured another fifteen hours without water as the train traveled east. Then it came to a halt. The men staggered out of the cars and discovered that their captors had abandoned them without money, food, water or shelter in the New Mexico desert. Local people saved their lives. In Arizona there were indictments and trials, but no one was ever convicted or punished for the Bisbee deportation, the largest mass kidnapping in the state's history.

Chapter Thirteen

AR15ONA

It was curious and revealing about Tucson that I had never met Wayne Belger before. We had both knocked around the same downtown bars and clubs for two decades. We made our living in associated professions. He was a magazine photojournalist and a fine art photographer. I was a magazine journalist and a writer of nonfiction books. I had lived for three years right around the corner from his warehouse studio living space and we had both frequented the same neighborhood dive bar. Not only had we never met. We had never even heard of each other. Tucson could be like that, especially in the creative fields. People tended to stay within their cliques or go it alone. Aloofness was more prevalent than inclusivity.

We finally met because we were assigned to the same magazine story. It was about a pioneering female archaeologist of the 1920s and 1930s named Ann Axtell Morris, who was now the subject of a movie called *Canyon Del Muerto*. Wayne gave me a ride to the house of her grandson in the Tucson foothills and talked the whole way. He was smart and funny, with a sunny Southern California affect and a hustler's charm. Aramaic letters were tattooed up and down his arms because he was into dead languages.

He told me that he was a surfer, a scuba diver, a big wall rock climber, a machinist and a patched-in member of an outlaw motorcycle club, all of which turned out to be true. I later found out that he had also been a licensed manicurist, a gigolo, a beauty supply store manager, a treasure hunter, a climbing instructor, a mascot for the Los Angeles Kings hockey team, a child recovery operative for the California Department of Justice, and a musician who played the didgeridoo and the Irish bodhran drum for a Tribal Celtic band called the Wicked Tinkers.

After we had interviewed and photographed Ann Morris's grandson, Wayne told me about his latest photographic art project. It was an undercover exposé of America's increasingly political and religious gun culture, in which the AR-15 had become a sacred object, a holy weapon like Excalibur. For all his projects, Wayne used his machinist skills to make a unique camera that was thematically linked to the subject. In this case he had built a pinhole camera out of gun parts, shell casings and F-16 fighter plane parts, with a Ku Klux Klan belt buckle underneath.

He was renting booths at gun shows, posing as a Second Amendment enthusiast and using the camera to take portraits of people with their firearms against one of three different backdrops: an American flag, a Three Percenter militia flag, or a flag that said "TRUMP: NO MORE BULLSHIT." He was also buying guns for the purpose of installing them in an art exhibit. One was an AR-15 pistol with three settings. The safety was marked "PEACE," the semiautomatic setting was "WAR," and the fully automatic setting was "GOD WILLS IT." It was all going to end up in an art gallery, in a show titled Thoughts and Prayers, and hopefully in a photographic book.

Wayne asked me if I was interested in writing the text for the book and tagging along to some gun shows to get a feel for the project. "I go all over the country, but Arizona is probably the most hardcore because we have such lax gun laws," he said. The project piqued my curiosity and I told him I was interested. Mariah expressed some concerns: "What if the gun nuts figure out that Wayne is bullshitting them?" Wayne's artist girlfriend Alanna was also worried. She was a Black woman from New York who didn't want to get anywhere near an Arizona gun show.

Wayne insisted there was nothing to worry about. "I've been doing this for a couple years now and no one has ever questioned me or challenged me. It's because I look the part. I'm an older white guy, I wear pro-gun shirts, I know a lot about guns, and I know gun jargon. I actually love guns, they're amazing machines, but the amount of firepower and gun violence in this country is absolutely insane." He had tried to scrub everything online that revealed his left-liberal politics, and when people at gun shows asked him about the weird-looking tattoos on his arms, he told them it was Aramaic, the original language of the Bible.

A few weeks later Wayne called. He had a booth reserved at a big gun show in Phoenix and a free-admission vendor pass for me. "Dress like a schlumpy middle-aged white guy so you don't blow my cover," he advised. "I'll be wearing jeans and a T-shirt with Mickey Mouse holding an AR-15." I selected a pair of jeans that had never fit properly, an ugly pair of blue running shoes, a brewery T-shirt and a sweat-stained

Carhartt cap. Aviator sunglasses and an accidental slip with the beard trimmer completed the look.

"Why are you dressed like that?" asked Isobel accusingly.

"I'm in disguise," I told her. "I'm going to be a spy at a gun show."

"Ooh, fun," she said. "But you look terrible."

On the drive up to Phoenix, I remembered the last gun show I attended. It was back in the early 1990s when Tucson had its one annual gun show at the county fairgrounds. I vividly recalled a 400-pound man with cross-purpose facial tics, wearing a pair of overalls and holding an AK-47. His gun was a shocking sight in those days, because most of the vendors had bolt-action hunting rifles, or vintage firearms for collectors. Now there was a gun show every month in Tucson and twice a month in Greater Phoenix, and the vast majority of the guns on sale, according to Wayne, were for "killing other humans as fast and efficiently as possible." Going to gun shows and owning high-powered assault rifles had become a lifestyle, driven by gun industry marketing and right-wing political rhetoric, both promoting the idea that owning big, powerful, military-style weapons made you an American patriot.

Arriving at the Veterans Memorial Coliseum in Phoenix, I estimated a hundred vendors outside the building, a hundred and fifty inside, and a few thousand people milling around. About 90 percent of them were white males. The rest were white women and children, and Black, Hispanic, Asian and Native men, a few with wives or girlfriends. A white-blond toddler brandished a toy revolver from his stroller. A six-year-old boy wore wraparound sunglasses and a black cap that read: "KILL IT." My first impression was that everyone was trying to be a badass, women and children included.

"Raising Wolves Not Sheep," declared the T-shirt of one crucifix-wearing mother, with a Bible quote on the back and two AR-15s making the sign of the cross. A young pudgy guy was wearing full military combat gear and could barely walk because he was so laden down with firearms. Signs everywhere said, "No Loaded Guns," so they were being worn as lifestyle accessories or symbols of tribal belonging.

By far the most popular slogan at this slogan-rich event was "Let's Go Brandon." It was on bumper stickers, T-shirts, hats, hoodies, capes, booty shorts. The phrase originated at a televised NASCAR race in Talladega, Alabama. The television audience could hear the crowd chanting, "Fuck Joe Biden," but the NBC sports reporter suggested they were chanting, "Let's Go Brandon," while interviewing the driver Brandon Brown. It was now a ubiquitous MAGA code phrase, and particularly useful for fundamentalist Christians who hated Joe Biden but weren't allowed to use the f-word.

I saw a few genuine badasses—a Latino gangster with prison tattoos, an ex-military combat veteran with chilling eyes, and a fantastically mean-looking biker with Aryan Nations tattoos and a T-shirt that read: "My First Two Wives Were For Target Practice." Not only was the act of killing glorified at the gun show. People also found it amusing. "All Lives Splatter," said a shirt illustrated with spraying blood from a bullet-exploded skull. Another popular yuk-yuk shirt and bumper sticker depicted a phallic-looking rifle bullet with the slogan "Just the Tip—I Promise."

Among the guns for sale was a .50 caliber AR-15 engraved with the words "You're Fucked" on the ejection port door. This was a good choice of weapon if you wanted to disable an armored personnel carrier or shoot down a plane, but it was not suitable for home defense, because the round would exit a human body with enough force to go through a wall into your neighbor's house.

There were thousands of guns for sale, mountainous stacks of ammunition, hundreds of different gadgets and accessories, blast mitigation devices, customizable stocks, conversion kits, military-looking vests, straps and helmets for your "tactical" lifestyle. A slick-talking salesman with a mustache was selling AR-15 mounts for your car, truck or combine harvester. An attorney in a blue suit was giving an amplified speech on how to avoid prosecution if you shot someone to death on purpose, whether it was self-defense or not.

You could buy body armor, a gold-colored AR-15 with the word *Trump* on the stock, a 12-gauge shotgun that folded up ingeniously for concealment, suppressors (as silencers are known) and fake suppressors just for show. Many vendors had signs reading: "Private Sale. No Paperwork," or "Cash and Carry. No Background Check." Under the private sale provision in Arizona gun laws, you can walk into a gun show and buy any firearm you want for cash, with no background check, no questions asked, and no registration process. This was how Wayne bought his AR-15 pistol, a Crusader model with "God Wills It" on the fully automatic setting (which was not enabled) and a flash suppressor so no one could see where you were shooting from at night. According to the manufacturer, Spike's Tactical, "We named it Crusader and engraved Psalm 144:1 on the lower receiver to hoist the flag of our faith and to make a statement, reminding our customers that we are here with you. The war is here. We have a duty to defend our homeland and our way of life."

―――

Wayne's booth was inside the coliseum. His anti-gun, anti-MAGA girlfriend Alanna had designed the banner that hung above the booth. It featured a mean-looking eagle and the slogan: "Show Your Pride with

Second Amendment Photography." In front of the table, mounted on a tripod, was the pinhole camera he had built. On the back of it was a cross flanked with .45 bullets and the words "GOD, GUNS AND COUNTRY." The body of the camera was machined from a block of aircraft aluminum and the aperture was in the primer of a military shell. Inside the camera was a piece of hammered-out brass from the one of the first 105 mm howitzer shells fired in the US-Afghan war—Wayne knew the guy who had fired it. The viewfinder was a gunsight that flipped up, and there was a small American flag that Wayne had stolen from Glenn Spencer's border militia compound in Southern Arizona.

Conceptually, and in practical terms, the camera was the key to the whole project. It was a representation of Wayne's views about American gun culture, which he saw as fear-based, delusional and inextricably linked to mass shootings, but it exerted a powerful magnetism on gun enthusiasts. "That is cool!" they said over and over again. If they asked about the soil in the glass chambers built into the camera, Wayne told them that it came from an American battlefield, which was true in a sense. He had collected it from sites of American mass shootings: Columbine High School, Sandy Hook Elementary School and the Emanuel AME Church in Charleston, South Carolina. Alanna had insisted on the KKK belt buckle that was underneath the camera, because she thought racism was an integral part of right-wing American gun culture. Only one person had been inquisitive enough to find it. He was a preppy-looking dude in a polo shirt and Wayne was worried that he would be offended, but he just gave a little smile and said, "That's great."

Wayne, who is a born hustler, was amazingly smooth and relaxed and engaging as he chatted away with people, told them about the camera and asked if they wanted to have their photograph taken, free of charge. He got them to sign a release waiver and asked them which of the three flags they wanted as a backdrop. Such was the national divide when it came to guns and flags that his subjects thought they looked tough and proudly American, whereas Wayne thought they symbolized the toxic masculinity and faux patriotism that defined the new American gun culture and was tearing the country apart.

The divide was particularly acute over the AR-15. The National Rifle Association was calling it "America's rifle," and there were calls from the right to enact this designation into federal law. Arizona was claiming it too, at least on the bumper stickers and T-shirts that said "AR15ONA." But these versatile, high-powered assault rifles, which could be equipped with high-capacity magazines, were also the weapon of choice in most mass shootings, so they were vilified and demonized by liberal gun control advocates, which only increased their popularity with pro-gun conservatives. And now the AR-15 had acquired a holy status as the preferred firearm of fundamentalist Christian gun owners, to defend themselves, in their minds at least, against tyranny and evil.

Wayne had recently spent a few days at the Rod of Iron Ministries outside Scranton, Pennsylvania. Its founder, Pastor Sean Moon—the son of Sun Myung Moon, the Korean religious leader whose followers were known as Moonies—preached that the AR-15 was the "rod of iron" from the Book of Revelations, a divine instrument for enforcing God's will. Pastor Moon wore camouflage suits and a crown of bullets, used a gold-plated AR-15 in liturgical ceremonies, and instructed his parishioners to bring their AR-15s into church to renew their marriage vows. At night, Wayne slept fitfully in the back of his truck with armed guards prowling around the compound. "Everyone was convinced that Communist Satanists were plotting to destroy America. It was really kind of amazing, and I felt privileged to be there and have the experience I was having," he said.

At one point he accidentally let slip that he had been vaccinated against COVID-19. "They all started panicking, saying, 'Oh no!' like I was about to melt into a puddle of goo. A woman told me not to worry, I was going to be okay. She was going to call a doctor who would give me a footbath that would reverse the magnetism in my blood, so I could no longer be tracked by satellites or whatever. She was really adamant about it and I kept saying, 'Thank you, that's great, but I've got to do this photo shoot first, and I'm sorry, we'll have to do it later, I have to go to lunch,' and so on. I'm good at letting people believe I'm a part of their belief system, but that place was a real challenge."

Wayne came away from there with some extraordinary photographs, taken with his phone and his Second Amendment Project pinhole camera.

"It's the only voice I have, the only thing I know how to do," he said. "I really don't see how this ends well for America, because the four million guns sold every month are not for hunting. They're for killing fellow Americans. Maybe if people look at my work and see how insane this really is, some minds will start to change. Or maybe not. But I'm not going to sit back and pretend that it's normal that American civilians own 46 percent of the guns in the world, or that we're averaging nearly seven hundred mass shootings a year, or that I can walk into a gun show in Arizona, buy an AR-15 for cash, and carry it loaded in public without a license. Even gun nuts in the rest of the country are astounded by that."

The ironic wrinkle in Wayne's project was that he personally loved owning and shooting guns, all kinds of guns, the bigger and deadlier the better. One of the reasons he was so persuasive at gun shows was that he could talk about guns all day long, with all the right slang, acronyms and technical knowledge. He had been going to gun shows for decades as an enthusiast. It was seeing America's gun culture change so dramatically in recent years that led to his Second Amendment Photography Project.

The eerie, gauzy, black-and-white portraits that he took with the pinhole camera in Phoenix that day—"a collaborative soft focus on a self-destructive American mythology," as he later described them—included one of the six-year-old boy in the "KILL IT" cap holding an assault rifle that looked enormous against his childish frame. Another featured a bearded man wearing body armor and holding up the AR-15 he had just purchased. Two scantily clad porn stars posed with AR-15s, working the sexy killer look. They were at the gun show handing out cards to their Only Fans site. Another of Wayne's photographic subjects was the gunsmith selling AR-15s at the booth next door.

He was a solidly built bearded guy in his mid-thirties named Mike Latham. His T-shirt quoted the part of the Second Amendment that was hard to argue about: "The right of the people to keep and bear Arms shall not be infringed." He was helpful, good-humored, generous, and he seemed highly intelligent and well-informed. He lent me an AR-15 so Wayne could take my portrait in front of the "TRUMP: NO MORE BULLSHIT" flag, and we both enjoyed his company and conversation. This was another thing that kept happening to Wayne at gun shows. He met people that he genuinely liked and wanted to be friends with, even though he was there under false pretenses which made it awkward. He didn't lie about what he was doing, and he tried to be as honest and open in conversation as he could, without revealing the whole truth. It was almost second nature to him now, after more than two years of working the gun-show circuit.

Mike showed us photographs of his arsenal at home—dozens and dozens of guns, including numerous machine guns. "I thought machine guns were illegal," I said to him. "Nope," he replied. "There's a process you have to go through, with background checks and fingerprinting and a $200 fee, but you can own a fully operational machine gun in Arizona and a lot of other states. Do you guys know about the Big Sandy Shoot?"

Neither of us had heard of it. Mike said, "It's the biggest machine-gun shoot in the world and it takes place twice a year near Wikieup, Arizona. Guys have .50-cals, artillery pieces, Miniguns." A Minigun, as Wayne explained to me, is six-chambered, rotates like a Gatling gun, fires up to 6,000 rounds a minute, and is often mounted in a helicopter gunship. "You guys should come along and check it out," said Mike. "It goes on for three days. You camp out or sleep in a vehicle. They have night shoots with tracers. If you want to get photographs of Americans with their machine guns, it's definitely the best place."

"We're there," said Wayne.

I had to leave the gun show before the end, so I missed the last act. As the dealers dropped their prices, hoping to unload more inventory, what Wayne described as "representatives of certain Mexican organizations" started buying up guns and ammo in bulk, and producing what appeared to be straw buyers for gold-plated .45 pistols, which Wayne presumed were for cartel bosses. It was well known to state and federal enforcement agencies that a river of guns flowed south from Arizona to the Mexican drug cartels, but since there were no laws regulating Arizona gun shows, they couldn't do much about it.

A few days after the gun show, I met Wayne at his local coffee shop in Tucson and he showed me the prints he had made. The porn stars and the "KILL IT" kid were the most striking. "But look at this one," he said, pulling out a photograph of me posing with an AR-15 in front of the "TRUMP: NO MORE BULLSHIT" flag. "You're the only one who actually looks scary," he said. "Congratulations my friend, you're the meanest-looking redneck at the gun show."

*I*n 1863, in the midst of the Civil War, Abraham Lincoln appointed a judge for the newly established Arizona Territory. He was a New Yorker named William T. Howell. Arriving in Tucson, he observed that "two out of every three people were barefooted" in his new judicial district and that the territory lacked a coherent set of laws. With the assistance of a former Wisconsin governor, Howell wrote a 441-page legal code, which was approved by the 1st Arizona Territorial Legislature in 1864.

Section 34 addressed "excusable homicides." These included an axe head flying off its handle and killing a bystander, and beating a child or a servant to death while using "moderate" force. Only when excessive force was used did it become inexcusable. Section 47 made it illegal to have "carnal knowledge of any female child under the age of ten years, either with or without her consent." In other words, nine-year-olds were considered capable of giving consent, and ten was an appropriate age for a girl to begin sexual relations.

Marriages between whites and Blacks were outlawed, and "No black or mulatto, or Indian, Mongolian, or Asiatic, shall be permitted to [testify in court] against any white person." Section 45 was mainly concerned with malicious deadly poisonings, but it also stipulated two to five years' imprisonment for anyone who procured "the miscarriage of any woman then being with child," by the use of "medicinal substances" or "instruments," unless it was a physician trying to save the life of the mother. No exceptions were made for pregnancies resulting from rape or incest.

This abortion ban stayed in place until Roe v. Wade in 1973. After the U.S. Supreme Court overturned Roe in June 2022, Arizona was thrown into confusion and uncertainty because the highly unpopular and politically explosive 1864 abortion law was still on the books. Two years later, the Arizona Supreme Court ruled that the old law did indeed apply, even though it was written for a society where most people were barefoot, only white males could vote, parents were allowed to accidentally beat their children to death, and it was legal to have sex with ten-year-olds. In 2024, after a bitter, emotional fight, the state legislature narrowly voted to repeal the law.

Chapter Fourteen

CITIES, FARMS, AND WATER

The Hotel Congress had retained its charm and character, and the Fox Theatre and the Rialto were still great live music venues, but no one would compare downtown Tucson to a Tom Waits song these days. While we were gone, a Keep Tucson Shitty movement had tried to prevent the development and gentrification, and it had failed. Large swaths of Tucson were still just as shitty as ever, if not more so, but the downtown was now full of modern apartment buildings, with some corporate hotels and office blocks to complete the new look.

The dive bars, artist lofts and small-stage live music joints were all gone, along with the cheap rents, the weird characters, the gritty feel, and the wig shop with sun-damaged mannequins in the window. The ramshackle musical instrument store in a landmark historic building was going to be a "pick-up" Starbucks, "exclusively designed for mobile orders through the app and a quick pick-up without the wait." There was a choice of juice and smoothie bars, but nowhere to order a greasy hamburger from a hipster junkie waiter at three in the morning. It all looked thoroughly prosperous, although there were still a few lurching street crazies and blanket-wearing jabberers in the mix.

When pandemic restrictions lifted and Mariah was finally able to go out downtown with her closest female friends, she came home with a verdict of "douchy." When I asked her what she meant, she cited bars and clubs full of TVs and novelty cocktails, door policies about neck tattoos, and too many women dressed up like Kardashians. "Don't they know it's Tucson and we wear black here?" she said sarcastically. "It was almost like being in Phoenix. Not quite, but almost."

―――――

Arizona's two largest cities don't feel competitive with each other. It's more like mutual disdain. Tucson looks at Phoenix as oversized, tacky and soulless. We tend to agree with Hunter S. Thompson, who wrote that Hell would be "a viciously overcrowded version of Phoenix—a clean well-lighted place full of sunshine and bromides and fast cars where almost everybody seems vaguely happy, except for the ones who know in their hearts what is missing." Edward Abbey called it "The Blob" because of its ever-expanding sprawl. Chuck Bowden used to joke that Maricopa County's favorite sports were golf, adultery and land fraud. A tongue-in-cheek Free Baja Arizona movement has long called for Tucson and Southern Arizona to secede from the evil empire controlled by Phoenix wealth and power. Phoenix looks at Tucson, if at all, as scruffy, small-time, liberal and irrelevant.

A few more overgeneralizations: Tucson prides itself on tolerance and celebrates its Hispanic history and heritage. In 2010 Phoenix politicians enacted the harshest anti-immigrant law in the nation, requiring law enforcement officers to stop suspected illegal immigrants and demand proof of citizenship, and this law was aggressively enforced by the showboating tough-guy sheriff Joe Arpaio and his deputies. Tucson has long voted Democratic. Phoenix, the home of Barry Goldwater and John McCain, has long been a bastion of conservatism, although it has recently undergone an important political shift. Thanks to an influx of liberal newcomers from other states, an expanding Latino vote, and a major defection of moderate Republicans and independents from the new Trump-aligned GOP, Maricopa County is now a vital swing district in national elections and the second largest voting district in the nation, after Los Angeles County.

Tucson's central neighborhoods are walkable and bikeable, with a high percentage of independently owned restaurants and businesses. Greater Phoenix is utterly beholden to the automobile and its retail landscape is dominated by chains, franchises and shopping malls. I know some excellent people in Phoenix, but I'm bad at visiting them because it means eight-lane freeways and aggressive drivers, traffic jams, air pollution, and endless boulevards of strip-mall mediocrity. Tucson is druggy and Phoenix is even druggier—number one in the nation for both cocaine and meth use, according to the American Addiction Centers. Phoenix has a chain of coffee shops in which the baristas wear bikinis. Tucson does not.

Tucson has a downtown neighborhood that harvests rainwater to grow native food-bearing shrubs and trees, with over a hundred edible species on a single block and community seed-milling events. Mesa, in Greater Phoenix, has a skate park that is landscaped and irrigated like a golf course, in which no Tucson skater would be caught dead. Tucson incorporates the plants and aesthetics of the Sonoran Desert into the city and tries to be responsible about water use. Phoenix, partly because it grew as an oasis city with abundant water from the Salt, Gila and Verde rivers, lives in denial or defiance of the desert with abundant lawns, swimming pools, fountains and artificial lakes, although less of them than there used to be.

Tucson is laid-back. With the exception of the overheated real estate market, business tends to happen at a languid, slightly disorganized pace, which often maddens entrepreneurial newcomers. The city of Tucson is notorious for wasting time and money hiring consultant firm after consultant firm when pondering mixed-use urban development proposals, whereas Phoenix gets shit done.

When I arrived in the 1990s, Tucson was a capital of slacker culture, with a strong residue of 1970s hippiedom. New Age spirituality was big and there was a lot of yoga, bodywork and healing going on. It was uncool to strive, or wear new clothes, or care too much about money. I knew drug dealers who disdained the idea of getting rich. Phoenix has always been far more dynamic and hungry for money, power and status. Tucson thinks that ostentatious displays of wealth are gauche. Phoenix thinks they kick ass, and when it comes to gaudy over-the-top mansions, its satellite cities of Scottsdale and Paradise Valley can go toe-to-toe with anywhere in the country. As Mariah said, Tucson wears a lot of black and that very much includes Latino and Native Tucson. Phoenix leans more toward the color palette worn by Senator Kyrsten Sinema, who strikes Mariah and her friends as a very Phoenix person.

———

On a cool windy morning in spring, we set off toward Phoenix on a family road trip. We planned to go camping in the desert on the other side of it, and along the way I wanted to take a look at the state's biggest water scandal. It had hardly rained in a year, the desert plants were parched and shriveled, and I was consumed by thoughts of water and its scarcity.

We drove through Marana, which I remembered as a scruffy little town in the desert outside Tucson, nicknamed Dogpatch by the *Tucson Weekly*. Now it was unrecognizable, with Phoenix-style subdivisions full of boxy tract homes, golf courses, shopping malls, and more than 50,000 residents. Like so much of Arizona's built landscape, it looked incongruous to my eyes—there was almost no attempt to harmonize with the natural surroundings—and it also looked temporary, a thin graft on an ancient landscape that would be here long after humankind was gone from the planet. In these deserts of dust and stone, where aridity has stripped the land down to its geology, I was keenly aware of geological time, in which the 300,000-year presence of *Homo sapiens* is a tiny blip. Dinosaurs were around for 170 million years.

A magazine editor in New York once asked me to name a quintessential Arizona activity. I thought of hiking through the saguaro forests outside Tucson, or riding a horse through the red rock buttes and towers of Monument Valley, or rafting the Colorado River through the Grand Canyon. Then I decided that nothing was more quintessentially Arizona than sitting in a vehicle eating a microwaved burrito in the parking lot of a convenience store, while looking, or not looking, at a rock formation that has been there for a billion years or more. The oldest visible rocks in the state, in the inner gorge of the Grand Canyon and in some of the mountains outside Phoenix, are nearly 2 billion years old.

Dust devils were parading across the desert north of Marana, whirlwinds like miniature tornadoes that sucked up dust and debris into columns hundreds of feet high. We nagged Isobel to put down her tablet and check them out. "Cool!" she exclaimed, giving them two seconds of her attention before getting back to her cartoon. It was a landscape of sparse flat rocky desert with low mountain ranges, until we entered the cotton and alfalfa fields of Pinal County.

Life was about to change for these farmers. They had been irrigating freely with Colorado River water since it first arrived in 1993, but their water supply was going to be cut by an estimated 30 percent, with deeper cuts expected in the following years. Their choices included leaving fields fallow, growing fewer water-intensive crops, irrigating more efficiently by using sprinklers or drip systems, pumping more water out of the depleted aquifer, or giving up farming and renting their land to solar energy companies, who would cover it with solar panels.

Most of these farmers hated the idea of giving up farming. It was what they knew and the Arizona desert was a fantastic place to farm when you had an unlimited supply of cheap water, because it had a year-round growing season. Here in Pinal County, in the agricultural zone between Tucson and Phoenix, they were accustomed to using over 300 billion gallons a year, or more than 800,000 gallons for every resident.

It seemed inevitable that there would be a fight over water between the cities and the farms, and that the cities would win. There's an old saying in the American West that water flows uphill to money, and this was certainly true of the Colorado River water in the Central Arizona Project canals. Soon after leaving the river, it was pumped over a mountain range and then it took thirteen more pumping plants, or lift stations, to move it uphill to Central Arizona. Statewide, nearly 80 percent of Arizona's water was going to agriculture, which Mariah thought was insane. "It's a desert!" she remonstrated. "We shouldn't be growing cotton and alfalfa here. We should grow them somewhere with plenty of rain." There was a sound logical argument that this irrigated farmland should be turned over to solar energy production, because nowhere in the country has more sunshine than the Arizona desert.

As the Pinal County farmers were looking at big cuts in their water usage, two national corporations were building the first phase of Superstition Vistas, an enormous master-planned city on 275 square miles of state trust land in the northern part of the county. It was slated to be the size of the San Fernando Valley in Southern California, and it aspired to house 900,000 people by 2060. Where was the water going to come from? There were confident assurances from the boosters and developers, and studies underway, but no one could say. If it was insane to grow thirsty crops like cotton and alfalfa in this desert, during the worst drought in 1,200 years, surely it was equally insane to build a huge new city. Nor, for that matter, did it make good sense that Arizona had over 370 irrigated golf courses. But this was America and you did what you could get away with, for as long as it made money.

The interstate took us through the Gila River Indian Community, a reservation that abuts the southern edge of the Phoenix metro sprawl. It's home to approximately 11,000 members of the Akimel O'Odham (formerly known as Pima) and Pee-Posh (formerly Maricopa) tribes. Once they were highly successful desert agriculturalists who relied on the Gila River, but non-Native farmers and Phoenix had hogged all the water. In the mid-nineteenth century, large riverboats plied the Gila. Now it was a river of sand that trickled when it rained.

The tribes operated three casinos, a 500-room luxury resort with thirty-six holes of golf, a motorsports park and a farming operation. And thanks to an extremely favorable decision in Congress, after a thirty-year campaign by tribal lawyers, they controlled the rights to Arizona's single largest allotment of Colorado River water—a whopping

650,000 acre-feet per year, most of which they were storing in an aquifer for future use, sale or trade. Tucson, by comparison, gets less than 150,000 acre-feet a year, and Phoenix gets 311,000 acre-feet. (An acre-foot is the quantity of water required to cover an acre of land one foot deep.) Going forward, the Gila River Indian Community was going to be a major player in Arizona's future. If it decided to sell most of its water to Phoenix, which was by no means certain, the city could continue its growth. If not, Phoenix might have to do the thing it hated to do, and limit its ambitions.

Leaving the reservation behind, we entered the great desert metropolis. Occupying some 17,000 square miles, more than twice the land area of New Jersey, Greater Phoenix was now more populous than Philadelphia or Oregon with 4.7 million people, in a place with seven inches of rain in an average year and some of the hottest temperatures of any city in the Northern Hemisphere. And Maricopa was the fastest-growing county in America, adding 60,000 people a year.

Academics and journalists had warned for at least forty years that the Phoenix business ethic of growth at all costs would one day lead to a reckoning with a finite desert water supply, but it had always seemed theoretical, comfortably distant in the future, and fixable by technology or engineering. Now there was widespread agreement, across both political parties, that the water crisis was real and imminent, but Phoenix had yet to slow down the runaway juggernaut of its growth machine. There was little will to stop it because it was the engine of the city's economy and it was what Phoenix had always done—suck in desert and farmland, and spit out subdivisions.

Greater Phoenix has similarities to Greater Los Angeles—it's a low-density urban landscape dominated by cars and freeways—but without the ocean, the beaches, the glamour, the talent, the cultural production and the pleasant year-round climate. It's balmy here in the winter, which explains its magnetic appeal to retirees from northern and midwestern states, but summer highs push 120 degrees and the city is regularly pummeled by violent rolling dust storms known as haboobs. Driving around Los Angeles, you looked at TV and movie stars on the billboards. Driving around Phoenix, you looked at accident attorney billboards—more of them than anywhere else I know. I assumed this was because Phoenix, the last time I checked, was the worst big city for traffic collisions and fatalities, averaging eighty-three crashes a day and a death every other day. Many Phoenicians are recent arrivals who don't know the city, the driving style is fast and aggressive with a lot of tailgating, and the freeways come to a very sudden stop when the traffic clogs up ahead, as we now experienced.

Crawling along in eight lanes of traffic under a brown cloud of pollution, we passed the omnipresent Rafi, whose accident attorney face grins at you from nearly a thousand billboards in Arizona. Then there was bearded, bespectacled Sweet James, also known as The Dense Beard of Justice. Another billboard showed a man with a tattooed face and arms, wearing a black tank top, a red baseball cap, and a gold chain. He was The Tattooed Realtor, "Let's Ink a Deal." Another had a gauzy photograph of relaxed, giggly, young professional women. This was for a marijuana dispensary. Then it was Law Tigers, The Husband and Wife Law Firm, and back to grinning Rafi again. As the traffic loosened up slightly, I told Mariah about the first time I came to Phoenix in the late 1980s.

I was probably twenty-six and traveling with two English friends. We had picked up a driveaway car in New York and driven it across the country to deliver to its owner in Phoenix. Then we were going to catch a bus to Nogales on the Mexican border, take the train to Guadalajara, Mexico, and keep going to the Yucatán. We were fresh out of Europe. We had never seen a city like Phoenix before, with no pedestrians or street life. Everything was spread out and looked the same, and there was nothing happening in the city center except dive bars and homeless people. We tried to find some nightlife, but we didn't know where to go. We tried a few bars but people seemed sour and bored and we couldn't find any fun. We gave up and slept in the car in an empty parking lot.

The next morning we cleaned the car, delivered it to its owner, and asked him for a ride to the bus station. He refused and slammed his front door in our faces. So we put on our backpacks and started walking through the curving suburban streets in the direction of the downtown bus station. We hoped to hail or call a taxi because it was eight or nine miles, but there were no taxis and no pay phones, just endless suburban ranch homes with carports and sprinklers going on the lawns. It seemed odd to us that there were no sidewalks.

Someone must have called the police. We had been walking for about twenty minutes when a patrol car pulled up next to us. "What are you doing here?" asked the cop. We explained about dropping off the driveaway car, and the owner refusing to give us a ride, and needing to get to the bus station. The cop said, "You can't walk here. I'm booking you for vagrancy." We were genuinely confused. "Why can't we walk? Isn't this a public street? How can it be illegal to walk?" The cop said, "Get in the car. You're under arrest."

On the way to the police station, we produced cash, traveler's checks and credit cards, and made the case that we were too solvent to qualify as vagrants. Reluctantly the cop agreed. He dropped us off near the bus station and told us never to walk in Phoenix again. "Seriously?" said Mariah when I finished the story. "Yup," I said.

———

Unlike Tucson, Phoenix was never a part of Mexico or New Spain. It was founded in 1868 by an ex-Confederate soldier named Jack Swilling, an alcoholic who was also addicted to morphine to ease the pain of old bullet wounds. Riding through the desert near the confluence of the Gila and Salt rivers, he came upon the ruins and silted-up canals of a large agricultural civilization that had been abandoned many centuries ago. It was built by the Hohokam people. Swilling saw that the canal networks had been fed by the Salt River, and he recognized the agricultural potential of the alluvial soil. He formed a company of men to start digging out the ditches, and six months later the first crops were harvested. The new settlement went through some name changes and had settled on Pumpkinville when an erudite Englishman named "Lord" Darrell Duppa, exiled by his family for his excessive drinking, came up with the name of Phoenix, suggesting a civilization rising from the ashes of another.

Many other ex-Confederates and southerners moved to Phoenix and brought their values with them. The city had legal segregation in the first half of the twentieth century. Blacks were confined to their own schools and neighborhoods, barred from most hotels, restaurants and swimming pools, forbidden to date or marry white people, and unable to work except as domestic servants or agricultural laborers in the irrigated cotton fields. It was like Mississippi without the rain, the humidity, and the Klan. Mexicans and Mexican Americans faced similar treatment in Phoenix, and it wasn't much better for them in Tucson.

Archaeologists don't know why the Hohokam suffered a population collapse and abandoned their settlements in the fourteenth and fifteenth centuries. One likely explanation is that salt levels built up in their fields over ten centuries of irrigation, which would have poisoned their crops, but there was also a migration into the area by Salado people fleeing drought farther north, which might have caused an upheaval. Researchers have also pointed to a drop in fertility, long periods of drought, the possibility of disease, and massive floods on the Salt and Gila rivers that likely destroyed canal networks.

The big question now was whether Phoenix, which has been described as the world's least sustainable city, was headed toward a similar fate. Temperatures were rising all across Arizona because of global warming, but they were rising much faster in Phoenix because of the urban heat island effect. Concrete, asphalt and buildings absorb and retain the heat of the sun in a way that desert and fields do not. The daytime highs are hotter than they've ever been, and the city doesn't cool off at night like it used to. The nights are roughly 9 degrees hotter than in 1948. Maricopa County, which has more than 4 million residents, is expecting another 2 million people in the next twenty years, and massive new master-planned communities are in the works to accommodate them. This can only worsen the heat island effect and put further strain on the water supplies.

A recent study projected that half of Phoenix's residents would need emergency medical care if the fragile power grid went out during a summer heat wave, and that 13,000 people would die. By 2060, according to another projection, extreme heat and water scarcity could make Phoenix one of the most uninhabitable places on the continent. But other experts predict that the city will learn to conserve, adapt, reuse, exploit far-flung aquifers, claim a much larger share of the CAP water and leave rural Arizona to wither, enrich the Gila River tribes by buying their water, and find other ways to keep going. I'm not in the future-predicting business, but I tend to agree with this assessment.

Phoenix is so improbable to begin with, so utterly dependent on air conditioning and vast hydrological engineering projects, but it has enormous wealth, power, determination and ambition. Tucson is talking about conservation, rainwater capture, scaling back development, planting a million trees, accepting the natural limits of a desert environment and living within them. Phoenix is talking about a big-ass canal from the Mississippi River and a massive desalinization plant in Mexico that will cause an environmental disaster. One way or another, so long as water keeps flowing to money and the electrical grid keeps the a/c blasting in summer, I expect that Phoenix will keep engorging itself on land and water for the rest of my lifetime, and maybe Isobel's as well.

We stopped for gas and snacks in Buckeye, which I remembered as a small, mostly Hispanic farming community in the desert west of Phoenix, beautifully described by Alfredo Véa Jr. in his novel *La Maravilla*. Now it was the western flank of the megasprawl and one of the fastest-growing cities in America, with over 100,000 residents and plans to grow to a million, although it was having trouble demonstrating to state regulators that it had a viable hundred-year water supply, which was required under Arizona law.

After Buckeye, we finally broke free of the last billboards, gas stations, auto dealerships, convenience stores and accident attorney billboards. We entered a barren hardpan desert that had once been the bed of an ancient sea. Its flatness was occasionally broken by low fanged mountain ranges that appeared to be made of iron. I appreciated its desolation and indifference, its lack of salesmanship and artificiality. Things out here were stark and direct. They were set out plainly.

I turned off the interstate and drove out to the remote Butler Valley in La Paz County.

Underneath the Butler Valley is one of the most valuable aquifers in Arizona, containing 6 million acre-feet of water conveniently located near the canal that brings Colorado River water to Phoenix. The aquifer, which formed during the last Ice Age, had been earmarked as an important future water source for Phoenix. But because groundwater is completely unregulated in rural Arizona, a Saudi Arabian company called Fondomonte was pumping massive amounts of water from this aquifer to grow alfalfa to feed to dairy cattle in the Middle East. Why had the Saudis come to Arizona? Because they had drained the aquifers in Saudi Arabia, growing feed for dairy cattle, and there were no laws preventing them from doing the same thing here.

Looking through binoculars from the side of the road, I could see bright green fields, irrigation ditches, and overhead sprinkler systems extending for miles. Fondomonte was able to pump as much water here as it wanted, without paying for a single drop, even though the Riyadh-based company didn't own this land. Since 2015 it had been leasing it in a sweetheart deal from the Arizona State Land Department, for an annual rate of just $25 an acre. Fondomonte was not disclosing how much water it was using, nor was it required to do so, but it was estimated at 22,400 acre-feet a year.

Fondomonte also owned a 10,000-acre alfalfa operation thirty miles away near Salome, and Al Dahra, a corporation from the United Arab Emirates, had another massive alfalfa farm in nearby Wenden. They were pumping out so much water that land was subsiding and municipal and residential wells were going dry. It was illegal to export water out of Arizona, but "virtual water," as some were calling this alfalfa, could be shipped to the Middle East. Fondomonte's spokeswoman in Arizona said that it was "xenophobic" to single out Fondomonte when farming is a global business and other farms in Arizona were also pumping groundwater and exporting their crops around the world.

The way I saw it, it was another self-defeating outcome that stemmed from Arizona's knee-jerk hostility to government regulations and religious devotion to the free market. Here in the Butler Valley, the most drought-stricken state in America was giving away vast amounts of its dwindling water supplies in order to enrich a foreign corporation and feed cattle on the other side of the world. It was outrageous, and by any reasonable standard, it was also insane.

*E*van Mecham was a twitchy-eyed, possum-faced Pontiac dealer from Glendale in the metro Phoenix sprawl. A Mormon and a paranoid far-right crank who belonged to the John Birch Society, he was elected as Arizona's governor in 1987, at his fifth attempt. In defense of the voters, many of them didn't know much about him—a staggering 50 percent of the electorate had moved to Arizona in the previous six years.

Once in office, he became convinced that he was being spied on. While searching in the ceiling of the governor's office for hidden microphones, one of his senior aides fell and broke a leg. Then Mecham accused the attorney general of using laser beams to listen in on his private conversations. His bigotry was completely unfiltered. He blamed workingwomen for the divorce rate and denounced a gubernatorial recall campaign as "a band of homosexuals." He said Japanese eyes "got round" when they saw Arizona's golf courses, and defended the use of "pickaninnies" as a legitimate term for Black children. This inspired an Arizona bumper sticker, "Pickaninny: What we did for Governor."

When Mecham canceled the state holiday for Martin Luther King Jr. Day, the NFL withdrew the Super Bowl from Arizona, thirty conventions were canceled, and a boycott ensued, costing the state tens of millions of dollars. After a little more than a year in office, Governor Mecham was indicted on six felony charges. These included borrowing $80,000 from a state fund to rescue his auto dealership, and taking an unreported campaign loan of $350,000 from a developer he had just met. He was facing up to twenty-two years in prison when he became the first Arizona governor in history to be impeached. But he was later acquitted in court on the felony charges, and he ran again for governor in 1990, placing a strong second in the Republican primary.

Chapter Fifteen

MONSOON SUMMER

Midway through our second summer, in 2021, a perfectly normal weather event took place, but it seemed miraculous. Cumulonimbus clouds bloomed up into the sky like cauliflowers, and they did not stall out and subside. They kept on climbing until they were dark ominous thunderheads and our hope was on tenterhooks. The sky boomed and flashed and the first fat raindrops came splatting down on the ramada roof. They kicked up little puffs of dust as they landed on the parched ground. Then forked lightning streaked across the sky, thunder crashed, and the rain came down in an almighty deluge.

In thirty minutes the temperature dropped from 104 degrees to 75 degrees. All over the city, people came out of their houses and stood in the rain, danced in the rain, howled in the rain. The street next to our house turned into a river of water, nearly a foot deep and flowing swiftly. Once the monsoon storm had passed over the city, taking its blessings north, we put on flip-flops and river sandals, made crude boats from aluminum foil, waded out into the warm current, and raced the boats against each other. This had been one of Mariah's favorite summer activities as a girl in Tucson, and it was gratifying to see that Isobel loved it too.

So began one of the wettest summers on record in Southern Arizona. It seemed as though the sky had finally remembered how to rain and now couldn't get enough of it. Our backyard transformed. In June, the two big beds were bare ground with small starter plants here and there. Now the plants were shooting upward and outward, filling in space and exploding with flowers, as if exuberantly drunk on rainwater. They attracted seven or eight different species of butterflies, including monarchs, queens, and swallowtails. More broad-billed and more Anna's hummingbirds arrived, plus a Costa's hummingbird and a rufous male, who glowed a gorgeous reddish-copper color. I thought he was as beautiful as Mr. Glamourzon, but Isobel strongly disagreed.

There was an almost perpetual whirring, buzzing, high-speed dogfight as the males battled for air supremacy and domination over the feeders and the choicest flowers. The efflorescence of life included a bumper crop of mosquitoes, gnats, flies, cockroaches, and other insects. All over the city the cicadas produced a high shrieking metallic whine. It was a characteristic sound of Tucson in summer, but we had never heard it so loud and insistent.

When we drove up into the Catalinas in August, the lower slopes of the mountains were as green as Ireland and we saw waterfalls cascading down the canyon walls. It was a similar story in the cactus desert west of the city: lush grasses, flowering vines, immense swarms of butterflies and other insects. One reason for the superabundance of insects, according to a biologist friend, was that bird and reptile populations had crashed in the terrible heat and drought of the preceding summers. Now the insects were feeding on the profusion of plant life generated by the rains, and reproducing over and over again with far less predation than normal.

In the Atascosa Mountains near Arivaca, botanists were finding plants growing that no one had seen there in forty years. The seeds had been lying dormant in the earth, waiting for a summer like this one, where it rained nearly every day, sometimes twice a day, and the landscape was taking on a tropical feel. I went hiking in the Santa Rita Mountains south of Tucson and had to push my way through chest-high grasses, vines, and flowering plants. In some ways it was an uncomfortable summer. I was often dripping with sweat from the high humidity, itchy from mosquito bites, and itchy-eyed and sneezing from pollen allergies. But if this was the price to pay for such glorious transformative rains, I was happy to pay it. And surely, I thought, all the rain had to be improving our long-term water prospects.

The experts kept saying that one good monsoon season was not going to fix twenty years of drought, that most of the rainfall was concentrated in Southern Arizona and not in the watershed of the Colorado River, where it was really needed to replenish reservoirs, and that the big monsoon rains, while welcome for the ecosystem, would make virtually no difference unless they started repeating year after year like they used to. I found this hard to accept, because rain is hope in the desert and it just kept on raining. The dry washes had become rushing streams. The Santa Cruz River was flowing with enough force and volume to dislodge the shopping carts in its channel, and its tributary the Rillito, which was normally sand and scrub, was churning with whitecaps and a few adventurous kayakers. And nearly every day I was out with Isobel racing boats and sticks on the river that flowed past our house.

————

She turned six that summer and moved out of her princess phase, except for the continuing expectation that she should be waited on hand and foot by her parents. She got rid of her tiaras and princess dresses and kept her scepters only because they were good for playing the Evil Queen. She threw away her collection of hair bows, which had been essential fashion items in Mississippi, but were not in vogue at her school in Tucson, or in keeping with her new fashion aesthetic. It pained Mariah's heart when Isobel refused to wear the pretty, chic French-looking dresses in which she had looked so timeless and adorable. Her new go-to outfit was faded denim shorts, black Dr. Martens boots with sparkles, and a black T-shirt with red roses and the legend *Rock Star*. "I'm into dark stuff now," she told us. "Vampires, demons, stuff like that. But not zombies. Zombies are still way too scary."

When people asked her what she wanted to be when she grew up, she said, "Fashion designer, vet and rock star." She did have an excellent sense of style, especially for grown-up clothes. Mariah and I routinely asked her what we should wear to social occasions, or if our outfits worked, because her judgments were instant and almost unerringly on the mark. It wasn't hard to imagine her ending up in some branch of the fashion world. In regard to her veterinary ambitions, it could be said that she loved animals, had a good rapport with most dogs, and a real talent for impersonating a puppy. Sometimes she would go along on all fours beside Savanna and Riley as we walked them through the neighborhood, sniffing at the curbside plants, panting with her tongue out and making little yips and barks.

We didn't have the heart to tell her she wasn't going to be a rock star. She was good at writing songs, like her bluesy rock anthem "Lady Prison" and a mournful new love ballad called "Oh My Horse Baby." But she didn't have the extrovert show-off charisma that rock stars need, and her singing voice left a lot to be desired. I loved her with all my heart, but it was all I could do not to clap my hands over my ears when she tried to carry a tune.

We wondered if she would grow up to be a writer or a wordsmith of some other kind, because she had a flair for language and an outsized vocabulary for her age. She would devise amazingly clever riddles, which we stupidly failed to write down or get on video and subsequently forgot, and she liked to make up oddball sayings as a way of playing with language. "I'm as old as a hedgehog in a slanted outhouse," she announced at the dinner table one evening.

"Are you sure?" said Mariah.

"Yes, Mama, I'm as sure as a candle lit with a fork. I'm as right as a duck swimming in spaghetti. And I'm as weird as a corkscrew stuck in a lemon."

Given the choice, she'd rather watch cartoons than read books, but she loved her books and invariably won the game we called Book Quiz, in which family members took turns asking a question about a small detail in one of Isobel's hundred-plus books. We were still reading them to her at bedtime, and she had started reading them by herself. One day that summer, she made a dramatic breakthrough and came bursting out of her bedroom to tell us about it. "I get it! I GET IT! Reading is amazing! It's just like you said. I started seeing it all in my mind like it was coming to life. It was like watching cartoons, only better. I get it! I get it! I finally get reading!" After that, she always had a book on the go, and never forgot to put one in her backpack for school. On weekends she got to read in bed as soon as she woke up.

Mariah, after working part-time at Crate & Barrel, was about to start a full-time job as an elementary school librarian, a position for which she had no experience. Since getting her master's in library science, she had worked only in college libraries. The school was on the south-ernmost fringe of South Tucson and about 90 percent of the students were Mexican Americans and Mexican nationals. The rest were Native American, with a few Anglos and African Americans. We drove down there to take a look at the school, passing the big casino owned by the Tohono O'Odham tribal nation, and the Raytheon missile and defense plant that employs 13,000 people—Tucson's second-largest employer after the university.

We turned into a neighborhood of trailers and derelict trailers, cars and the carcasses of cars, loose dogs, dirt side streets, heaps of rubble and old tires strewn about, plastic grocery bags caught on thorny plants and flapping like flags in the wind. It looked as poor as the poorest parts of Mississippi and reminded me of a small ranching town in Sonora. There were horses and cattle in some of the yards, a few nicer houses made of brick and stucco with wrought-iron fences, a brightly painted carnice-ria, or meat market, and a rustic-looking feedstore called El Suegro, the Father-in-Law. Some of Mariah's students would be coming to school on horseback and ATVs. Roughly half were learning English as a second language, and about 15 percent couldn't speak any English. It was a Title 1 school, receiving federal assistance because 80 percent of the students were "economically disadvantaged." Some of the other 20 percent, Mariah had heard, lived on fairly prosperous ranches to the south and were dropped off in big expensive vehicles.

The school stood in vivid contrast to its surroundings. It was bright and fresh and clean, with a blue and beige color scheme, small trees shaped into perfect ovals, larger mesquites and eucalyptus trees, and not a scrap of litter or disorder to be seen. The school looked proud and cherished, and this made sense to Mariah, because the people who interviewed her seemed highly motivated and well organized.

Academically the school was rated C, not bad at all considering the challenges it was facing. For the teachers and the new librarian, it offered a lot of hard work for pretty meager pay and benefits. When it comes to funding for public schools, teacher pay and educational outcomes, Arizona consistently ranks among the bottom five states in the country.

With Mariah working full-time, I would be taking Isobel to school, picking her up most days, and doing a lot more grocery shopping, cooking, cleaning, laundry and other chores. I worried about getting my work done and meeting my deadlines. Where was the time going to come from, especially if I wanted to exercise and walk the dogs as well? Then Isobel's school announced that it was no longer providing aftercare, and students would need picking up at three p.m. Now I started to panic and curse, and rifle through options.

The Jewish Community Center (JCC) was conveniently located and its aftercare program had excellent reviews, but we weren't Jewish. I called up my friend Aaron Levinson in Philadelphia and explained the predicament. "What should I say if they ask if we're Jewish?" I asked. "Tell them you practice the Jewish values of tolerance, rationality and education in your home," he said. "We actually do practice those values," I said. "You see?" said Aaron. "You're more Jewish than you thought."

Mariah had worked at the JCC as a teenager, when its members were exclusively Jewish. Now, as I discovered to my relief during the application process, it was welcoming people from all creeds and backgrounds while promoting Jewish culture and values. That was fine by us. We had a solution to our aftercare problem, as well as access to a gym and a swimming pool, and Isobel would get to learn about one of the world's great thought systems. Once enrolled, we began getting several emails a week about Jewish religious and cultural customs. I welcomed these emails as a learning opportunity and tried hard to memorize the information they contained. But I soon became overwhelmed by all the Torah references and Hebrew phrases, and gave up my learning journey into Judaism with a sense of guilt and failure. "Now you feel like a bad Jew," said Aaron. "Join the club."

Then we found out, via Isobel, that the person sending out many of these emails wasn't Jewish. He was a Christian who was learning about Judaism in order to teach it at the JCC. When I told this to Aaron, he exploded with delight. "Where else is this going to happen?" he crowed. "Where is the Sunday school that hires a Jewish guy to teach Christianity to their kids? Where is the madrasa that hires a non-Muslim to teach Islam? I *love* this. It makes me proud of my people."

The JCC became an important part of our daily lives in Tucson, and we were highly impressed by its competence and commitment to tolerance and good works. The staff regularly bused in handicapped people for activities programs. During Ramadan, they collected money and food for poor Muslim families in Tucson. We signed Isobel up for the gymnastics, swimming and basketball programs, and enrolled her in the summer and winter camps. By joining the JCC—and this hadn't occurred to us when we enrolled—we also exposed ourselves to potentially dangerous anti-Semitism for the first time. A Christian community center wouldn't have needed security guards, but they were always stationed outside the JCC and sometimes armed, depending on the threat level.

I was working out in the gym one afternoon, with Isobel downstairs in aftercare, when Pima County sheriff's deputies came through with a sniffer dog. Someone had called in a bomb threat, for the second time that year. A nearby synagogue had been vandalized recently, graffitied with swastikas and a misspelled anti-Semitic slur. A thirty-year-old man named Nathan Beaver—blond crew cut, pig face, elongated earring holes—was arrested and charged for this crime. Two other synagogues in Tucson were also vandalized that year.

Right-wing political violence had come too close to our family with the shotgun attack at Isobel's sister school. Then there was random violence: Jill's son was still processing the fact that his math tutor had been shot and killed for no apparent reason by a complete stranger. And a young dental hygienist jogging in the neighborhood next to ours was shot in the neck in another random attack. Having thrown in our lot with the JCC, we also had to take on the threat of anti-Semitic violence and more fully understand that it was always there for Jewish people and had been for a very long time.

————

Sometimes Mariah came home from her new job in tears. Sometimes she collapsed on the bed with exhaustion. Sometimes she wanted a cocktail, and sometimes she was happy and eager to talk because her day had gone well, or she had made a meaningful connection with a student, or someone had been kind to her, like the two little girls who approached her shyly and asked if they could volunteer to help in the library.

Mariah needed all the help she could get. There were hundreds of books that needed shelving and hundreds more that were shelved incorrectly. She needed to order new books and catalogue them, there was a pile of old computers to clear out, and the library needed new furniture and repainting. But Mariah had very little time to work on these projects because she was also required to teach multiple classes every day in the library, and on weekends she had to prepare detailed lesson plans for those classes, which were focused on books, reading and research. She also had to pitch in with morning duty, lunch duty and bus duty. All in all, it was a tough job. With no training or experience as a teacher, she struggled to control the unruly students. Even the veteran teachers were saying they had never seen such bad behavior problems, which they attributed to the pandemic. These students were finally coming back to school in person after nearly eighteen months at home.

Culturally, the school was familiar to Mariah. She had grown up around Mexican Americans and Mexican nationals, and they had been in the majority at her high school. She told her students that she didn't speak Spanish, but she knew enough to call them out when they said *pendejo,* a mildly vulgar word meaning asshole/idiot. "Miss!" they said in shocked tones, "I thought you didn't speak Spanish." Once she knew all their names, gained a better understanding of what worked and what didn't, and stopped covering her face with a mask, she found it easier to both take charge of the room and convey her kind, sympathetic nature.

Sometimes she was able to spellbind the students with stories that she read to them, or fully engage them with research projects. Sometimes she got compliments, hugs, and sweet little notes. After two months, there were still some really bad days and consistent disruptive behavior from some students, but she wasn't coming home in tears anymore. "So many of the problems actually could be solved by throwing money at them," she said. "If the teachers had an aide in the classroom, it would make all the difference. We're all trying so hard, but we're stretched so thin."

There was a refreshing lack of petty politics among the staff at the school, and a real commitment to achieving better results. Many of the teachers and staff lived in the district and sent their own children to the school. "I know we all love this school and love working here," one of the district administrators said in a speech at the beginning of the year. "But we need to face the reality that our test scores are not where they need to be, and a lot of our students are failing."

The biggest challenge was the high level of poverty in the district. Study after study has shown that low-income families tend to read and talk less to their children, value education less, and put less pressure on their children to do well at school compared to higher-income families. Low-income communities experience the most social dysfunction, and at this school, it was also fairly commonplace for a student to go through the trauma of losing a parent to deportation.

Mariah was impressed by the care and love and support that most parents put into their children—the elaborate perfection of the girls' hairstyles, the carefully packed lunches, and the parents' engagement at teacher-parent conferences. And she also wondered about the home lives of those students who came to school in dirty clothes with unwashed hair, or with a big bag of candy to eat but no other food, or completely exhausted because no one had prevented them from playing video games all night. What challenges were those parents facing? The great majority of the students seemed like normal, healthy, well-adjusted kids, but there was a sizable minority with ADHD, autism and other learning disorders. It was unquestionably the hardest job Mariah had ever had. Sometimes it was brutally exhausting and sometimes it was incredibly rewarding: she got to inspire a young mind with the love of books and reading. And it came with a spectacular bonus: summers off, for as long as she could deal with the rest of it.

———

Mariah was gone before we woke up in the morning, and then it was a race against the clock to get Isobel dressed and fed, win the teeth-and-hair battle, unload the dishwasher, pack her lunch, fill her water bottle, throw on some clothes, drink a triple espresso to counteract the sleep deprivation, and get out the door. On the drive to school, we counted dogs and chatted, and I tried to keep her eyes averted from the f-bomb bumper stickers and flags that we regularly came across in traffic: "Fuck Gun Control," "Fuck Your Feelings," "Fuck Around and Find Out," "Do I Look Like a Fucking People Person?" "Fuck Biden," "Fuck Biden and Fuck You for Voting for Him," "Zero Fucks Given," "#gfyourself."

There were many hard questions to answer on those drives to school. "How long does it take a snail to climb to the top of a gazebo?" was in one category of difficulty. "Dada, what's an adult shop?" was in another. I told her it sold boring stuff for adults like tools and uniforms. She wanted to know why people made war, why they were mean to animals, why they were destroying the planet, and what was wrong with them. One morning she surprised me by asking, "Why did Donald Trump put kids in cages?" She must have heard about the Trump administration's family separation policy at school, because we certainly didn't tell her. I tried to explain the rationale for the policy, that separating children from their parents and in some cases locking the children in chain-link enclosures was supposed to deter foreigners from coming to America illegally, but she couldn't get her head around it: "Why would anyone do that to a family? That's the worst thing I've ever heard."

When we reached the school, she would scamper off and hail her friends, and I would drive home and attempt to ignore all the chores that needed doing, and the ever-beckoning internet, and get some work done. I was trying a new system in which I would knock out a household chore every time I took a break from writing. It seemed like the most efficient use of time, but it didn't help my writing or my general mood. Work and life went better when I took myself on long walks, read books, made trips into the desert, socialized in the evening, or went out for lunch with friends. But it was impossible to find the time to do those things and keep up with everything else.

I was living the kind of life I had sworn to myself I would never live, ruled by responsibilities and money demands, clogged up with chores and drudgery, with almost no freedom to spend my time as I wanted. If I took a day off and went hiking, I got further behind on writing and had to work harder to catch up. I often felt trapped, because I was utterly trapped. I still struggled with my restlessness and the call of the open road. In the bleak, angry, wounded aftermath of our mercifully infrequent marital fights, I invariably fantasized about living by myself in a vehicle again, but I knew I wasn't going to do it. It was a bad idea and I couldn't bear the thought of inflicting that much pain and sadness on Isobel, whose love for me was so pure and deeply trusting.

Parenthood had changed me profoundly, just as everyone said it would. I was no longer a self-contained individual, pursuing my own interests and desires. My daughter had the upper hand over my emotions. She could destroy the pleasure of a delicious meal in a restaurant by refusing to try anything on the menu, or fill me with joy by dancing around the living room to Earth, Wind & Fire, a band she had loved since she was a baby. Once, when I was suffering from an acute injury to my worn-out spine, she reached her hands up and started to lean backward, expecting me to grab her hands as any father would. But I just stood there, because in that moment my body decided to guard its injury, and she fell backward and landed hard on the wooden floor with the back of her head. Even though she wasn't concussed or badly hurt, the look of shock, pain and betrayal on her face was like a nail hammered into my heart. Hours later I was still struggling not to weep.

As a younger man, when I vowed to myself that I would never settle down and have children, I didn't fully understand how much love a family can generate, even though I grew up in a loving and reasonably happy family myself. Or maybe I just didn't care. The desire for a life of constant travel and personal freedom was so powerful that I was inclined to dismiss anything that might get in its way. It had taken decades to get that out of my system, and I wouldn't trade those decades for anything, but now, as I approached sixty, the keys to my happiness were held by a six-year-old girl and her mother.

*T*he small town of Quartzite in the far western desert is unusual in two ways: seasonal demographics and glorification of camels. During the long inferno of summer, in the hottest part of the state, its population is around 2,400. But in the mild sunny winter months, more than a million people—the chamber of commerce claims two million—arrive to fill up the RV parks and camp in the surrounding desert. Most of them are retirees in motor homes.

A carnival atmosphere prevails, with swap meets, parades, a gem and mineral show, potluck suppers, balloon rides, and a five-day celebration called Camelpalooza. It features camel rides, camel educationals, and a movie screening of *Legendary Ottoman Camel Driver Hi Jolly*, about the man who cemented Quartzite's relationship with these humped animals and is buried here in a pyramid tomb topped with a metal camel silhouette.

In 1856, Secretary of War Jefferson Davis (future president of the Confederacy) imported seventy-five camels to transport freight and people across the newly acquired desert Southwest. The lead camel driver with the new U.S. Army Camel Corps was a Greek Syrian Muslim named Hadji Ali. Americans called him Hi Jolly. He successfully completed a round-trip journey from Texas to California. The camels performed admirably, but they made the horses and mules fearful, panicky and difficult to manage. Under heavy pressure from the mule lobby and consumed by the impending Civil War, Congress declined more funding for the Camel Corps. The animals were auctioned off and some ended up feral in the desert.

Hi Jolly moved to Arizona, married a woman in Tucson, and ended up in Quartzite, which later decided to fashion its identity around him and the short-lived camel experiment. Images of camels are all over town. Live camels move around in horse trailers. Town council members have little camel statues next to their nameplates.

Chapter Sixteen

BIG SANDY

The landscapes of Arizona come in a magnificent variety and are nothing like the flat sandy desert that outsiders often imagine. In the southeast are the savanna-like grasslands and sky island mountain ranges. West of Tucson and across the Tohono O'Odham reservation is saguaro-studded upland Sonoran Desert, the wettest and most biodiverse desert in the world. On the high escarpment known as the Mogollon Rim (pronounced *Muggy-yawn*) is the largest Ponderosa pine forest on the continent, extending for two hundred miles. The San Francisco Peaks near Flagstaff rise to 12,600 feet and are snowcapped for much of the year. North of them is the Colorado Plateau, land of red rock spires and buttes, the Hopi mesas and the Navajo Nation, Monument Valley, the Painted Desert and the Grand Canyon. None of that rich variety was on display, however, as I drove up through western Arizona to join Wayne Belger at the world's largest machine-gun shoot. Apart from a Joshua tree forest I had forgotten about, it was scrubby hardpan desert and low jagged mountain ranges for five hours straight.

217

I stopped in the middle of nowhere to photograph Nothing. Founded in 1977, it once boasted a population of four, who described themselves on a sign as "staunch citizens" and "dedicated people" who had "faith in Nothing, hoped for Nothing, worked at Nothing, for Nothing." Now it consisted of an abandoned, vandalized building and a sun-battered sign saying NOTHING.

Twenty miles up the road was Wickieup, population seventy-one, unambitiously named after a style of temporary Native American hut. Eleven miles more and I turned off the highway on a dirt road, crossed the Big Sandy River without getting my tires wet, and followed the signs to the Big Sandy Shoot. I tried to shift out of tenderhearted father and husband mode, and get ready for three days of violent aggression and what promised to be earsplitting noise. For protection, I had bought a pair of fairly expensive electronic earmuffs designed to mute the sound of gunfire and amplify human speech.

I felt uneasy and apprehensive. If anyone asked what I was doing at the shoot with a notebook and no machine gun, I would tell them I was writing about Wayne's Second Amendment Photography Project, which was true. But he was misrepresenting the project, and I was going along with it. What if angry gun nuts found out we were impostors? Wayne was using his real name, and despite his scrubbing attempts it only took a few minutes on the internet to find his sympathetic portrayals of the Standing Rock pipeline protestors, far-left Zapatista rebels in Mexico, Palestinians in the West Bank, and Syrian refugees arriving in Greece. It was obvious from these images where his political sympathies lay.

I picked up the vendor pass he left for me at the entrance gate and drove up to a dusty, windswept, flattened ridge overlooking a canyon. A small mountain on the other side of the canyon acted as a backstop for the bullets. The canyon floor was littered with oil drums and wrecked cars and trucks—these would be used as targets. More than a hundred RVs were parked along the ridge, and many of them were fronted by vendor booths. Along the rim of the canyon was a quarter-mile firing range with hundreds of perfectly legal, fully automatic machine guns set up and ready to fire, plus mortars, military cannons, rocket-propelled grenade launchers, antiaircraft guns and a great big Sherman tank. American flags were flying. Jimi Hendrix was blaring from the speakers. Once again, Arizona was taking it to extremes. There was more than enough firepower here to annihilate a small army.

The atmosphere was markedly different to the gun show in Phoenix. A few people had right-wing slogans on their shirts or hats—"Unborn Lives Matter," "God Guns Trump"—but it didn't feel nearly as surly or politicized. Wayne broke it down for me when I found his booth, with Alanna's banner—"Show Your Pride with Second Amendment Photography"—rattling in a strong wind. "There's less attitude, less assholery, less macho stancing, and less aggressive Christianity," he said. "No one here is talking about commie Satanists. Normally I have to explain to people what a pinhole camera is. Not here. They know. They remind me of guys who are into vintage cars, except they're into hardcore weapons of war."

It was a new aspect of American gun culture for Wayne, and the imagery was powerful and irresistible. He was excited to photograph it, but he also felt conflicted. "I don't think they should have this stuff, but they seem like decent guys. And I really, really want to shoot a machine gun."

They were mostly older white men with large amounts of disposable income. Some were dressed in military regalia, others in khakis and polo shirts, and most somewhere in between. Arizona was heavily represented, but the shooters were from all over the country, and a few were from Europe, Mexico and Australia. I talked to a Jewish doctor from Dallas who withheld his name. He had approximately $100,000 worth of guns and was planning to shoot off "a good six figures" worth of ammunition, which is extremely easy to do with a machine gun. A single round for the hulking .50 caliber guns, which are designed to take out planes and armored personnel carriers, cost $5 at the vendor booths, and the .50 cals, as everyone called them, could shoot 1,200 rounds a minute, or $6,000 a minute at vendor prices. Even the vintage twin-drum Thompsons shot $1,000 worth of ammo in less than a minute, and the Big Sandy Shoot went on for three days.

It began with a hats-off, hands-on-heart Pledge of Allegiance, followed by a lone howl of "Let's Go Brandon!" and a safety talk by Ed Hope, the eighty-year-old general manager of the event. You could shoot handguns, but you couldn't wear them. Ear protection was mandatory. When shooting at the model planes that would be flying through the canyon, resist the urge to keep following them with your gun barrel, so as not to endanger the shooting line. Also beware of target fixation that led you above the horizon, because on the other side of the mountain was public grazing land. When shooting mortars and grenades, try not to set the mountain on fire, although there was a fire crew for that eventuality. "We've never had a serious accident and let's keep it that way," he concluded.

Then the shooters went to their guns, a horn blared, a red flag was run up a pole, someone yelled, "Fire in the hole!" and all the machine guns opened up at once. Even with ear protection, I found it horrendously loud. I could feel the concussive pressure waves from the .50 cals inside my lungs and my skull, which sent my body into clenched distress mode because it had never experienced anything like it. The loudest rock concerts were like lullabies compared to war machines. The Miniguns made a rude, dirty, outrageous sound like a massively amplified raspberry. The boom from the artillery pieces was like getting punched in both ears at once and the howitzer seemed to jolt my eyeballs in their sockets. In addition to the oil drums and wrecked vehicles, there were "reactive targets" that exploded when you hit them with machine-gun fire. I took cover behind the RVs, where it was still loud as hell with ear protection, and looked at my watch. Three hours and forty minutes to go until they took their first break.

———

I found Ed Hope, the general manager, and interviewed him on the far side of the ridge, behind all the RVs and the catering tent. Conversation was possible there unless the .50 cals or the Miniguns were going off. His hearing aid—all the older guys had hearing aids—was wirelessly connected to his cellphone, so he'd be looking at me, answering my question, and then he'd come out with an apparent non sequitur because his calls went straight into his ear: "The shoot has been going for thirty-three years, seventeen years at this range, and we do it in memory of Bob Farris, who was an icon in this community, and . . . Hey, yeah, Kent'll take care of that, sure thing, bye. Now where was I?"

"Bob Farris," I said.

"Right," he continued. "Bob was an old gentleman and a bachelor with no kids because he was so completely focused on firearms. After he died we put him in a big green dinosaur full of explosives, set him out there on the range, and blew him into dust, which was his wish."

"It's as not as political here as we were expecting," I said. "Is that deliberate?"

"Yes. I'm a liberal Democrat and nearly all these other guys are brainwashed Trump Republicans, so we try to keep politics out of it."

"You're a liberal Democrat? With machine guns?"

"That's right. I'm a retired schoolteacher from Flagstaff. I taught auto mechanics. I have thirty-six machine guns and more than three hundred other firearms. I hate the NRA, even though I'm a lifetime member, because they gave my personal information to the Republican Party, because Wayne LaPierre belongs in jail, and because I want more gun control. If we keep doing nothing when a mentally ill teenager gets an AR and shoots up his classmates, we're feeding ammunition to the anti-gun people."

"What sort of gun control do you support?"

"We need to start policing this, with strict gun licenses and harsh punishments for gun crimes. Otherwise they're going to start taking away our machine guns, even though they're not the problem. These guns have never been used in a mass shooting, and they're tightly regulated with background checks by the FBI and fingerprinting and a whole lot of paperwork, which is how it should be."

"Are there any other Democrats here?"

"Let's see, we've got about a hundred and fifty shooters. I'd say maybe twenty are Democrats, and they're keeping it quiet. The guys who come here aren't militia types. They're dedicated collectors and most of them are professionals or gun dealers. Working people can't afford the guns or the ammo. We estimate there are $10 million worth of guns at the shoot, and these guys will shoot about 3.5 million rounds. We have the shoot twice a year because it takes that long to accumulate the ammo. I'll shoot $5,000 worth in a few minutes and I won't even care. It's just so much fun."

———

Like me, Wayne was astonished and delighted to learn that the man in charge of the world's largest machine-gun shoot was a liberal Democrat.

It was one of the things that Wayne and I had in common: both of us loved seeing stereotypes upended. "I get a lot of shit from left-wing people for hanging out at gun shows and Second Amendment rallies," he said. "They think that all gun nuts are evil crazy racists, and they're offended that I engage with them. It's the exact mirror of what I hear at gun shows about liberals, that they're all evil crazy communists. If we hadn't come out here and started interacting with these people, we'd never know that a guy like Ed Hope or his viewpoint existed, or that the guys who are into machine guns, the deadliest guns of all, are basically hobbyists and collectors."

Wayne had been walking up and down the firing line, meeting people, watching them shoot, asking them about their weapons, which of course they loved to talk about, and inviting them to have their photograph taken later at his booth. The noise and jolting explosions didn't bother him. His ears were far less sensitive than mine, which he attributed to years of punk rock concerts and shooting guns. He was thoroughly enjoying himself until a guy yelled, "Fuck you, nigger!" as he raked the canyon floor with machine-gun fire. "It wasn't one of the registered shooters," Wayne said. "It was a new guy who just showed up. There was some embarrassed laughter. It made people uncomfortable. But I share my life with a Black woman, you know what I mean?"

Wayne conceived the Second Amendment Photography Project because he was so upset and disturbed by the relentless mass shootings in modern American life, and the way they were being enabled by the new extremism around the Second Amendment and the mass marketing of assault rifles. He thought it was insane that the most popular weapon for the mass murder of innocent Americans, including schoolchildren, was being called "America's rifle" by the NRA and sanctified as a holy weapon by fundamentalist Christians.

"I was thinking, 'Fuck these people. I'm going to go full Borat and expose how sick and crazy this whole thing is.' But I love people. I'm fascinated by them. Once I started meeting them and talking to them, the project turned into more of an exploration of a uniquely American mythology. It's been an amazing journey."

It was a foundational belief in right-wing gun culture that armed citizens would have to defend their country against foreign invaders or a tyrannical government. That was the true purpose of the Second Amendment, in their interpretation, and it was why they needed so much firepower. Wayne thought this was completely delusional. Early in the project he would say, "Don't you think the government would use Apache helicopters to take you out from five miles away, and AC-130 gunships and drone strikes?" To which the usual answer was "They wouldn't do that to American citizens." Instead of saying what he wanted to say—"Oh, so the tyrannical government is going to play nice and use limited firepower so you can defend yourself more effectively?"—Wayne had learned to say, "I hear ya," a simple phrase that he now employed all the time at gun shows. It was respectful and encouraged people to keep talking without directly agreeing or disagreeing with them.

He thought the U.S. Army, the most powerful military force in the world, could handle a foreign invader, and that it was mythological fantasy to believe the U.S. government could be defeated by citizens with assault rifles. "Sometimes I wish they'd be honest and come out with the real reason why they need an AR-15," Wayne said with a grin. "Sometimes I wish they would say, 'I have toxic masculinity issues and I need this rifle as my support puppy.'"

It was true what Ed Hope said about machine guns. They were tightly regulated and had never been used in a mass shooting, but Wayne still thought it was potentially very dangerous for civilians to have them: "What if one of these guys gets robbed? A Minigun could take out thousands of people at a sports stadium in a couple of minutes. What if one of these guys goes nuts, or has a really bad day and wants to go out with a bang? What if a domestic terrorist with no criminal record wants to go through the process to get a .50 cal machine gun? He could take out planes coming in to land at LAX."

In the break between the morning shoot and the afternoon shoot, Wayne was in his booth showing people the camera, explaining the project, keeping his views to himself, and taking portraits of Americans with their machine guns. He was having trouble with the wind, which was making his flag backdrops move around too much and blurring the images. I asked why he couldn't dispense with the flag backdrops and he explained their importance.

When he was ten years old, watching television with his family in California, a news story came on about a young woman named Patty Hearst who had been kidnapped and brainwashed by the Symbionese Liberation Army. "I saw her standing in front of a flag with a gun," he said. "It was the first time I understood the world wasn't safe. The image is burned into my memory and when I started this project, I used the same composition."

He decided it was too windy to photograph and we wandered the vendor booths. He bought a .50 cal SLAP (saboted light armor penetrator) round as a component for an art installation. The vendor assured him it would penetrate three inches of solid steel. She was a young woman, tattooed, brassy and talkative, wearing a tank top and a bandanna in her hair. She was selling ammo, guns and gun parts with her husband, who looked wary and shifty. They were living in a slightly battered motor home, traveling around the western states to gun shows, rallies and shooting events.

"I like to blow shit up," she said raspily. "I'd never shot a .50 cal before I came here. If I had a weenie, it'd give me a hard-on. My husband is brilliant with guns. He can turn anything into a fully automatic."

Her husband shot her a look that said, *Quit talking about illegal shit.*

They were from Oregon, but they were spending most of their time in Arizona now, because it had so many gun events and such gun-friendly laws. It wasn't everywhere you could drive around in a motor home full of machine guns, ammo and gunsmithing tools without sweating a traffic stop. "We got pulled over outside Bullhead City and it was no fucking problem," she said. "The cop thought our guns were cool."

The tank had come to Big Sandy from Las Vegas, where it was rented out to tourists for rides and car-crushings. It fired massive 105 mm shells, weighing 23 pounds each. The tank guys, who were young, friendly and dressed in military garb, invited Wayne and me to climb aboard and go for a ride through the desert. Sometimes you wake up in the morning and have no idea what the day has in store for you. I had met a liberal machine-gun enthusiast, had my ears assaulted by the loudest noise I had ever heard, and now I was riding on a tank that was demolishing desert vegetation and turning with impressive agility. When the tank ride ended, they offered us a blast on their Minigun. Considering that the Minigun burned through $100 of ammunition in a single second, this was a generous offer, and it seemed churlish to refuse.

But first they loaded one of those massive shells into the tank's main gun. Shooters and spectators gathered around for this Big Sandy highlight. When the massive ground-shaking boom came, the crowd whooped and roared. Afterwards I fired the Minigun and some other machine guns. The thrill of harnessing all that power, violence and explosive force was more than counterbalanced by the pain it inflicted on my ears and the inside of my head. Wayne, on the other hand, couldn't get enough of it.

The night shoot struck us both as the most American spectacle we had ever seen. It was like the Fourth of July combined with *Apocalypse Now*. The machine guns were shooting tracer rounds in red, white and blue at lit-up model airplanes and reactive targets that exploded with white flames. There were fireworks in the sky and grenade explosions, flares going off, fires on the mountain, fires in the canyon, smoke everywhere, the fire brigade deployed. Booming artillery, the murderous rattle of the .50 cals, the dirty thunder of the Miniguns, all-American cries of "Fuck yeah!" and "Dayum bitches!" On and on it went, hour after pulverizing hour. Wayne and I slept in our vehicles that night, and from the ringing in my ears, I was pretty certain that they'd sustained permanent damage.

————

The following day, a Saturday, the shoot filled up with hundreds of spectators, and now it felt more like the Phoenix gun show. These were mostly working people from Northwest Arizona, the reddest part of the state, and by some metrics the reddest place in the nation. The parking lot below the ridge was a phalanx of pickup trucks, and I guessed that most of them had a handgun inside, since they weren't allowed up here at the shoot.

It was single men and families, with children as young as three and four, which I found hard to fathom. Arizona's fast-growing population of African Americans was not well represented. The majority of the men wore full beards and T-shirts and caps emblazoned with slogans: "Let's Go Brandon," "We the People Are Pissed," "FU46," "Do Whatever Da

Fuck You Wanna Do," "I Smell Commies," "Zero Fucks Given," "Ready
For War," "No One Needs An AR-15? No One Needs A Whiny Little
Bitch!" "Pedophile Hunter," "Guns Don't Kill People, I Kill People." A
few wore the insignia of the Three Percenter militia movement. There
were bikers and their old ladies, a few old cowboys in Wranglers and
straw hats, a couple of ex-con hard cases with Aryan Nations tattoos.

In midafternoon they formed a loose crowd around the tank as it
prepared to fire. I was in the back of the crowd, scribbling in my notebook. When I looked up, there was a man in my face.

"The fuck are you doing?" he said.

We were both wearing ear protection, so his voice came through
like a tinny recording. I pointed to my vendor badge. He shook his
head slowly and glowered at me. I ignored him and went back to taking
notes, wondering if he would escalate or let it go, keeping my eyes on
the page. Then came the cry of "Fire in the hole!" from the tank crew,
followed by the colossal boom, which I used to make a swift exit.

I went to my vehicle, shut myself inside, ripped off my disappointing
ear protection. I needed a break from the noise and the scene. I drove to
the gas station convenience store in Wickieup. It was busy on a Saturday afternoon. People were dressed much the same as the spectators at
the Big Sandy machine-gun shoot, but with one significant difference.
There was no rule against wearing sidearms here. About half of the
men and women in the store and getting in and out of cars and trucks
in the parking lot had semiautomatic pistols holstered on their belts.

On the way back to the shoot, I stopped on the dirt road, walked up a
dry wash for a few hundred yards, sat down on a rock, and drank a cold
beer with my ears ringing in the blessed silence. All around me were
low desert hills with catclaw, creosotes, a few mesquites and ocotillos,
and mountains on the skyline in all directions. A red-tailed hawk soared

overhead and made its shrill cry. In the fine sand of the wash were the tracks of coyote, fox, rabbit, ringtail cat, kangaroo rat, snake and lizard.

If you turned the kaleidoscope of the Big Sandy Shoot, you could see a mutually supportive community of responsible hobbyists and collectors, a celebration of violence and war, an extraordinary freedom granted by a government to its citizens, an unparalleled method of converting money into noise, and the desecration of a place that probably looked like empty wasteland to most of the shooters—"nothing out there but desert." I thought about kit foxes, who had evolved their large delicate ears to become acutely sensitive in the desert silence, and the unfathomable quantity of lead that had been blasted into the canyon and the mountain and was now presumably leaching toxic chemicals into the soil and the aquifer.

———

Back at the shoot, we bumped into Mike Latham, the Phoenix gunsmith who first told us about Big Sandy. Once again the three of us fell into an easy rapport, and we gave him an early supper of canned soup and beer before the night shoot. Occasionally he talked about communists being in charge of the anti-gun states. My definition of a communist was apparently very different from his, but that was fine. I don't need to agree with people to value their company. Mike was a fourth-generation Arizonan, and I asked him how he would describe the state's basic attitude. "It's not too friendly," he said, and I couldn't tell if he thought this was a good thing, a bad thing, or just the way things were.

Earlier that day I met a man wearing a shirt that read: "Happiness Comes from Guns, Not Relationships." He told me, "I've got ex-wives because of machine guns." I asked Mike if that was a common story in his world. "Guns can definitely be an obsession," he said. "Especially when you get into World War II and World War I guns, and the stories that go with those guns. My own collecting is pretty obsessive."

"I'm like that with Harleys," said Wayne. "My girlfriend doesn't understand why I need another one."

"How many Harleys do you have?" asked Mike.

"I have three and I want more."

"I have over two hundred guns," he said, and the statement hung there in the air for a moment before he continued. "My gun safe is a whole room that I built onto my house. I have a thirteen-year-old daughter who loves to shoot and is good at it, which I think is good for her general confidence. I'm not married. I'm looking for a woman who won't run from the guns, but it's hard. Most of them see that room and they want out."

Mike started shooting guns when he was five. His father was a firearms enthusiast and had been a gunsmith. As Mike told us about his gun-centric upbringing, I thought, *Are we all just products of our environment with a few small variations and anomalies?* "I wanted to get into the firearms industry, but I couldn't find a way. Then I found out about a two-year gunsmithing course at Yavapai College, and I enrolled and became a gunsmith."

He was stunned to learn that Ed Hope was a liberal Democrat who wanted more gun control. "That makes no sense at all," he said. Mike took the standard NRA position: any concessions on gun control would lead to more gun control. "Arizona passed a law saying we won't enforce any new gun control regulations, and we won't fund any agencies that enforce them," he said. "This is how we want it. So leave us alone."

I told him my thoughts about gun control. "It's possible they might raise the age limit on assault weapons to twenty-one, and there might be more background checks, but America is still going to be armed to the teeth, and we're going to keep getting mass shootings and a sky-high murder rate because of it. There's 400 million guns in this country already. The government isn't going to take them away from people, because it would be total mayhem if they tried."

"That 400 million figure is a very conservative estimate," he said. "It doesn't include all the guns sold before background checks came in. Those guns are still here. The real figure is probably closer to 600 million. And now you've got the Ghost Gunner 3-S. How do you regulate a gun that anyone can build in their kitchen in two hours with a block of aluminum and a 3D printer?"

It was getting dark now and the night shoot was imminent. We followed Mike down to his spot on the firing line, and he showed us the machine guns he had brought. "This PPS-43 was the pinnacle for the Russians at the end of World War II and the beginning of the Cold War . . . This is a 1914 Hotchkiss, the main heavy machine gun for the French and Americans in World War I . . . That one's a 20 millimeter. Big boy gun. Those bark really loud and will take out a light tank . . . Here's the .50 cal, the elephant in the room. It's something I built myself using the barrel from an armored personnel carrier. It's cheap and janky-looking and works great."

He had at least a dozen more. When the night shoot erupted, my jaws and body instinctively clenched against the violence and loudness, which was that of a pitched battle in wartime, but Mike looked perfectly calm and relaxed as he loaded up his machine guns and blasted away at the targets, and he was exceptionally generous in giving us a turn with any gun we wanted to shoot. My ears were in a lot of pain when he offered to load up the .50 cal for me, so I declined, which Wayne couldn't believe. "Oh, come on, man! When will you ever get the chance to shoot a .50 cal again?" Wayne was massively amped, coursing with excitement and adrenaline.

After the night shoot, a bonfire was built and we sat around it. Wayne really wanted to get himself a machine gun, and he was wondering if he could use his machinist skills to make one, even though it would be highly illegal. He and Mike had a long conversation about specifications, chambering, and other technical stuff I couldn't follow at all. Gradually Wayne came down off his machine-gun high, and Mike said just to call him if he ever wanted to shoot one again.

Later that night, Mike started talking about his dream for the future, the thing he had always wanted, the reason he had to stop spending all his money on machine guns and ammo. It struck me as a quintessentially Arizonan dream: "I want a long piece of land where I can shoot by myself."

*J*oseph Stedino was a Mafia associate, ex-con and FBI informant who went undercover in 1991 to expose the rampant corruption in Arizona politics. Working with the Phoenix district attorney's office, he posed as Tony Vincent, a flashy, big-spending mafioso who would attempt to buy lawmakers' votes with cash to get casino gambling legalized in Arizona, with the clear implication that the mob would run the casinos.

Accustomed to bribing politicians back east, he couldn't believe how easy and inexpensive it was in Arizona. Don Kenney, the conservative Mormon chair of the state house judiciary committee, took $55,000, even though gambling was prohibited by his religion, but others sold their votes for as little as $660. Chuy Higuera, a Democrat from Tucson, said he'd do it for the shrimp concession at the casino. Stedino felt bad for Higuera, knowing how cheap he would look when it all went public, and urged him to take some money. A number of lawmakers said they'd vote Stedino's way if he brought them prostitutes, but to his frustration, the DA's office wouldn't allow it.

Stedino, who was wearing a wire the whole time, exposed and recorded a political culture ruled by greed, corruption, lust and cynicism. Male legislators jockeyed for seats that gave them the most revealing views of their female colleagues. Lobbyists peddled bogus "studies" tailored by unscrupulous faculty members at Arizona State University, and pestered Stedino to "rub out" rival lobbyists. "There's not an issue in this world I give a shit about," said state representative Bobby Raymond, a Democrat from Phoenix. "I do deals . . . My favorite line is 'What's in it for me?'" Stedino borrowed that line as the title of his highly entertaining book about the whole sordid affair.

Eighteen people were convicted in the so-called AzScam bribery sting, including two state senators, five representatives and one former representative, five lobbyists, two Democratic Party officials, and one justice of the peace. Stedino dispensed over $300,000 in bribes to reel them in and came very close to landing the house and senate majority leaders, both of whom took his money and wriggled free.

Chapter Seventeen

THE LIONS OF THE RIGHT

I wanted to meet politicians and get a better understanding of the political scene. After many decades as a Republican stronghold, Arizona was America's newest swing state, voting narrowly for Joe Biden in 2020 and sending two Democratic senators to Washington. A 2014 Harvard study found it to be the most politically corrupt state in the country—both in terms of government officials providing benefits in exchange for illegal gifts and cash, and for legal campaign donations—but it seemed less corrupt than it used to be.

Every four years when the election results were announced, Chuck Bowden bet me a bottle of wine that the incoming governor would be impeached or sent to prison. That was a good sporting wager in the era of Evan Mecham (impeached for swindling and corruption) and Fife Symington III (convicted on seven counts of bank fraud, later pardoned by Bill Clinton). Since Symington's resignation in 1997, however, all the governors had managed to serve out their terms without being indicted.

I particularly wanted to meet Republicans and understand what was happening with the Arizona GOP. Once an election-winning machine, it now appeared to be locked into a feverish doom spiral. Not only was it losing the big races to centrist Democrats, but its finances were a shambles and it was fixated on paranoid conspiracy theories. MAGA populists had taken over and were viciously attacking traditional conservatives, who were leaving the party in droves, further weakening its ability to win elections. Arizona, not for the first time, had become a national joke on the late-night talk shows, and attracted incredulous media coverage from all over the world, because state Republicans had initiated a complete recount or "forensic audit" of the 2020 elections, and hired a blatantly partisan and farcically inept company called the Cyber Ninjas to do it.

In Mississippi, a state that reveres writers and sociability, I was spoiled for access to politicians. The governor invited me to lunch at the mansion and told me to call him anytime. I met all the members of the state house of representatives when they passed a resolution commending one of my books, and Senator Roger Wicker asked me to sign fifty copies to give to his Republican colleagues in the U.S. Senate. I socialized regularly with former governor William Winter and various state senators and representatives, and I could get my calls and emails returned by any politician in the state.

Arizona was almost the opposite. Of the fifteen politicians in both parties that I contacted and recontacted, only one responded. This was Mark Finchem, a member of the Oath Keepers militia and a MAGA stalwart who was at the Capitol during the January 6 insurrection. He was on the leading edge of the efforts to undo the results of the 2020 election in Arizona and called himself the "Election Integrity Patriot." His nickname was the Kalamazoo Cowboy because he had a droopy mustache, wore cowboy hats and silk string ties, and had moved to Arizona from Kalamazoo, Michigan. Finchem was a state representative and the leading Republican candidate for secretary of state, the office that oversees all of Arizona's elections. The prospect of a hardcore election-denier taking charge of elections in a vital swing state was freaking out liberals all over the country.

When I emailed his office, he replied promptly and told me to call his cellphone that evening. Once we connected on the phone, I thanked him for talking to me, and in a strong Michigan accent he said, "I believe in God's dance card, and your timing is perfect. I didn't ask for this battle, but my constituents asked for a champion and I'm not a coward. I was born a sheepdog and I will die a sheepdog. My friends and colleagues keep telling me, 'You've got to tell this story.' So that's what I'm doing—I'm writing a book and I need some help. Is that something you could do?"

I said we could definitely talk about it, and he suggested meeting for margaritas at five-thirty the following day. "I've got a fundraiser that evening. It'll probably do me good to have some polish on me." Then he gave a deep sigh and his mood shifted. He said, "You know, it's an exceptionally painful thing what this country is going through."

"I couldn't agree more," I said. I thought he was referring to the bitter political divisiveness.

"Every one of our institutions has been corrupted by a communist insurgency, and it all goes back to Nikita Khrushchev in 1956. He said, 'We will take your nation without firing a shot. We will destroy you from within.' Now we're seeing the culmination of Khrushchev's plan. Even law enforcement has been co-opted by Bolsheviks. They're everywhere. They're *everywhere*."

I couldn't think of a good response, and I didn't need one because

Finchem was off and away. He monologued for nearly an hour about the communist-infiltrated federal government and plots for world domination that involved the Party of Davos gang, the Chinese Communist Party, the Catholic Church, and "madman" Bill Gates. I wondered if Jewish bankers might put in an appearance, but they did not. At one point he said, "I'm not a conspiracy theorist, I need evidence." At another, "I don't have the evidence yet, and the moment I have the evidence, it will disappear."

As I listened to Finchem, I kept thinking about the historian Richard Hofstader's famous essay "The Paranoid Style in American Politics," which I had just reread. It was one of the best descriptions of the MAGA movement I had come across, despite the fact that it was written in 1964: "heated exaggeration, suspiciousness, and conspiratorial fantasy . . . America has been largely taken away from them and their kind, though they are determined to try to repossess it and to prevent the final destructive act of subversion. The old American virtues have already been eaten away by cosmopolitans and intellectuals; the old competitive capitalism has been gradually undermined by socialistic and communistic schemers; the old national security and independence have been destroyed by treasonous plots . . . at the very centers of American power."

Finchem belonged to an American political tradition that Hofstadter traced back to the 1790s. The following day he canceled our margarita date and we met instead for breakfast in Oro Valley, an agglomeration of suburban subdivisions and retail plazas northwest of Tucson with a high proportion of well-off white Christian retirees. Trump's former advisor Steve Bannon had bought a $1.55 million house there and it was Finchem's district. He was already seated when I arrived at the restaurant, wearing his trademark cowboy hat with jeans, boots, a polo shirt and a blazer. He was more measured and possibly more sober than he had been on the phone at nine p.m., but he could still talk the ears off a mule.

We began with his "election integrity" crusade, the issue that now defined him as a politician. "I'm a rural guy, a man of modest means, not interested in the limelight, but once I insisted on election integrity hearings, I was immediately launched into the position of being a champion of the people."

He said it was "impossible" that Trump lost Arizona, and his constituents felt the same way. "It's always been a red state. I don't even know anyone who voted for Biden," he said, even though heavily Democratic Tucson was only ten miles away.

I offered my help with his book, thinking it would be a weird and fascinating project, but I said that I would need to get paid for my time, which seemed to dampen his enthusiasm considerably. I asked about his candidacy for secretary of state: "Are there any circumstances in which you can see yourself certifying a Democratic victory in Arizona?" He said, "I get asked that all the time. It's simple. The law is the law. I will follow the law, unlike the crooks and clowns that ran the last two elections."

Again he stressed that he wasn't a conspiracy theorist, but by the time the bacon and eggs arrived we were back to Nikita Khrushchev and the Bolshevik takeover of America's institutions—the federal government, the justice system, the education system, law enforcement, "even the churches." He tore into the Chinese, the City of London banks who had directed "every war, every taxation, they want wars because they fund both sides," and the United Nations, which was in cahoots with the Mexican drug cartels and "leading caravans to invade the U.S. and flood the zone with illegal voters."

I asked, "Is this a coordinated effort between these different entities, or are they operating separately?" He replied, "The lust for power is the root of all evil, and that's a battle between God and Satan." He gave me a searching look that seemed to say, "Do you get it now?" Then he wiped off his droopy mustache with a napkin and took a bite of heavily buttered toast.

A highly placed lobbyist had told me that some Arizona Republicans were pushing election fraud narratives that they knew were total bullshit, because it was a great way to raise money, blow up on social media, ingratiate yourself with Trump, and get on Fox News. But Finchem did not appear to be one of them. He was a Pentecostalist who worshipped at the Assemblies of God church, and his faith in election fraud seemed as unshakable as his faith in God and Satan.

I asked him to describe his personality. "I'm a sheepdog and a honey badger," he said. "I've never backed down from a fight or pulled my punches. My name, Mark William Finchem, has meaning behind it. Mark is a servant of God, and William is a noble, resolute protector. I worked for twenty-one years as a firefighter, law enforcement officer and paramedic. I delivered six babies. My background is in farming and ranching, but I ended up working for a software company doing fraud countermeasures. I'm also a constitutional scholar, and the federal government has no legal authority to control any national forest or national parks in Arizona. The Grand Canyon should be a state park. Imagine the receipts."

I paid for his breakfast, thanked him for talking to me, and asked if he could put me in touch with U.S. congressman Paul Gosar or any other leading Arizona Republicans. "Sure thing," he said, but that didn't happen and neither did our book collaboration, because Finchem was soaring into MAGA stardom, flying all over the country, making speeches and TV appearances, and raking in campaign donations. We stayed in touch though and I encouraged him to take daily notes on what was happening, in case he got around to writing that book. He was elated to get the coveted Trump endorsement in the race for secretary of state, but it turned out to be a mixed blessing. Finchem lost to his Democratic opponent by 120,000 votes, and then, true to form, he filed an unsuccessful lawsuit alleging that election fraud had taken place.

————

On social media I saw a promotional ad for a sunset boat cruise on the Colorado River with Paul Gosar and "90 patriots." Special guests included Kelli Ward, the ultra-MAGA head of the Arizona GOP, and Sonny Borrelli, Republican state senator, majority whip, and superspreader of election fraud claims. It seemed worth the $100. If I could meet the lions of the right in a social-fundraising setting, maybe I could set up a meeting or an interview with them at a later date. At the very least, I would get a sense of them and a unique experience. It wasn't every day that the opportunity of a sunset cruise with Paul Gosar presented itself.

A firebrand dentist who had moved to Arizona from Wyoming, he was arguably the most right-wing congressman in America. Even within the House Freedom Caucus, the furthest-right bloc in the House Republican conference, there were concerns about Gosar's extremism, racism and grasp on reality. According to ex–Freedom Caucus member Denver Riggleman of Virginia, Gosar was a "blatant white supremacist" with "serious cognitive issues." He also suffered from an undisclosed neurological condition that caused his head to sway oddly, his speech to slur, his hands to twitch and spasm, and his legs to pump up and down when he was sitting.

To meet him, I drove up through western Arizona to Bullhead City, a strip of subdivisions, condos, and Jet Ski rental shops along the Colorado River. A monster truck roared up and down the main drag with twin "Fuck Biden" flags. I stopped at the River Dog Bar for a burger and a beer, and sat among bikers, boaters, construction workers, retirees and casino workers. Across the river from Bullhead City was Laughlin, Nevada, with eight casino hotels, including one shaped like a nineteenth-century riverboat. As I was leaving the bar, a man walked in wearing a picture of Joe Biden on his shirt. It surprised me until I read the legend: "I Could Shit A Better President."

I drove across the river to the casino resort where Gosar's boat cruise would begin. A hot gritty wind whipped across the desert and into my face as I walked across the enormous parking lot. It was over 100 degrees and hordes of people on Jet Skis and speedboats were churning up and down the river. At the casino's boat ramp, I stood in line with a small group of MAGA Gosar enthusiasts. One was a middle-aged man with strange staring eyes, ranting about vaccine mandates in Israel. The rest of us ignored him and endured the heat. More people were arriving, but as the launch time neared, their numbers were closer to thirty than the promised ninety. Their average age was about seventy, and most of them seemed to work for the Mohave County Republican Party.

Paul Gosar arrived in a navy blazer, accompanied by Kelli Ward in white slacks and a navy blouse. Sonny Borrelli, the majority whip, a former U.S. Marine rodeo champion with an Italian American accent and a low-rise pompadour, was dressed like a cowboy with a gold chain around his neck. We all climbed aboard the casino's riverboat and I went directly to the air-conditioned bar on the lower deck to cool off. I ordered a gin and tonic as a conversation starter with the man next to me, who was also drinking a gin and tonic. He was a retired insurance man from the Upper Midwest named Bill Hardt, running for state representative, and we had a thoroughly pleasant and convivial conversation about Arizona politics, although he seemed disturbed that I lived in Tucson. "Isn't it full of liberals?" he asked. I said, "Majority liberal, but plenty of conservatives and independents too." He filled me in on the recent redistricting of the electoral maps, which favored Republicans, then introduced me to Sonny Borrelli. "This guy's writing a book about Arizona and wants to know about our politics."

"You heard the latest, right?" Borrelli said to both of us. "They found over 733,000 votes that were never counted. And we can't decertify the election? Gimme a break." I gave him my card and asked if we could get together and talk about those missing votes. "Anytime," he said. "I'll be in touch."

I bought a fresh round of gin and tonics and sat down with Bill Hardt to continue our conversation, but it took a turn that made me feel deflated and weary. "We know there were 400,000 illegal votes in Arizona at least, and Zuckerberg is said to have given $50,000 to the Maricopa County supervisors. Of course the real problem is we're being invaded by the Communist Party of China. They've infiltrated our government and our school systems. And the globalists who run the United Nations . . ."

I excused myself and went to find Paul Gosar. He was up on the top deck, looking thin, haggard and unwell, but still determined and venomous. I told him that he was going to be in my book and I didn't like writing about people who I hadn't met and didn't know, because it forced me to rely on media portrayals. He said, "Everything goes through Penny. Give her your details and we'll see what we can do."

"I will, but let me ask you something. How does it feel to have gone through everything you've gone through in so short a time?" Gosar had led the first charge to overthrow the 2020 election with his march and rally in Phoenix. He was giving a speech in the House at the U.S. Capitol, objecting to the certification of Arizona's election results, when the January 6 insurrection began and they all had to scurry and hide. He had been censured and stripped of his committee assignments for posting an anime-style video of himself attacking Joe Biden and killing Alexandria Ocasio-Cortez. He had been pilloried for appearing at the white nationalist, anti-Semitic AFPAC convention. To name just the highlights. He flashed a smile and looked pleased with himself. "The way I look at it is, 'Why not me? Why not now?' Penny is right over there. I'll introduce you."

I talked to Penny, Gosar's district director. She said she would be in touch but that seemed doubtful. Then I introduced myself to Kelli Ward, the head of the Arizona GOP. I gave her my card and asked what I should know about her. "I'm a fighter," she said. "Paul Gosar is a fighter. We're not going to let this go. I'm going to keep fighting. Now you'll have to excuse me. I've got some people I need to talk to." The one thing I had never doubted about Kelli Ward was her pugnacity, so she had advanced my understanding by a measurement of zero.

She summoned everyone to the lower deck for a prayer, followed by the Pledge of Allegiance and the national anthem, after which Sonny Borrelli shouted out the obligatory, "Let's go Brandon!" Now the speeches began, and there were some big numbers flying around—400,000 illegal votes, plus 733,000 that were never counted. "They call us liars, they call us crazy," said Borrelli. "But the evidence is the evidence. How can you argue against it?" *If the evidence is the evidence,* I thought to myself, *why has every single lawsuit alleging election fraud and malpractice failed in the courts, both in Arizona and the country at large?* Mark Finchem the Kalamazoo Cowboy thought it was because communists had infiltrated the judiciary.

Kelli Ward stood up and claimed 100,000 to 200,000 ballots in Maricopa County had no chain of custody—nice round numbers with a broad spread. Paul Gosar, who had just returned from a meeting with Trump at Mar-a-Lago, had to clutch one of his hands to stop it from twitching and jumping, but he was full of fire on the microphone. He rattled out conspiracy theories and apocalyptic predictions, called for bounties on the heads of enemy politicians, and warned that the Chinese were about to knock 60 percent off the dollar with their cryptocurrencies. When he finished, Kelli Ward took the mic again and got down to the real point of the sunset cruise.

"Paul Gosar has enough money for reelection to Congress, but some of it is still in your pockets," she said. "Give. Him. Money. Give him cash, get your credit cards out. I know you haven't maxed them all out, and God bless you if you have."

I had checked the campaign finance numbers. Gosar, running for his seventh term, already had far more money than any of his primary challengers. But you can never have enough money in American politics, and small contributions from retired individuals like the people on this boat were one of his main sources. Nor did he stand the slightest chance of losing in the general election in November. Six of his own siblings had tried to unseat him in 2018 by appearing in campaign ads endorsing his Democratic opponent. "He's just not fit for that office and needs to be removed," said one, but he won by an enormous margin. Now the siblings were calling for his removal from Congress for his lies about the election and January 6, but here in Mohave County, the reddest county in Arizona, that was far more likely to gain him votes than lose them.

In his six terms in office, Gosar had achieved almost nothing in terms of legislation. Now, as a legacy project, he wanted to deliver a new source of water to Arizona, perhaps a pipeline from the Mississippi, but he seemed incapable of compromising and building alliances, and he wasn't taken seriously by the diminishing group of lawmakers who actually get things done in Washington, D.C. How did he expect to get a multibillion-dollar pipeline built across half the country when he couldn't even bring himself to say the words *President Biden*?

Gosar was essentially a performer in the right-wing media space, where the most attention went to those who staked out the most extreme positions. The more offensive you were to liberals, the more you got attacked by the liberal media, and the more popular you became with your own people. This was surely why Gosar had gone to the white supremacist convention, for the deluge of controversy and publicity that followed. It was a major symbolic victory for him. He never talked to journalists outside the right-wing media, and he had nothing to gain from a writer like me. The ensuing silence from Penny, despite my follow-up efforts, came as no surprise. Nor did I ever hear back from Kelli Ward or Sonny Borrelli.

———

On the way home, I went through the unincorporated community of Golden Valley—a few stores and businesses strung along the highway and hundreds of prefab homes, trailers and RVs straggling out into the surrounding desert. This was where Timothy McVeigh had lived on and off, hung around with the local militia types, and planned the 1994 Oklahoma City bombing. It was the deadliest homegrown terrorist attack in American history, killing 168 people, including 19 children.

The motive was hatred and suspicion of the federal government, which has not subsided in the least in Mohave County. If you want to build an off-the-grid compound, stockpile weapons and food, wear a gun at all times, join a militia, or give free rein to sick impulses, Golden Valley is a good place to do it. A local man had just been arrested after 183 animals, including dogs, rabbits, birds, turtles, snakes, and mice, were found in a freezer. Many of them had been frozen alive.

I slammed on the brakes when Great American Pizza and Subs came into view. The building was painted with an American flag design and flanked by painted shipping containers in the parking lot depicting a coiled rattlesnake and the USS *Arizona* battleship with guns blazing. I parked and walked up to the front door, which had a message taped to it. In red capital letters it said: "WARNING!!! GOVERNMENT OFFICIALS PLEASE BE ADVISED," and underneath, "I am aware that you are only here to 'do your job' but I am WARNING you to not proceed any further. You are attempting to deprive me of my rights under the color of law and are also committing an act of domestic terrorism by attempting to 'intimidate' or coerce me." Reading on, it became evident that some clash had occurred with health department officials over Arizona's short-lived mask mandate, and the author of the message—Robert Hall, the owner of the business—was threatening lawsuits and property confiscation and hinting at the death penalty if they messed with him again.

Hall was standing in the middle of the restaurant when I walked through the door, a stocky middle-aged man with a white goatee and a holstered pistol on his belt. Several of his customers also wore handguns, including a long-bearded desert rat with a shirt saying "Abort or Deport Democrats." I ordered a sub, regretted my decision when I saw the pizzas, and told Hall I was writing about Arizona politics.

He said he'd be happy to talk after the lunch rush. The interior of the restaurant was full of patriotic murals, decorations, objects, and Second Amendment slogans. The AR-15 hanging on the wall would be given away on Saturday for a charity fundraising event.

Hall sat down across the table. My instincts told me that he had a short fuse and a bad temper, but he was courteous and engaging. I told him I was coming from the boat cruise and I asked him what he thought of Paul Gosar. "How long has he been there? Six terms? And the border is still wide-open and the election was stolen right underneath our noses. God bless him, he's a good man, but he hasn't done anything."

I asked what other issues were important to him. "What we need from the government is what's in the preamble to the Constitution and we're not getting it," he said. "We're not getting a more perfect union. We're not getting justice and domestic tranquility. The government is not promoting the general welfare and we're not securing the blessings of liberty."

He said he hated to see the country so divided, especially over race. "I love my Black brothers and sisters and I love my Hispanic brothers and sisters," he said. "I want all Americans to come together and I relate it to pizza. The crust is our foundation. We're all in the sauce together, but we're different, like pepperoni and peppers and onions and olives. And the cheese sticks us all together. That's how America should be, but now we've got Black Lives Matter, and the Democrats want to spend money on special programs to help Black people. They're dividing us. What Black people need is opportunity like every other American."

The main reason why people moved to Golden Valley, he said, was affordability, with like-mindedness about liberty and gun rights as a close second. "Everybody I know carries a gun. Everyone in this restaurant is carrying a gun, even that guy over there who's a Democrat. If you can't see their gun, it's concealed. Mine's open because if anyone wants to come in here and rob the place, or try to kill a bunch of conservatives—we've had so many death threats and obscene messages—I'm the first person they'll aim at, which is how I want it. I might get killed, but their chances of getting out of here alive are almost zero."

He said that libertarianism and conservatism were the dominant creeds in Golden Valley, and people looked out for each other. "My buddy José's house burned to the ground recently, when he and his family were at work. We put a donation jar here in the restaurant, and in two weeks we had so much money for that family, because everyone knows them. There's a bad element here too like everywhere. Not a lot of murder, but people get their shit stolen all the time and there's drugs and weird stuff happens."

I was still processing the phrase *not a lot of murder* when he started talking about the two local militias, and slowly it dawned on me that he belonged to one of them. "Our militia here is pretty strong, very strong as a matter of fact, and in tune with the sheriff. He could call anytime and say, 'I need active people,' and there'd be 150 of us deputized just like that. The sheriff told me he'd never call us unless he really needed us. We're trained, we're well organized, with two-way radios. If something goes down, we're ready to go, and we don't mind dying for our gun rights. I'd rather go out in a blaze of glory than give up my defense and protection for my family."

Robert Hall grew up in Oklahoma, spent much of his adult life in desert California, where he worked in real estate development, and moved to Mohave County seventeen years ago, first to Bullhead City and then Golden Valley because he could afford to own more land here. He couldn't imagine moving again. "I'm hooked on the people. This is where I belong." I told him truthfully that I had enjoyed meeting him and hearing his views. As a parting gift he gave me a slice of brisket that he had slow smoked to perfection and a pocket copy of the U.S. Constitution.

"I always tell people, I'm a super nice guy, but I'm twice as mean as I am nice," he said. "Come back anytime."

*H*aphazard improvisation, one of Arizona's core characteristics, shows up in its place names. In the desert west of the Tohono O'Odham Nation is the small town of Why, Arizona. Some locals say the town originally sat on a Y junction and the residents would say they lived at the Y. To get a post office, however, a community must have at least three letters in its name, so the residents came up with Why, which sounds the same. Others say the town named itself after the most common question asked by tourists passing through: "Why would anyone live here?" To which the usual reply is "Why not?"

In the 1930s the Civilian Conservation Corps was mapping the area around Sedona. An engineer pointed out a canyon and asked a local man for its name. The man replied, "Damned if I know." The engineer misheard him and wrote down Damfino, which is still the name of the canyon today.

In the pine forests of the White Mountains in eastern Arizona is the town of Pinetop, but its name has nothing to do with trees. It memorializes a tall, bushy-haired bartender who worked at Walt Rigney's saloon in the 1890s. The nearby town of Show Low began as a 100,000-acre ranch founded in 1875 by Corydon Cooley and Marion Clark. They soon decided there wasn't room enough for both of them and agreed on a poker game to decide who would get the ranch. The game went on for many hours without a winner. Clark finally said, "If you can show low, you win." Cooley threw down the deuce of clubs and said, "Show low it is." It's been Show Low ever since, and the main street is called Deuce of Clubs.

Tonto *is the Spanish word for idiot, yet Arizona has the Tonto National Forest. It's named after the Tonto Apache tribe, who were called People Without Minds by the Chiricahuas, possibly for their willingness to live near whites. They call themselves Dilzhe'eh, which originally meant "people with high-pitched voices."*

Chapter Eighteen

WALK IN BEAUTY

W e were going on a family road trip to the red rock canyon country of the Colorado Plateau, which is one of my favorite places
on earth, although not for culinary reasons. A half-decent burger or
second-rate Mexican was about the best you could hope for, so I was
loading up the car with bread, wine, coffee, nuts, olives, beef jerky,
food bars, and a cooler full of sliced meats, cheeses, condiments, salad
vegetables and fruit. We weren't bringing any camping gear because
it was midsummer and blistering hot. It seemed inconceivable that I
used to live in Arizona without air conditioning and go camping in
the full summer heat.

Isobel was helping me pack, and I was telling her about the trip.
"We're going to see some amazing scenery, and meet some Navajos, and
go on a jeep tour into my favorite canyon, and visit a Japanese friend
who has three kids you can play with." She stood there unimpressed,
squinting into the sun. "Will we get gas station snacks?" she asked.
"Skittles? Doritos?" When I said yes, she squealed and started chanting,

"Gas station snacks! Gas station snacks!" They were the highlight of every road trip for her.

She had been more agreeable and cooperative lately than we had ever seen her. The strong-willed defiant side of her personality had gone into partial retreat, as if gathering its strength for the teenage years ahead. Or maybe she was just older now and more reasonable. We had recently crossed an important threshold between little kid and big kid. After months of insisting to her skeptical school friends that Santa Claus, the Tooth Fairy, and the Easter Bunny were real, Isobel finally asked us point-blank. We gently told her the truth and assured her that Christmas and Easter would still be fun. She thought about it deeply for a long time. Then she said, "But magic is still real, because love is magic, and books are magic because they come to life when you read them." That was a beautiful sentiment, we thought, and hard to disprove.

With everything packed up, we drove north through Tucson to Mark Finchem's district in Oro Valley—retail plazas, medical and dental offices, churches, golf courses—and finally emerged into rocky cactus desert. The sky was a deep rich blue with small white clouds spaced apart at regular intervals, like an old Warner Bros. cartoon of the Southwest. Vultures were soaring and turning upward in a gyre.

On a two-lane highway we drove through a long stretch of desert with a few small historic mining towns. Piles of tailings and smelter smokestacks stood as grimy monuments to the glory days. At Globe, where the copper mine was producing again, we delighted Isobel by stopping for gas station snacks, and then drove on to the Salt River Canyon. In most states it would be considered a showstopping scenic wonder, but it didn't get much attention in Arizona because it was dwarfed by the Grand Canyon.

On switchbacks and hairpin turns we descended more than 2,000 vertical feet from the rim to the flowing river, which marks the border between the San Carlos Apache Reservation and the White Mountain Apache Reservation. We ate roast beef and horseradish sandwiches at a riverside rest area and drank cold sparkling water in the 100-degree heat. We were three hours from Tucson with another two to go, and for nearly all of that journey no buildings would be visible. Arizona is bigger than the UK—England, Scotland, Wales and Northern Ireland put together—with roughly a tenth of its population. And 90 percent of the people in Arizona live on just 2 percent of the land. Driving across big open spaces is an integral part of travel here, and thankfully Isobel didn't mind it. She was perfectly content riding in her car seat with her tablet and headphones, her stuffed animals, drawing projects and crunchy snacks.

The road led up and out of the canyon and kept on climbing until we were in mountain pine forests and meadows. Apache ranchers in cowboy hats were driving pickup trucks with livestock trailers, confounding Western movie tropes. We saw elk moving through the pines and caught glimpses of Mount Baldy, or White Mountain, as the Apaches call it, an extinct volcano rising above the tree line to 11,400 feet.

The White Mountain Apaches were able to retain this Delaware-sized portion of their ancestral lands, with abundant timber, water and wildlife, because they gave up raiding and fighting and provided scouts to the U.S. Army during the Apache wars. Their economy is now based on ranching, forestry, outdoor recreation for tourists and a large casino. The Chiricahuas, by contrast, resisted the spread of American power into their homelands with extraordinary courage, skill and determination, and ended up shafted and betrayed with no land of their own. At a safe remove, we tend to valorize Geronimo and his diehards, but many other Apaches thought their intransigence was futile and a mistake, and Geronimo himself was not widely liked by his people.

Leaving the reservation behind, we came into Show Low. I wanted to stop at The Trumped Store, a coffee shop specializing in gaudy Trump souvenirs and memorabilia, but I was noisily outvoted by my family. A long slow descent from the pine-clad high country brought us down onto the high ocher desert of the Colorado Plateau. The light had a polished gleaming quality and you could see for at least a hundred miles. In midafternoon we reached Holbrook, an old Route 66 town with an air of faded Americana. Once it had been a notoriously wild and violent frontier cow town, and until 1913 it was the only county seat in America without a church. We drove past enormous concrete dinosaur sculptures, rock shops selling petrified wood, boarded-up buildings on Bucket of Blood Street (named for a mass killing in a saloon in 1886), and a still-functioning motel of concrete wigwams built in 1950.

Once again, it struck me as the most improbable place for a Japanese sake master to end up, but my friend Atsuo Sakurai was happy in Holbrook, and the local people were proud of him and supportive—a credit to small-town Arizona. Even more improbably, the sake that Atsuo had brewed in his Holbrook garage, using California rice, yeast, water and the grain fungus known as koji, won a gold medal at the prestigious Tokyo Sake Competition, where it was voted as the best sake produced outside Japan. It went on to win another gold medal at the Los Angeles International Wine Challenge. I had written about his unlikely triumph for a magazine, which is how our friendship began.

In 2008 Atsuo was working at a sake factory in Akita in the north of Japan and giving tours of the facility to visitors. One day a twenty-five-year-old Navajo woman arrived at the factory for a tour. She was living in Japan and teaching English. Her name was Heather Basinger. "It was a feeling right off the bat, I just knew," she told me about that first encounter. "My sister was with me that day and she noticed it too. It was love at first sight."

They got married in Japan and had two children there. Atsuo completed the seven years of training and passed the exam that certified him as a first-grade sake brewer. He was frustrated by his lack of opportunities. "My dream was always to have my own sake company and make my own sake," he said. "But in Japan I would always have to work for an established company, because it was impossible for me to get a license, and no innovations are allowed. The government has laws against it."

He moved his family to coastal Oregon, where the climate is similar to Japan's, but he couldn't get a loan or a license there, and Heather was homesick. So they moved to Holbrook, Arizona, where she grew up. For Atsuo, it seemed like an impossible place to start a sake company. It was small and remote, with no business infrastructure. It had the wrong climate and no sake drinkers. It did have good clean water, however, and a local man persuaded Atsuo to give it a try.

The Holbook city council was happy to grant him a permit, and the high desert turned out to be an excellent place to brew sake. Purity is the sake-maker's goal and in Japan's humid climate this means constant vigilance against unwanted molds, yeasts and other contaminants. In the parched air of Northern Arizona the age-old problems evaporated, and it was much easier to brew fresh, clean sake. The business took off quickly, and eighteen months after completing his first batch, Atsuo flew back to Japan to collect the prestigious gold medal at the Tokyo Sake Competition.

———

We met up with Atsuo and his family at Petrified Forest National Park east of Holbrook, where Heather was working as a ranger. It was excellent to see him again and be back in his deep, kind, thoughtful presence. In his early forties, he was wearing long white shorts and a camp-collared plaid shirt, looking vaguely like a character in a Jim Jarmusch movie. Heather was getting their two sons and daughter out of the car, making sure they had snacks and water bottles in their backpacks. The children were bilingual in English and Japanese, but they didn't speak any Navajo.

In the scorching hot afternoon sun, we hiked out into the red stony desert, through glittering fossilized trees that had toppled over more than 200 million years ago. Heather explained how they had become almost solid quartz: "This was a wet swampy area and the trees were buried deep in water and mud, so they didn't decay in the normal way. Over time the wood absorbed minerals like silica from the water. Gradually the minerals replaced the organic matter in the trees and crystallized." A line from a book jumped into my head. The English writer J. B. Priestley had described Arizona as "geology by day and astronomy at night."

The Sakurai children were polite and reserved. They generously shared their snacks with Isobel, but didn't say much, and she was feeling shy and overheated. No chatter or games ensued. We hiked for an hour or so, and then drove to the Painted Desert overlook. In a vast engulfing desert silence we gazed out at red, pink, purple, orange, brown and cream-colored domes and eroded mesas, lit by late afternoon light streaming through distant thunderstorms. We were looking at one portion of the Painted Desert, a multicolored badlands formation that extends for 150 miles across Northern Arizona. "Ice cream rocks," said Isobel. "I see strawberry, peach, cherry, vanilla and butterscotch, blueberry mixed with vanilla, *mmm* chocolate."

Back in Holbrook, Atsuo grilled steaks in the backyard and poured us glasses of his delightful sake. Isobel met her first pig and learned that he didn't have a name because he was going to be eaten, which she took in her stride. There were chickens, a turkey, a vegetable garden and, inevitably, swarms of flies. Atsuo, an avid reader of literary fiction, talked books with Mariah and then brought me up to date on his Arizona Sake operation. He was brewing it in a small white "sake house" on an empty lot by the Super 8 motel with help from an assistant named "Hillbilly Steve." His sake was being served in the Japanese consulate in Los Angeles, and sake connoisseurs were making the pilgrimage to Holbrook from all over America and the world. He wanted to expand his operation, but only modestly.

"I like the simple life, as you know," he said. "I wish people wanted less. I don't think economic development brings happiness. It brings the desire for more and more, which cannot be satisfied and destroys nature."

I asked what Arizona meant to him. "Here I can make my sake however I want to make it. I have a sake infused with the Navajo tea plant to bring together my culture and Heather's culture. I love to spend time with my in-laws on the reservation. Here I have freedom and independence and I'm my own boss. My friends in Holbrook say I am a samurai in a cowboy hat, or that I wear a cowboy hat like a samurai helmet. I love this. Arizona is where my dream came true."

———

The following day we drove into the Navajo Nation, which is the size of Ireland or West Virginia, with 170,000 inhabitants. The field of vision was still dominated by the intensely eroded and distinctive landscape of the Colorado Plateau. Buttes, mesas and canyons. Slickrock layer cakes studded with piñon pines and junipers. Red rocks carved by wind and water into goblins, hoodoos, spires, battlements, whales and other fantastical shapes. Long horizons and high forested mountain ranges in the distance. But there were indications that we had crossed into a different cultural zone.

As we drove north, the occasional clusters of houses on the west side of the road were facing east, as normal, but the houses on the other side of the road also faced east and put their backs to the highway. The custom of the Diné, as the Navajo call themselves, meaning "The People," is to welcome the rising sun into the front of their homes. We saw loose dogs and loose horses on the unfenced highway, a few of the traditional hut-like dwellings called hogans, a teenage girl out herding sheep on a red desert valley. It was like being in Arizona and somewhere else at the same time, an autonomous zone that lay within the state's geography and outside its dominant culture. Walking into a gas station to buy snacks for Isobel, it felt like a different country. The swagger and tension and surly undercurrents were gone. No one was wearing a pistol or a belligerent slogan on their shirt. No one looked pissed off. People were calm, relaxed and patient, with an easy grace and soft voices.

The state of Arizona does not recognize daylight saving time, because nobody tells us what to do and in summertime we yearn for the sun to set, not stay up for an extra hour. But the Navajo Nation, which is mostly in Arizona but extends into Utah and New Mexico, does recognize daylight saving time. So you have to adjust your watch when crossing into this sovereign nation. But if you enter the Hopi reservation, which consists of two parcels of land inside the Navajo reservation, you have to adjust your watch back again, because the Hopis stay on regular Arizona time.

The fact that the Navajos and the Hopis can't agree on the time of day is emblematic of their broader relationship. The two tribes do not get along, mainly because of a long-standing and bitter land dispute over the government's drawing of the reservation lines, and also because of prejudice. Most Hopis will tell you that the Navajo are recent arrivals who migrated down to Arizona less than a thousand years ago, borrowed some of their religion from the Hopi, and then borrowed sheep and horses from the Spanish, because they don't have their own ancient traditions and culture like the Hopi do. The Navajos, in turn, stereotype the Hopis as arrogant and untrustworthy, and dispute the migration story, because their oral traditions tell them they emerged from previous worlds into the Southwest.

We checked into a hotel in the small reservation town of Chinle, and a Navajo friend of mine named John Tsosie drove down from his house just over the New Mexico line to meet us for lunch at the hotel's restaurant. As usual, he looked crisp and clean in a new baseball cap and sneakers, with a turquoise ring and a thin gold necklace. Unflappable and good-humored, like most of the Navajos I had met, he was coproducing movies set on the reservation and running a nonprofit to raise awareness of domestic violence issues, both on and off the reservation. Mariah appreciated the way he shook her hand and Isobel's hand as well as mine. That doesn't usually happen when a man meets another man and his family, she told me afterwards.

John ordered a Navajo burger—two patties inside fry bread—and we started talking about the similarities and differences between the Navajo Nation and the rest of Arizona. I said, "It seems like you buy the same products and like a lot of the same things—pickup trucks, basketball, shopping, watching TV—but you don't have the rugged individualism. Isn't it the opposite of that in Navajo culture?"

John said, "Pretty much. We don't think of ourselves as individuals in the same way. We're members of the tribe, and we all belong to clans, which are basically kinship networks."

There are more than a hundred clans and every Navajo belongs to four of them. The first is the mother's clan, the second is the father's, third is the maternal grandfather, and fourth is the paternal grandfather. When you're introducing yourself, you give your name first and then your clans, for example, "I am born to Towering House (mother's clan), born for Water-Flows-Together (father's clan), etc." The Diné are forbidden to marry anyone with matching maternal and paternal clans, even if there are no blood ties, so it's obligatory on the first date to ask the other person for their clans. "Many a romance has been foiled that way," John said. "And if you meet someone who has two or more of your clans, you automatically become related, so you might have twenty-eight uncles."

Perhaps the biggest misconceptions about the Navajo stem from the poverty and hardship that dominates media coverage of the tribe, and is obvious to people driving across the reservation on the way to Monument Valley and the Grand Canyon. They see the broken-down trailers, primitive hogans and depressing government housing, the junked cars and loose dogs, the lack of amenities. Roughly 40 percent of people on the reservation have no running water, and 10 percent live without electricity. Factor in the grim history of racism and military defeat, the government's attempts at forced assimilation, the lack of jobs and the high rates of alcoholism, and it becomes very easy to cast the Navajo into the role of downtrodden victims.

I had spoken with the president of the Navajo Nation, Jonathan Nez, on several occasions and one of the first things he said to me was this: "We don't want your pity. We're a very resourceful, adaptable, resilient people. Despite everything that's happened to us, we're still here on our land. We still have our traditions and ceremonies and our own way of being in the world. We have a robust tribal government managing our resources. Our language is still spoken and our children are learning it in the schools and now through movies dubbed into Navajo. Our story is one of resilience, not victimhood."

———

The next morning we were picked up at the hotel by a tour guide named T. J. Hunter. He wore plaid shorts, a T-shirt illustrated with a turtle and his long black hair in twin braids. More than anything else on this trip I wanted Mariah and Isobel to see Canyon de Chelly (pronounced *Shay*), the sacred heart of the Navajo Nation and one of the most beautiful canyons in the Southwest. Outsiders are not allowed to go into the canyon without a Navajo guide, and T. J. worked for a family-owned tour company called Beauty Way. As we took our seats in an open-topped jeep, he explained the company's name: "As Navajos, we try to walk in beauty. Don't break a branch if you can get around it, don't step on a bug, walk the narrow path that leads to beauty all around you and harmony with nature." It struck me as the opposite of the Big Sandy Machine-Gun Way.

The floor of the canyon was broad, flat and sandy, with cottonwood trees, willows and invasive Russian olive trees, first brought to the United States as a landscaping and windbreak tree and now spreading out of control in the Southwest. The red ocher sandstone walls began modestly and then rose higher and higher as we drove deeper into the canyon. T. J. stopped to examine the fresh tracks of a large male bear. "Everything is people with us," he said. "Bear people, tree people, sky people, rock people, rabbit people. Navajos are five-fingered people, and all the other people joined them in the Fourth World, which is the one we're living in now." An important thing to know about Navajos, he added, is that they're usually kidding around and teasing each other. "The old saying about laughter being the best medicine is true. There's a medicine man who uses laughter to heal the sick, because it's powerful."

He stopped again to point out rock art and cliff dwellings left behind by the Anasazi, or Ancestral Puebloans, as archaeologists now call them— the ancients who lived here before the Navajo, built a complex civilization and abandoned it in the fourteenth century, probably because of drought. Isobel was amazed that you could see the stone granaries where people stored their corn a thousand years ago, and she asked the obvious question: Why did they live high above the ground in cliff dwellings? "They were probably afraid of other people coming to take what they had," said T. J. "If bad people came into the canyon, they could pull up their ladders and be safe." We watched a raven fly past and its shadow move across the canyon wall. We shouted and listened to the echoes.

For T. J., the canyon was full of memories and stories. He had spent much of his childhood here and his extended family still lived in the canyon. He pointed out a small farmhouse where a Navajo lady with an M16 rifle shot a bear and a mountain lion who were preying on her sheep. To illustrate the effectiveness of ancient hunting weapons, he pulled out an atlatl and a feathered arrow that he had made himself. He limbered up his shoulders for a few minutes, then hurled the arrow at least ninety yards in a perfect arc against the wind and put two more arrows right next to it. The Grant family was highly impressed, especially its youngest member.

The smooth sandstone walls of the canyon kept getting higher, with rippling patterns and rock towers appearing. I feasted my eyes on the bold color scheme: red ocher rock, bright green cottonwood leaves, cobalt blue sky. T. J. pointed to a small field with a house on it. "There's my auntie's place, one of my many aunties. She makes blankets the old way, with natural dyes from plants." He was unable to answer my question about the spirits that dwelled in the canyon—that knowledge was not for outsiders—but he did touch on the chindi, or ghosts, left behind by the dead. "We won't go near the dead, or places where people have died, because the chindi can make you sick. We stay away from cliff dwellings for that reason."

Before turning around and driving back out of the canyon, he stopped in the shade for twenty minutes to tell us in vivid precise detail about the time he saw a skinwalker, which he described as a witch that turns into an animal, roams at night, and is capable of moving at superhuman speeds and killing people in gruesome ways. "I wasn't sure if skinwalkers existed until I saw one that time," he said. "It was right over there."

I looked at Isobel, who was scared and fascinated and also slightly doubtful, looking to us for clues as to how she should respond. When the tour was over and we were back at the hotel, she wanted to know more about the chindi and the skinwalkers. I told her that the Navajo have a different belief system to ours, and that the world contains a multitude of different belief systems. "Imagine how boring it would be if everyone thought the same way," I said.

"Skinwalkers are really scary. Are they real?"

"They're supernatural beings like zombies or werewolves. They're certainly real to T. J., but you don't have to worry about them. The Navajos are the only people who have trouble with skinwalkers, because they're the only people who believe in them."

"A skinwalker could still be in my dream and turn it into a really horrible nightmare," she countered.

"That's not going to happen," I said firmly, and thankfully it never did.

*S*edona is Arizona's capital of New Age spirituality, alternative healing and wellness. Mysterious cosmic forces are said to emanate from its red rocks. Swirling centers of energy known as vortexes promote healing, meditation and self-exploration. Needless to say, all of this has been thoroughly commodified into a thriving local industry.

Native Americans enjoy extraordinary prestige as paragons of spiritual wisdom who live in harmony with nature, and their images command big money in the local galleries, as a conflicted Native artist once explained to me in a bar. He was from the Pacific Northwest, where he had graduated from art school with high honors. "My art was angry and political," he told me. "I made a painting of a Native guy being dragged through a laundry wringer by his hair. I called it Assimilation. My professors loved it but nobody wanted to buy it and put it on their wall."

He drifted down into Arizona and New Mexico. "I couldn't believe how clichéd the art was in the galleries. Indians in traditional dress. Kachinas and sunsets. Swirly New Age shit with rainbows and peacock tails." In Sedona, he decided to paint a parody of southwestern art and see what happened. "Dude, I had an Apache shaman with a headband, sitting cross-legged by his fire, with his spirit zooming up on a rainbow into a UFO. I sold it for thousands of dollars, and I've been here ever since, painting bullshit and making great money."

He bought another round of drinks. "But I don't know how much longer I can stand it. I keep trying to push the parody further and further, and they just keep giving me more and more money."

Chapter Nineteen

HEATSTRUCK FOR TRUMP

Wayne Belger and I met up in the parking lot of the 6,000-seat Findlay Toyota Center in the heavily Republican town of Prescott Valley. Neither of us had been to a Trump rally before and we wanted to see the defining politician of the era perform live in Arizona, where he got more adulation than almost anywhere. The event website said the doors would open at 2:00 p.m. but to get there early, because admission was first come, first serve, and huge crowds were expected. We got in line at 12:30 p.m. with a few hundred people, many of them wearing the American flag in one way and another.

Micki Larson-Olson, aka QPATRIOT, was parading around the parking lot in a red wig and skintight Captain America costume. Soon to serve 180 days for resisting arrest at the Capitol during the January 6 insurrection, she belonged to a deeply weird breakaway QAnon cult led by a demolition contractor called Michael Protzman, also known as Negative 48, with over 100,000 followers on his Telegram channel. He made outlandish predictions based on the ancient Hebrew numerology system called gematria, and prophesied the imminent return of famous dead people. Rapt devotees had waited with him for months in Dallas to witness the resurrection of John F. Kennedy and his son JFK Jr., who Protzman says is descended from Jesus and destined to be Trump's vice president. So far Protzman's predictions had an accuracy rate of zero, but it didn't seem to be hurting his popularity with his followers, who were here at the Findlay arena in large numbers.

Wayne and I took turns holding our place in line and checking out the merchandise on sale, which was an onslaught of flag-, gun- and Trump-themed shirts, stickers, hats, fridge magnets, sunglasses, plus QAnon slogans, Confederate flags, and "Show Me Your Boobies" buttons. There were posters of Trump as Rambo, Trump as Jesus, Trump as Aragorn from *Lord of the Rings,* Trump as "The MAGA King," wearing a golden crown and ermine robes. The whole carnivalesque scene, with its traveling vendors, festive costumes, inside lingo and the promise of communal cathartic release, reminded Wayne of a Grateful Dead concert, with "Let's Go Brandon" shirts instead of tie-dye, and aggressive Christian nationalism instead of peace and love.

It was brutally hot. The official temperature was 97 degrees, but that was measured in the shade and there was no shade in the parking lot, just full-blast Arizona sun, heat-absorbing asphalt and humidity from the rain the night before. People were collapsing from heatstroke and heat exhaustion. We saw three big middle-aged women go down within a twenty-yard radius of where we stood in line. By 2:00 p.m., when the doors were supposed to open, several thousand people were waiting in the broiling sun, and at 2:15 a security guard announced a delay, producing a huge collective groan. Event staff were now handing out bottles of water as fast as they could. The water wasn't cold, but it helped.

We watched groups of VIPs walk straight from their vehicles into the cool, dark, air-conditioned arena. I was too hot to do anything but breathe slowly and calmly, drink water and endure, but Wayne stirred himself to photograph a smirking young dude from Glendale with a QAnon tattoo on his bicep. We asked him why he got the tattoo. He said, "Because I'm that friggin' hardcore," and my desire to continue the interview faded away. To rally its flagging spirits, the crowd started up a chant of "Let's Go Brandon!" Cheers rang out when Mike Lindell, the election-conspiracy-obsessed pillow magnate, appeared and invited people at the front of the line to take selfies with him.

Now the crowd was getting restive, yelling and chanting, "Open the doors! Let us in!" People were fanning themselves with scavenged pieces of cardboard, trying to stay in the shade cast by one another's bodies. Many were spectacularly sunburned and paramedics were treating what appeared to be dozens of people with heat-related illness. Why couldn't they just open the goddamn doors?

An old man collapsed and split his head open, just a few feet away from me, as more VIPs pulled up in expensive vehicles and strolled into the air-conditioned building. It seemed like an apt metaphor for Trump's brand of politics. He presented it as an anti-elitist movement for working people, but his greatest achievement, apart from stacking the Supreme Court, was record tax cuts for wealthy Americans, like the ones walking straight into the air conditioning while the working stiffs were kept outside waiting for hours in the heat. Kari Lake, the pixie-cut former newscaster running for Arizona governor, arrived in a purple dress with a sheriff's escort and waved at us. People cheered and shouted, "Kari, let us in! Get us out of the sun!" But she didn't. Finally, about 3:15 p.m.—Wayne and I had been waiting in the sun for nearly three hours—the doors opened and the long, slow check-in process began. Proud Boys were trying to recruit new members just inside the entrance.

Later Trump would tell us what dedicated patriots we were for waiting hours in the hot sun to see him. But the same thing happened the last time Trump came to Prescott Valley in 2020: long unexplained delays for a crowd waiting in full summer sun and sixty people treated for heat-related illness. In 2017, fifty-six succumbed to the heat while waiting outside a delayed Trump rally in Phoenix. Wayne was convinced it was deliberate. He thought it gratified Trump's narcissistic ego to keep his adoring fans waiting and suffering and collapsing for him in the heat. I thought it was equally likely that he just didn't care.

We took our seats high in the amphitheater. The dazed, nauseous, heatstruck feeling gradually subsided as my body temperature cooled. A sentimental memorial video about Ivana Trump, who had died a few days ago, played on the big video screens, followed by hard-sell commercials for Trump products and a short film about an illegal immigrant who had murdered an American family. Then it was time for prayers, the pledge, the anthem, and "Let's Go Brandon!"

The atmosphere was like a religious revival meeting crossed with a Mussolini rally and a World Wrestling Entertainment event. But it was even weirder than that, because QAnon cults were in the arena and livestreaming themselves. Protzman and his followers were claiming that Michael Jackson, Prince, Whitney Houston, John Lennon and other dead superstars were going to perform here tonight. I spotted ex-sheriff Joe Arpaio, former scourge of brown-skinned motorists, taking photos with Mike Lindell, former crackhead turned pillow impresario. America felt like a pirate ship adrift on the high seas.

The speeches were dumbed down to the simplest slogans. The crowd responded with roaring cheers, loud angry boos like a wrestling crowd when the villain does something unfair to the hero, or repeated three-syllable chants: "Build the wall! Build the wall!" for example. Kelli

Ward, the pugnacious head of the Arizona GOP who had given me the brush-off on Paul Gosar's boat cruise, marched up to the microphone in a red dress and reactivated the ear pain I'd sustained at Big Sandy by screaming as loudly as she could, "Stand up if you're ULTRA MAGA!!! ULTRA MAGA!!!!" Senate candidate Blake Masters laid into Arizona senator Mark Kelly, a former astronaut: "He's the worst senator in America." *Boo!* "Send him back to space!" *Yay!*

Kari Lake got up there to wild applause and delivered a warning to her enemies: "When Mama goes MAGA, it is game over. For the cartels. For the swamp rats. For the RINOs and radical leftists." *Kari! Kari!*

She said, "I believe we have two sexes, and we've got the alpha men in our group." *Yeah! Yeah!*

She pointed to the "filthy fake news" filming the event, and the crowd booed. *Fake news media! Fake news media!*

She continued, "On day one in office, after I take my hand off the Bible, I will blow up the drug tunnels and shoot down the cartel drones." *Shoot 'em down! Shoot 'em down!*

It went on like this for three hours with multiple speakers until an intermission. It reminded me of a line from George Orwell: "Let's all get together and have a good hate. Over and over."

Trump kept us waiting for another hour and a half, but we got to watch a video about his plane getting painted gold. Then the sound system started blasting "Y.M.C.A." by the Village People, and at least half the crowd got up and started dancing, whooping and waving their arms in the air. As novice Trumpers, Wayne and I were surprised by the MAGA enthusiasm for gay disco anthems, but apparently "Y.M.C.A." and "Macho Man" were always played at Trump rallies.

Finally the MC announced Donald J. Trump the forty-fifth president, and he slow-walked his way to the podium as "God Bless the

USA" played on the sound system and the crowd roared and cheered on its feet. Trump was clapping his hands as he walked, pointing to individuals, flashing the odd smile, touching his heart, feasting on the love and adoration.

"Wow," he began. "And a very big hello to an incredible place. Arizona!" He briefly talked up the MAGA candidates he had endorsed in the state, "this incredible slate of America First Republicans," all of whom would go on to lose to Democrats. Then he started laying into Joe Biden, who had destroyed all of Trump's "incredible achievements" and was more dangerous than "the five worst presidents in history put together." Arizona's southern border, under Trump's administration, was "the best in history." Now it was "the most unsafe border of any country in history," and the people crossing it were "the worst criminals the world has ever known." In Biden and his radical leftists, America was facing "the most menacing forces and vicious opponents the world has ever seen . . . I truly believe our nation is doomed to become another Venezuela."

As I listened to Trump's rhetoric, I jotted down a note every time he hit a classic fascist trope. Demonization of the opposition. Contempt for democratic institutions. Debasement of the truth: experts can't be trusted, facts and reality are what we say they are. We will bring back the glorious mythic past. We support the family; they are deviants. We are hardworking; they are lazy and want to take advantage of us. We need a law-and-order crackdown because they are criminals (Trump was calling for drug dealers to be executed). We are the true patriots, and only by supporting the strongman will we save our nation from destruction by its enemies.

I was uncomfortable using the term *fascist* to describe the MAGA movement, mainly because it favored free market capitalism rather than a state takeover of the economy, but I was growing increasingly comfortable with *fascistic*. Of course we all have our own perspectives. The right saw the left as fascistic for imposing its woke ideology in schools, universities, corporations, mainstream media and Hollywood; for censoring conservative viewpoints and crossing the line into violence with Antifa and the lawless elements at the Black Lives Matter protests. I thought that was a legitimate viewpoint, and that the far left and the far right were remarkably similar in terms of zealotry, tribalism and oppressor-victim thinking. But the MAGA right vastly outnumbered the woke left and posed a far greater threat to democratic norms, with a far greater potential for political violence.

Looking at Trump perform, I saw a hustling, braggadocious, all-American showboat version of a wannabe authoritarian strongman. The MAGA faithful saw the hero who could save their imperiled nation. And Michael Protzman saw JFK Jr., alive and well, and wearing an unconvincing Trump mask. As Protzman said to his 100,000 followers, "The mask didn't look the best and he will start to make it more obvious."

By the time Trump concluded his speech with "We will make America proud again, we will make America strong again, and we will make American great again," he had been going for nearly two hours. Until I saw him live, feeding on the crowd and commanding its emotions, I hadn't appreciated how thoroughly Trump enjoyed himself at his rallies, and how hard it was for him to get off the stage. "Ah, there's nothing like a Trump rally, isn't this the greatest thing in the world?" he said.

———

We got out of there at 10:30 p.m., ten hours after we first stood in line. There wasn't a hotel room to be found in Prescott or Prescott Valley.

Wayne drove the two hundred miles back to Tucson, but I didn't have the energy for it. I made it to Phoenix and pulled into a Drury Inn. The bar was conveniently close to the check-in desk. As I ordered a beer, a middle-aged couple a few barstools away invited me to join them. They said they were Hopi and down in Phoenix for a Native basketball tournament.

For the next hour and a half, I drank beer with this warm, friendly couple, Denise Bekay and Bruce "Jay" Koyiyumptewa. They talked about Native basketball, and the importance of praying and singing to your corn plants in a place with no irrigation and little rain, and the kachina spirits who dwell in the San Francisco Peaks near Flagstaff, and many other aspects of Hopi life and culture. "The man has the field and the clothes on his back," said Jay. "The woman gets the harvest and everything else."

"If you're a woman, you have to make the piki for ceremonies," said Denise. "It's a lot of work. First you grind up blue corn and mix it with water and a special ash. Then you smear it paper-thin across a hot stone with a fire underneath it so it gets real thin and crunchy. It burns the shit out of your hands. A good Hopi woman has got all kinds of scars and burn marks on her hands. But that's how we do it."

Jay was curious about Great Britain. "Over there, do you get knighted with swords and shit like that?" he asked. I set him straight on that question, and asked him if the Hopis were still doing the traditional Snake Dance with live rattlesnakes. "Yeah, but you'll never see it," he said. "There's a lot of songs and ceremonies that happen in the kiva that outsiders can't see or hear."

Native basketball, he said, had its own unique style, and it evolved because every reservation had a hoop, but the court was often rough ground. "So the ball stays in the air most of the time and we play the game superfast, way faster than regular basketball. The first time a regular team plays against a Native team, they don't know what to make of it."

Jay talked about all the New Agers in places like Santa Fe and Sedona, who revere the Hopi for their spirituality and want some of it for themselves. "All they see is the green leaves on the tree," he said. "They don't really see the trunk, or understand that the roots go way down into the earth, that this knowledge has been passed down over a long, long time. I don't mean to be rude, but white people have no idea what they're doing to the earth."

"We're a smash-and-grab people," I said. "Dig out the copper and gold. Log the forests. Kill all the buffalo. Use up the rivers and pump out the groundwater."

"You really have no idea what you're doing and it's kind of amazing to us," he said.

The cluelessness of my people did not prevent Jay and Denise from inviting me to Hopi, as they called the reservation. "Come up anytime," he said. "There's nothing to do and it's illegal to drink beer, but you might find it interesting."

That night I slept well for once, and as I drifted off, I felt soothed and comforted by the fact that Arizona contained multitudes, that I could go to a Trump rally and make Hopi friends on the same evening, that I would find it interesting to visit Jay and Denise on the Hopi mesas, that there was more than enough in Arizona to keep me interested for the rest of my days.

*S*ometimes all you need to break into show business is a cute face, a botched stagecoach robbery and some feminine wiles. Pearl Hart was five foot two and weighed less than a hundred pounds. She grew up in Canada reading dime novels about the American West before coming to see it for herself. In Arizona she worked as a waitress, a cook and a prostitute before taking up with a miner and con man named Joe Boot in 1899.

He said they could make easy money by robbing the stagecoach on the road between Florence and Globe. They managed to get $400, but they hadn't planned an escape route and were swiftly caught by a posse. Boot surrendered meekly. Hart fought like a wildcat.

In the Tucson jail she persuaded two gentlemen to help her escape, but she was caught again by a lawman who recognized her. At her trial she wore a pretty dress and flirted with the all-male jury, lifting up her skirt at one point to show them her ankles. They found her not guilty. The judge was furious and ordered another trial on federal charges. By this time Pearl Hart was famous, signing autographs and posing for photographers. The eastern newspapers had dubbed her the "Girl Bandit," and they howled with outrage when she was sentenced to five years in the notoriously tough Yuma prison.

The territorial governor refused to discuss the reason for her early release in 1902, but his secretary later wrote that Hart had told the prison warden she was pregnant. And it was thought that only two men had been alone with her: the warden and the governor. Telegrams flew between the prison and the capitol, resulting in her immediate release, and she went into show business in Kansas as the Arizona Bandit.

Pearl Hart hadn't been pregnant. She had outsmarted the governor and the warden and won her freedom with a ruse.

Chapter Twenty

FOREST PEOPLE

Isobel kept asking for what she called an "Isobel Daddy camping trip." Mariah gave the idea her blessing and the preparations began. At this stage of my life I was completely reliant on lists, and Isobel thought they were fun. She loved stationery and it was a way to play with her notebooks and pens. We sat at the small round dining table, both working on our lists. She wrote: "Stuffies (3), books, pajamas, hairbrush . . ." I wrote: "Water, cash, beer, beef jerky . . ." Glancing over, she said, "You like beef jerky?"

"Yes I do," I replied.

"So do dogs," she said disdainfully.

I went back and forth on the question of adding "gun" to my list. I had been meaning to buy a compact, lightweight, semiautomatic handgun for camping trips—I was concerned about predatory humans, not bears or mountain lions—and I kept not getting around to it because I didn't want to spend the money, or research the best make and model, and I wasn't in the habit of carrying a gun unless I was hunting for meat. So once again, my camping list ended up firearm-free. While I was packing, I threw in a can of bear spray for emergencies, human or ursine, and a short-handled axe that would be useful for splitting firewood but could also be weaponized. Through the ether I could hear my gun-loving friend Bo Weevil mocking me in Mississippi: "Good luck with that axe if the shit hits the fan."

We said our goodbyes to Mariah and drove down through the grass-lands to a sky island range near the Mexican border. On a bumpy twist-ing dirt road we climbed up to a National Forest campground above 6,000 feet. I put my cash in the little Forest Service envelope, pushed it through the slot in the metal pole, and started pitching the tent next to a small stream in the oaks, pines and junipers. To the south through a gap in the trees was an enormous view across cloud-dappled plains to the pale blue ranges of the Sierra Madre.

As I hammered in the tent stakes with a rock, Isobel scampered about and chatted away in a long stream of non sequiturs: "I wonder what it's like to be a bug. Ooh, look at this blue rock. If a princess went camping, I bet she'd set up a castle with air conditioning and velvet furniture and Wi-Fi. Daddy, do real princesses have pink gowns? Ooh, a purple rock." Once I had the tent set up, the sleeping pads inflated, and the sleeping bags and pillows inside, she carefully arranged her books and belongings.

"All the stuffies I brought are wild animals, since we're camping," she said, placing Tigey the wildcat, Wolfie the wolf, and Teddy the bear on her pillow. "See you tonight for snuggles!" she told them. Fairly often on camping trips she grumbled and whined and found fault with everything, but this time she was starting out in a very upbeat mood. We unpacked her folding camp chair, which was styled as a yellow caterpillar. We had bought it in Mississippi, and now the nylon fabric was starting to shred and fray. "I can't believe my camping chair is decomposing!" she exclaimed.

We went exploring along the rocky stream bank. The footing was tricky, so I advised her not to commit all her weight on her front foot until it was solidly planted. As usual, she disregarded my advice on principle, because she hated me telling her what to do. She insisted that tiptoeing was the best method and tried it for a few minutes before taking my hand for support and walking flat-footed again. Her eyes scanned the ground for colored rocks. She had a plan to make a rainbow of rocks on the ground with all the right colors. "A sunset rock!" she said, holding up a small round orange-pink pebble. "I found the prettiest rock in the entire world!"

The only other people around were a few birders who had come here from Colorado and Texas to see rare warblers and flycatchers and the extraordinary diversity of bird life in this mountain range. Hundreds of bird species can be observed here. It was a good place for colored rocks too, and Isobel had nearly all of the rainbow made when she decided she'd rather read in the tent. We lay there side by side for nearly two hours with a faint breeze rustling the tent and the sound of birdsong.

———

I was reading a newly published book by Chuck Bowden, but it was difficult to concentrate because it kept dislodging memories from their resting places, and it felt like he was talking to me from beyond the grave. Chuck had died nearly eight years ago. He was not gunned down by a cartel assassin or tortured to death. He died of a heart attack in Las Cruces, New Mexico, after feeling unwell for a couple of weeks. He was sixty-nine years old.

People talked about how much living he had packed into his time on earth, and the vast quantities of alcohol and cigarettes that he had consumed. All that was true, but he had also produced a gargantuan amount of work and never stopped or slowed down. The book I was reading, *Dakotah,* a beautifully chiseled meditation about his childhood in Illinois and the history, culture and meaning of the Great Plains, was one of eight book manuscripts that he left behind. They were being published by the University of Texas Press.

The last time I spoke with him, I was calling from a remote farmhouse in the Mississippi Delta and he was in a remote farmhouse near Patagonia, Arizona, where he often went to write and think by himself. Chuck didn't like to talk about his work in progress because it stanched the flow, but he told me he was writing "a long tone poem" about birds and animals and nature, which were the things he loved most in the world. He had been intending to write a nature book for decades.

He said he was living on very little money and spending a lot of it on birdseed. He had no possessions left except his laptop, his binoculars and some clothes. "It's better this way," he said. "No more bullshit and nothing left to lose." He had burned his bridges in the New York media world by telling magazine editors they were publishing shit. I don't know how or why he had accumulated so many unpublished book manuscripts, except that he couldn't stop writing. It was absolutely essential to his existence.

He mentioned that he was working on something else too, about his childhood in Illinois, and that was the book I was now reading in a tent on a mountain with my child next to me.

I was born to be erased.
And accept this fact.
The ground under my feet has always meant more
to me than the people around me.

I was living in the Mississippi farmhouse when I got the news of his death. I sat down in silence for a long time, absorbing the blow. Then I drove forty minutes to the supermarket in Yazoo City, where I bought six yellow bell peppers, onions, carrots, celery, potatoes, and chicken stock. I drove to the liquor store and bought a bottle of the cheap Australian Shiraz that was Chuck's everyday wine. Then I went home and charred the peppers on the flames of the gas stove until they were black all over. I put them in a plastic bag to steam the skins loose. I was making a soup that Chuck had learned at Marcella Hazan's cooking school in Venice and taught to me. It was for special occasions, and he often served it around Christmas.

Peel the peppers with a thumbnail, collect the clear juices and slice up the flesh. Sauté the onions, celery and carrots until soft. Add the sliced peppers, salt, diced potatoes, chicken stock and water. Cook for 20 minutes until the potatoes are soft. Then puree and serve in bowls, drizzled with olive oil and the clear pepper juice.

Tasting the soup was a sensory reminder of his best prose—rich, bold, uncluttered, full of flavor, mesmerizing. Tasting the wine, I remembered the look of innocent pleasure on his weathered face as he watched the birds, the unabashed sexuality as he plunged his face into the crotch of a flower and inhaled the scent, the scabs and lacerations on his legs after his long marches across the desert. I never understood why he walked through the vegetation, rather than around it. Maybe he stubbornly refused to alter his course. Maybe he enjoyed the sensation

Richard Grant

of thorns and twigs raking across his skin. Maybe it helped him shed the horrors he was marching away from.

Even as he catalogued the bloody dystopia of Juárez and prophesied the bleakest of futures, his love of the world was undiminished, his outlook was not depressive or pessimistic, and this was partly because his senses were so alive. He could take tremendous pleasure in the color of a hummingbird's throat, the feel of a woman's thigh under his fingertips, the rain falling like arrows on the desert as the sky convulsed in thunder. The man loved storms, the bigger and more violent the better. He would stand there grinning joyfully, maniacally, as the wind and rain lashed him. Sometimes he would let out a guttural roar.

———

Isobel was down at the stream giving "spa treatments" to her colored rocks. I was drinking a beer while warming up pinto beans for myself and arranging charcuterie on a blue enamel plate for Isobel. There were storm clouds in the western sky and one of them was rimmed with bright flaming gold. "Isobel," I called out. "You have to see this."

"Hold on," she said. "The blue rock isn't finished with her treatment."

"I'm serious. Turn around and look at the sky."

She turned around and then ran up to me. "Oh my gosh, we have got to tell Mama about this cloud. Could it be any more gorgeous?" I tried to photograph it with my phone, but it failed to capture the brightness of the gold.

After dinner, I lit a fire. A day in the fresh air away from screens had liberated Isobel's imagination, and now as she sat by the fire it seemed to go into overdrive. "Sometimes when you watch the wood burning in a fire, you can make out shapes, and it feels like you're in a story," she said. "Look, the hero is fighting his dog who has a very long nose, because they got in an argument, and now they're hanging over a pit with dragons and the dragons are trying to jump up and eat them. There's a squid dude with green stripes and he's cackling, he's evil. Ooh! Look, Dada! Now the hero is riding the dog with a very long nose, and they're fighting the squid dude."

"I love your fire story," I said, writing it down in a notebook. She corrected me: "It's not *my* story, Daddy. The fire is telling the story and I'm telling it to you."

She carried on telling it for the next forty-five minutes, with the same characters going through highly dramatic narrative twists and turns as the glowing coals shifted and the firewood rearranged itself. Finally I called a halt because we were past her bedtime. We lay down in the tent and read our books by lantern light for ten minutes. Then I turned off the lantern and asked, "Do you want a song? A 'Gun Street Girl' or a 'Blackjack Davey'?"

"No," she said. "I'll listen to the crickets for my music tonight." There was a lovely quiet, pulsing rhythm in the cool night air, made by what sounded like cicadas. After she fell asleep, I crept out of the tent. I had been taking notes here and there, and had scribbled furiously as she told the fire story. Now, with the light of a half-moon shining down, I wrote down everything else I could remember about that enchanted day, so I would never forget it. Then I poured myself a whiskey and finished *Dakotah*.

The book is shot through with vignettes of pivotal moments in the lives of historical figures, including Lewis and Clark, Wild Bill Hickok, Walt Disney and various twentieth-century musicians. The book ends with the last words of Daniel Boone, as he lay dying in Missouri, and they also read as Chuck's goodbye to life, typically blunt and assertive: "I'm going now. My time has come."

———

In the morning we drank strong black coffee and milky hot chocolate and kindled the fire back into life. Breakfast was hard-boiled eggs and hot sauce for me, cereal and milk for her. She had been warned in advance that there would be a hiking component in this camping trip, and she had agreed to it, but that didn't mean it wouldn't put her in a grumbling sulk. She loaded up her backpack with blueberry bars, challah from the JCC and an apple, and we set off up an old logging road that led to a trail.

Small flies with striped abdomens buzzed around our faces. I had a knife on my belt and used it to cut two small leafy branches. I showed her how to use a branch to fan her face and keep the flies away, and for once she took my advice. There were thickets of manzanita on both sides of the road, with shiny reddish-brown bark and waxy mint-green leaves. "It looks like a mint chocolate bar for animals," she observed.

The flies kept after us. I could tell that she was trying very hard not to complain about trudging uphill while trying to swat pesky flies away from her face with a leafy branch. I was proud of her for not complaining. After an hour of hiking, we left the flies behind and reached the rim of a big canyon of weathered granite with rock towers and battlements. Birds were flying hundreds of feet below us, and below them was a creek flowing with monsoon rain. We stopped and ate our lunch in this ancient place.

On the way back down to camp we were hailed by a birder who looked unsettled. She had come here from Texas with her husband. Like many birders, they could identify a rare flycatcher from a partial glimpse in a thicket a hundred yards away, but they knew very little about mammals. "A large cat was just here," she said. "We threw stones at it and it's over there now. Could it be a bobcat?"

I pulled my hands apart to show her the size of a bobcat.

"No," she said. "Much bigger than that. Maybe six feet long."

I told her it was unquestionably a mountain lion, and she should call back her husband, who was trying to photograph it. "I'm glad you have your knife, Daddy," said Isobel. "You could cut its head off." I didn't tell her that wasn't true, because I wanted her to feel safe, and I wished I had that pistol I kept failing to buy. I couldn't shoot a mountain lion unless it was attacking, but I could certainly scare one off by shooting above its head. The woman started shouting her husband's name and the lion bounded away and vanished, as they nearly always do around humans. We caught a glimpse of its tawny color flashing through the vegetation. In thirty years of camping and hiking in the American West, it was only the second time I'd seen one, although I'd seen their tracks many times. When I got back into phone service, I looked up mountain lion attacks in the United States. There had been 126 since 1890, with 27 fatalities. Children are particularly vulnerable to lions, but statistically they're in far more danger from lightning strikes.

Back at the campsite, as if programmed by the deep human past encoded in her DNA, Isobel came up with the idea of playing hunter-gatherers, although she didn't know that term. She called it Forest People. She made us doll-sized clothes out of bark and pine needles and asked if I knew which plants along the stream could be eaten. I said we could definitely make a salad from the dandelions, and if we could find yucca flowers, we could eat those too. She picked some dandelions, rinsed them in the stream, and found pieces of bark for plates. "It's probably best to make this a pretend salad, because the stream water might have parasites," I said. I was worried she'd object and get upset, but she readily agreed.

"Now we need to make tools to hunt animals," she said, and started sharpening the end of a stick by rubbing it against a rock. "I'm making a spear. You make a bow and arrow." I braided some long grasses into cordage and tied them to two ends of a curved branch. She finished her spear and made a slingshot from a stick and a hair tie. "We need a knife," she said. I handed her a sharp rock.

She pointed to a big boulder in the stream. "Let's hunt that cow." She stalked up to it and stabbed it with her spear, and I tried to shoot an arrow at it with my bow. "It's dead," she said. We lit a pretend fire underneath it and used twig utensils to eat the pretend meat. After we had finished our pretend meal, the game ended and she said, "It's really fun to pretend you live outdoors and make stuff out of what you find in the forest. Can we get a book about which plants we can eat?" Then I remembered that you can make a tasty vitamin-rich tea out of pine needles. We collected some and I chopped them up fine, let them steep in boiling water for five minutes, and poured us both a cup of pine tea. She drank some and said, "Yeah, not bad, but it's got nothing on hot chocolate."

She got out one of her notebooks and her invisible ink pen and started writing spells. The first two were rain spells, which seemed fitting for an Arizona child. "This one makes it rain, and this one keeps the rain away from our campsite so we can have a fire and cook s'mores." Then her imagination led us into a realm called Magic Country, where flying plates delivered weather forecasts and the clouds in the sky were all our friends. She looked up at the clouds and greeted them: "Hello, Miranda! Hi, Bessie! Hi, Stormy! Hi, Cloudy!"

We calculated that she had now been in Arizona for nearly half of her life, and so had I. "Do you feel like a Mississippi girl, an Arizona girl, or both?" I asked. "Arizona girl," she said. I asked what Arizona meant to her. "This," she said. "Going camping. Playing Forest People. The mountains and the sky. That cloud was literally gold, Daddy. I wish Mama could have seen it."

That night the fire told us another long story about dogs and monsters and heroes and princesses, and we roasted our marshmallows on twigs. At bedtime, as she lay on my chest listening to me read a story, she said, "I miss Mama. Can we go home in the morning? Can we bring Mama next time and go on a longer camping trip?"

"Of course we can," I said. "That's exactly what we'll do."

NOTES

Vignette: George Warren

1   *George Warren:* Colorized postcard of George Warren, Postcards of the Past, 2021.7.21, Bisbee Mining and Historical Museum, https://bisbeemuseum.org /postcard_archive/2021-7-21-pc/.

1   *one-ninth of a mother lode:* Ron Dungan, "Inglorious Arizona: How a Down and Out Miner Wound Up on the State Seal," *Arizona Republic,* March 31, 2016.

1   *sweeping floors and cleaning spittoons:* Tom Zoellner, *Rim to River: Looking into the Heart of Arizona* (Tucson: University of Arizona Press, 2023), 251.

1   *state seal:* Colorized postcard of George Warren, Bisbee Mining and Historical Museum.

Chapter One: Going Home

4   *"You can't spell CRAZY":* author interview of Jon Talton, January 2022.

4   *60 percent:* Howard Fischer, "About 60 Percent of Arizonans Weren't Born in the State," *Phoenix Daily Independent,* November 4, 2019.

4   *"Father of four":* Kiri Blakeley, "'The Devil Made Me Do It': Father of Four, 42, and Owner of BBQ Company, 'Sacrifices Family Poodle in Meat Smoker Because He Didn't Like Daughter's T-Shirt,'" *Daily Mail,* May 16, 2016.

5   *"A naked Apache Junction man":* Charles Bowden, *Desierto: Memories of the Future* (New York: W. W. Norton, 1991), 29.

5   *dead last in the nation:* Tom Zoellner, *Rim to River: Looking into the Heart of Arizona* (Tucson: University of Arizona Press, 2023), 121.

5   *more than half:* Zoellner, *Rim to River,* 121.

Vignette: Human Body Parts

13   *Buckets full of human heads:* Harry Cockburn, "'Like Frankenstein': Woman's Head Attached to Man's Body Found Lying Next to Bucket of Human Parts in Lab," *Independent,* July 19, 2019.

13   *"human chop shop":* Meagan Flynn, "Human Chop Shop That Sold Body Parts for Experiments Without Consent Ordered to Pay $58 Million to Donors' Families," *Washington Post,* November 20, 2019.

13   *dumping 24 limbs:* Associated Press, "Man Sentenced to 6 Years in Prison for Dumping Body Parts in Arizona," *Arizona Republic,* October 31, 2022.

Chapter Two: Coming into the Country

22   *"The sound tightens now":* Charles Bowden, *Blue Desert* (Tucson: University of Arizona Press, 1986), 10.

Vignette: Saguaros

25   *saguaro cactus:* See *A Natural History of the Sonoran Desert,* edited by Steven J. Phillips and Patricia Wentworth Comus (Tucson: Arizona-Sonora Desert Museum Press, 2000), 184–93.

25   *saguaros are people:* "Saguaros Are People, Too," Saguaro Discovery Trail, Tohono Chul (Tucson, AZ), https://tohonochul.org/wp-content/uploads/2013/12/SDT -Saguaros-are-people-too.pdf.

25   *David Grundman:* "A Menace to the West," *The Ancient and Esoteric Order of the Jackalope* (podcast), April 6, 2020.

Chapter Three: Desert Limbo

27   *they grow only: A Natural History of the Sonoran Desert,* edited by Steven J. Phillips and Patricia Wentworth Comus (Tucson: Arizona-Sonora Desert Museum Press, 2000), 184.

29   *"maimed stone god":* Charles Bowden, *Frog Mountain Blues* (Tucson: University of Arizona Press, 1987), epigraph.

Vignette: The Naming of Arizona

40   *Arizona was named:* Donald T. Garate, "Who Named Arizona? The Basque Connection," *Journal of Arizona History* 40, no. 1 (Spring 1999): 53–82; see also Donald T. Garate, "Arizonac: A Twentieth-Century Myth," *Journal of Arizona History* 46, no. 2 (Summer 2005): 161–84.

Chapter Four: Big Empty

43 *"dark prince"*: Tom Zoellner, *Rim to River: Looking into the Heart of Arizona* (Tucson: University of Arizona Press, 2023), 314.

51 *"a long avenue"*: Raphael Pumpelly, *Travels and Adventures of Raphael Pumpelly, Mining Engineer, Geologist, Archaeologist, and Explorer,* edited by O. S. Rice (New York: Henry Holt and Company, 1920), 187.

53 *Hia Ced O'Odham:* See Gary Paul Nabhan, Wendy Hodgson, and Frances Fellows, "A Meager Living on Lava and Sand? Hia Ced O'odham Food Resources and Habitat Diversity in Oral and Documentary Histories," *Journal of the Southwest* 31, no. 4 (Winter 1989): 508–33; see also Charles Bowden, *Killing the Hidden Waters* (Austin: University of Texas Press, 1977), 43–45.

54 *songs and dances:* Bowden, *Killing the Hidden Waters,* 44.

54 *federally recognized:* Scianna Garcia, "Hia-Ced O'odham Seek Federal Recognition as a Tribe," *Arizona Daily Star,* January 26, 2023.

Vignette: Desert Thirst

56 *W. J. McGee:* Bill Broyles, B. W. Simons Jr., and Tom Harlan, "W. J. McGee's 'Desert Thirst as Disease,'" *Journal of the Southwest* 30, no. 2 (Summer 1988): 222–27.

56 *3,378 border crossers:* Jerome F. Koleski et al., "Border Crosser Deaths in the Arizona-Mexico Desert: Data on Remains 2001–2020," *Journal of Health Care for the Poor and Underserved* 33, no. 1 (2022): 398–406.

Chapter Five: Brick House

57 *"essential services"*: Bryan Bender, "In Arizona, Liberty Trumps the Virus Fight. How's That Going?" *Politico,* April 2, 2020.

58 *Paul McCartney's 151-acre ranch:* As told to Jerry Wilkerson, "Contractor's First Job: Renovating Paul McCartney's Tucson Ranch," *Arizona Daily Star,* July 5, 2023, 1.

62 *Harris's hawks:* Joshua Sokol, "Zoologger: The Only Raptor Known to Hunt in Cooperative Packs," *New Scientist,* September 30, 2015.

Vignette: Thieving Thirteenth

68 *The thirteenth session:* Marshall Trimble, "The Notorious Thieving 13th," *True West,* October 9, 2023, https://truewestmagazine.com/the-notorious-thieving -13th/.

68 *bullwhip and a monkey wrench:* Trimble, "The Notorious Thieving 13th."

Chapter Six: Risk

69 *"No man ever":* Joseph Conrad, *Lord Jim* (New York: W. W. Norton, 1996), 51.

72 *relatively new development: A Natural History of the Sonoran Desert,* edited by Steven J. Phillips and Patricia Wentworth Comus (Tucson: Arizona-Sonora Desert Museum Press, 2000), 61.

75 *Marion "Suge" Knight:* Steve Gorman, "Onetime Rap Mogul Marion 'Suge' Knight Sentenced to 28 Years for Manslaughter," Reuters, October 4, 2018.

79 *robbing freight trains:* Louis Sahagun, "Brazen Rail Bandits on the Border," *Los Angeles Times,* July 23, 1995.

81 *Ciudad Juárez:* Molly Molloy, "Last Call," *Journal of the Southwest* 61, no. 1 (Spring 2019): 107.

82 *El Sicario:* Charles Bowden and Molly Molloy, eds., *El Sicario: The Autobiography of a Mexican Assassin* (New York: Nation Books, 2011). Documentary film *El Sicario, Room 164,* directed by Gianfranco Rosi, 2010.

Vignette: State Capitol

84 *the state capitol complex:* Tom Zoellner, *Rim to River: Looking into the Heart of Arizona* (Tucson: University of Arizona Press, 2023), 151–52.

84 *unbuilt masterpieces:* Frank Lloyd Wright Foundation, "Never Before Seen Look at Frank Lloyd Wright's Unbuilt Arizona Capitol 'Oasis,'" *The Whirling Arrow,* November 20, 2020, https://franklloydwright.org/oasis-state-capitol -quarterly/.

Chapter Seven: Home at Last

85 *Ts-iuk-shan:* Will C. Barnes, *Arizona Place Names,* revised and enlarged by Byrd H. Granger (Tucson: University of Arizona Press, 1960), 630.

86 *worst drought in 1,200 years:* Chelsea Harvey and E&E News, "Western 'Megadrought' Is the Worst in 1,200 Years," *Scientific American,* February 15, 2022.

86 *hottest May on record:* Ariana Brocious, "Tucson Sees Hottest May on Record," Arizona Public Media, June 1, 2020.

93 *hottest summer:* Daniel McFarland, "Tucson Has Set a New Record for 100-Degree Days in a Year at 100," kvoa.com, September 30, 2020.

93 *108 days:* Cuyler Diggs, "2020 Climate Summary and 2021 Outlook," KGUN, January 8, 2021.

93   *53 days:* Danny Shapiro, "Here's a Look Back at the Phoenix Weather Records Set in 2020," ktar.com, January 4, 2021.

93   *Two hundred and twenty-seven migrants died:* Samuel Gilbert, "2020 Was Deadliest Year for Migrants Crossing Unlawfully into US via Arizona," *Guardian,* January 30, 2021.

93   *323 heat deaths:* "Heat-Associated Deaths in Maricopa County, AZ: Final Report for 2020," Maricopa County Public Health, https://www.maricopa .gov/ArchiveCenter/ViewFile/Item/5240.

93   *spread to 115,000 acres:* Rebecca Sasnett, "Tucson's Bighorn Fire: Less Wind, More Humidity to Help Fight Massive Blaze Today," *Arizona Daily Star,* June 30, 2020.

94   *spreading more rapidly:* Jeremy Duda, Isaac Stanley-Becker, and Chelsea Janes, "How Arizona 'Lost Control of the Epidemic,'" *Washington Post,* June 25, 2020.

Vignette: Grand Canyon

97   *the conquistador Francisco Vázquez de Coronado:* "Stories: The Mythical Seven Cities of Cíbola," Coronado National Memorial, Arizona, June 7, 2021, https:// www.nps.gov/coro/learn/historyculture/stories.htm.

97   *Looking down at the Colorado River:* See Pedro de Castañeda et al., *The Journey of Coronado,* translated and edited by George Parker Winship (New York: Dover Publications, 1990), 22.

97   *left unexplored:* "The Early Spanish Explorers," Grand Canyon National Park, Arizona, September 21, 2019, https://www.nps.gov/grca/learn/historyculture /explorers.htm.

Chapter Eight: To Please the Trigger Finger

103   Jim Kane: J. P. S. Brown, *Jim Kane* (New York: Dial Press, 1970).

103   Forests of the Night: J. P. S. Brown, *Forests of the Night* (New York: Dial Press, 1974).

107   *"To refuse a drink":* Carlos Mario Alvarado Licón, *Tarahumara, una tierra herida: análisis de la cultura de la violencia en zonas productoras de estupefacientes en Sierra de Chihuahua* (Chihuahua, Mexico: Talleres Gráficos del Estado de Chihuahua, 1996).

109   *a hundred Chiricahua Apaches:* See Douglas V. Meed, *They Never Surrendered: Bronco Apaches of the Sierra Madres, 1890–1935* (Tucson: Westernlore Press, 1993). See also Neil Goodwin, *The Apache Diaries: A Father-Son Journey* (Lincoln: University of Nebraska Press, 2000). See also Neil Goodwin, *Like a*

Brother: Grenville Goodwin's Apache Years, 1928–1939 (Tucson: University of Arizona Press, 2004).

109 *hunted down by Mexican ranchers*: See Goodwin, *The Apache Diaries*, and Helge Ingstad, *The Apache Indians: In Search of the Missing Tribe*, translated by Jeanine K. Stenehjem (Lincoln: University of Nebraska Press, 2004).

Vignette: George Hand

114 *"a city of mud-boxes"*: J. Ross Browne, *Adventures in the Apache Country: A Tour Through Arizona and Sonora* (New York: Harper and Brothers, 1869), 131.

114 *"Murderers, thieves, cut-throats"*: Browne, *Adventures in the Apache Country*, 22.

114 *kept a daily diary*: George Hand, *Whiskey, Six-Guns & Red-Light Ladies: George Hand's Saloon Diary, Tucson, 1875–1878*, edited by Neil Carmony (Silver City: High Lonesome Books, 1994).

114 *"Everybody got drunk"*: Hand, *Whiskey, Six-Guns & Red-Light Ladies*, 59.

114 *"John Dawson (drunk)"*: Hand, *Whiskey, Six-Guns & Red-Light Ladies*, 69.

114 *"The church was busy"*: Hand, *Whiskey, Six-Guns & Red-Light Ladies*, 107.

114 *"I was drunk early"*: Hand, *Whiskey, Six-Guns & Red-Light Ladies*, 60.

Chapter Nine: The Chiricahuas

116 *mega-dairy operation with more than 200,000 cows*: Debbie Weingarten and Tony Davis, "A Mega-Dairy Comes to the Desert," *High Country News* 53, no. 8 (August 1, 2021).

117 *capital-rich corporations*: Noah Gallagher Shannon, "The Water Wars of Arizona," *New York Times*, July 19, 2018.

117 *once moved like the wind*: David Roberts, *Once They Moved Like the Wind: Cochise, Geronimo, and the Apache Wars* (New York: Simon & Schuster, 1993), epigraph.

118 *no white people*: Grenville Goodwin, *Western Apache Raiding and Warfare, from the Notes of Grenville Goodwin*, edited by Keith H. Basso (Tucson: University of Arizona Press, 1971), 41.

118 *"Our people used to go"*: Goodwin, *Western Apache Raiding and Warfare*, 43.

119 *War parties*: James L. Haley, *Apaches: A History and Culture Portrait* (Garden City, NY: Doubleday, 1981), 166–21.

119 *notoriously inventive torturers*: Roberts, *Once They Moved Like the Wind*, 43–49.

119 *A chief named Eskiminzin*: Charles D. Poston, *History of the Apaches*, Manuscript, University of Arizona Special Collections, 53.

119   *Other methods included:* Roberts, *Once They Moved Like the Wind,* 46

119   *The worst fate:* Goodwin, *Western Apache Raiding and Warfare,* 284. Roberts, *Once They Moved Like the Wind,* 46.

120   *The boys trained:* Roberts, *Once They Moved Like the Wind,* 106.

120   *They learned to ride:* Roberts, *Once They Moved Like the Wind,* 107.

120   *As a kind of graduation:* Roberts, *Once They Moved Like the Wind,* 107.

120   *Lozen:* Sherry Robinson, *Apache Voices: Their Stories of Survival As Told to Eve Ball* (Albuquerque: University of New Mexico Press, 2000), 4–15.

120   *When her palms tingled:* Roberts, *Once They Moved Like the Wind,* 178.

121   *wickiups:* Haley, *Apaches: A History and Culture Portrait,* 80.

124   *five consecutive days:* Goodwin, *Western Apache Raiding and Warfare,* 50.

124   *"My legs were like automobiles":* Goodwin, *Western Apache Raiding and Warfare,* 55.

124   *pouches of food:* Sebastian Junger, *Freedom* (New York: Simon & Schuster, 2021), 38.

125   *Nana:* Stephen H. Lekson, *Nana's Raid: Apache Warfare in Southern New Mexico, 1881* (El Paso: Texas Western Press, 1987).

125   *fifty miles a day:* Roberts, *Once They Moved Like the Wind,* 194.

Vignette: Massai

128   *remove the Chiricahua warriors:* David Roberts, *Once They Moved Like the Wind: Cochise, Geronimo and the Apache Wars* (New York: Simon & Schuster, 1993), 295.

128   *A young warrior named Massai:* Sherry Robinson, *Apache Voices: Their Stories of Survival as Told to Eve Ball* (Albuquerque: University of New Mexico Press, 2000), 88–100. Jason Betzinez, with Wilbur Sturtevant Nye, *I Fought with Geronimo* (Harrisburg, PA: Stackpole Co., 1959), 143–45.

Chapter Ten: Violence and Delusion

129   *Robert Norwood:* Tim Steller, "A Year After Election, Tucson and America Risk More Political Violence," *Arizona Daily Star,* November 1, 2021.

130   *George Floyd protest marches:* Ray Stern, "Phoenix Police Arrested More than 200 Protestors Following Ducey's Curfew Order," *Phoenix New Times,* June 1, 2020.

130   *gunshot shattering the window:* Zachary Evans, "Gunshot Fired into Republican Field Office in Arizona During Campaign Event," *National Review,* May 29, 2020.

130 *arsonist:* Yvonne Wingett Sanchez, "Police Arrest Former Activist Suspected of Arizona Democratic Party Headquarters Arson," *Arizona Republic,* July 29, 2020.

131 *epicenter of QAnon activity:* Jerod MacDonald-Evoy, "Arizona Has Deep QAnon Ties, Including Its Politicians," *Arizona Mirror,* September 22, 2020.

131 *author Tom Zoellner:* Tom Zoellner, *A Safeway in Arizona: What the Gabrielle Giffords Shooting Tells Us About the Grand Canyon State and Life in America* (New York: Viking, 2011), 127.

131 *nearly 30 percent:* Stuart A. Thompson, "QAnon Candidates Aren't Thriving, but Some of Their Ideas Are," *New York Times,* July 25, 2022.

131 *armored truck:* MacDonald-Evoy, "Arizona Has Deep QAnon Ties, Including Its Politicians."

131 *In Sedona:* MacDonald-Evoy, "Arizona Has Deep QAnon Ties, Including Its Politicians."

131 *a couple in Gilbert:* MacDonald-Evoy, "Arizona Has Deep QAnon Ties, Including Its Politicians."

131 *Austin Steinbart:* MacDonald-Evoy, "Arizona Has Deep QAnon Ties, Including Its Politicians."

132 *artificial penis:* MacDonald-Evoy, "Arizona Has Deep QAnon Ties, Including Its Politicians."

132 *hired as a political campaign manager:* David Gilbert, "A QAnon 'Time Traveler' Is Running a GOP Congressional Campaign," *Vice News,* June 23, 2022.

132 *road rage:* Ashlee Valentine, "States with the Most Confrontational Drivers," *Forbes Advisor,* August 28, 2023.

132 *road rage shootings:* Sarah Robinson, "New Statistics Show Arizona Ranked Second in Road Rage Shootings," *Arizona's Family,* August 17, 2023.

132 *convenience stores:* Eddie Celaya, "Gunfight at Tucson Store Leaves Man, 12-Year-Old Boy Dead," *Arizona Daily Star,* September 26, 2023. "Arizona Store Shootout Ends with Robber, Bystander Dead," Associated Press, July 3, 2020.

132 *strip malls:* "Teen Girl Killed, 8 Injured in North Phoenix Strip Mall Shooting, Police Say," *Arizona's Family,* June 4, 2022. "Multiple People Shot at East Phoenix Strip Mall," *Arizona's Family,* November 17, 2023.

132 *outlet malls:* "Police: 5 Shot, Including 3 Kids, at Arizona Outlet Mall," *Arizona's Family,* March 23, 2022.

132 *A woman hiking was stabbed:* Graeme Massie, "Lauren Heike: Arizona

Esthetician Murdered on Desert Hiking Trail After Being Attacked from Behind," *Independent,* May 4, 2023.

133 *affluent teenagers:* Robert Anglen and Elena Santa Cruz, "Brass Knuckles, Beatings, Fear: Random Attacks on Teens Loom over Preston Lord Murder Case," *Arizona Republic,* December 14, 2023.

133 *A twenty-year-old incel:* Erica Stapleton, "Dark Side: The Westgate Shooting," 12news.com, February 18, 2021.

133 *Fentanyl overdose:* Chorus Nylander, "N4T Investigators: Fentanyl Leading Cause of Death for Pima County Teenagers," kvoa.com, March 3, 2022.

133 *In Tucson, two teenagers:* KOLD News 13 Staff, "Police: Arizona Teens Charged After Developmentally Disabled Man Beaten to Death with Baseball Bat," KOLD News 13/Gray News, November 18, 2022.

133 *A thirty-year-old math tutor:* Carol Ann Alaimo, "Teen Suspect Facing Murder Charge in Shooting of University of Arizona Alum," *Arizona Daily Star,* May 13, 2021.

134 *hundreds of suspicious Trump supporters:* Mark Bowden and Matthew Teague, *The Steal: The Attempt to Overturn the 2020 Election and the People Who Stopped It* (New York: Atlantic Monthly Press, 2022), 43.

134 *carrying AR-15s:* Simon Romero, "With Arizona Too Close to Call, Trump Supporters Gather at a Vote-Counting Site in Phoenix," *New York Times,* November 5, 2020.

134 *armed county sheriffs:* Bowden and Teague, *The Steal,* 87.

134 *nation's first Stop the Steal rally:* Robert Draper, *Weapons of Mass Delusion: When the Republican Party Lost Its Mind* (New York: Penguin Press, 2022), 7.

134 *"Patriots!":* Draper, *Weapons of Mass Delusion,* 9.

134 *Jake Angeli:* Richard Ruelas, "How Jake Angeli Went from Being a Phoenix Character to a Face of the U.S. Capitol Raid," *Arizona Republic,* January 17, 2021.

135 *"Reality must be defeated":* Tom Zoellner, *Rim to River: Looking into the Heart of Arizona* (Tucson: University of Arizona Press, 2023), 232.

136 *162,000 chickens:* Bill McCarthy, "Fowl Play? Social Media Users Falsely Claim Arizona Ballots Were Destroyed in Chicken Farm Fire," *Politifact,* May 25, 2021.

136 *Gateway Pundit:* Joe Hoft, "After Finding Shredded Ballots in the Dumpster Earlier Today—a Mysterious Fire Breaks Out at Maricopa County Official's Farm," *Gateway Pundit,* March 6, 2021.

136 *Arizona Patriot Party:* Will Sommer, "A Treasure Hunter, a Satanism Expert,

and Mike Lindell Fight to Overturn Biden Win in Arizona," *Daily Beast,* March 22, 2021.

136   *"You need to get out of here":* Tim Steller, "A Year After Election, Tucson and America Risk More Political Violence," *Arizona Daily Star,* November 1, 2021.

137   *"'Trump won'":* Steller, "A Year After Election, Tucson and America Risk More Political Violence."

137   *Journalists later discovered:* Steller, "A Year After Election, Tucson and America Risk More Political Violence."

Vignette: Tombstone

138   *Prospector Ed Schieffelin:* Thomas E. Sheridan, *Arizona: A History* (Tucson: University of Arizona Press, 2012), 151.

138   *In addition to 110 saloons:* Marshall Trimble, *Arizona Oddities: Land of Anomalies and Tamales* (Charleston, SC: History Press, 2018), 21.

138   *gin fizz toddy:* Trimble, *Arizona Oddities,* 21.

138   *"horizontally employed":* Trimble, *Arizona Oddities,* 86.

138   *Big Minnie Bignon:* Trimble, *Arizona Oddities,* 86.

138   *buried in Tombstone:* Lynn R. Bailey, *Tombstone, Arizona: "Too Tough to Die": The Rise, Fall, and Resurrection of a Silver Camp, 1878 to 1990* (Tucson: Westernlore Press, 2004), 214–15.

Chapter Eleven: Patterns of Life

139   *Tucson's allocation:* Associated Press, "Tucson May Forego Some Water to Help Keep Lake Mead Level Up," *Las Vegas Sun,* April 15, 2024.

140   *1,000-mile pipeline:* Ciara Nugent, "Arizona Faces an Existential Dilemma: Import Water or End Its Housing Boom," *Time,* January 20, 2023.

Vignette: Colorado City

154   *Colorado City:* Tove K. Danovich, "The Forest Hidden Behind the Canyons," *Ringer,* June 24, 2019. Timothy Egan, "Polygamous Community Defies State Crackdown," *New York Times,* October 25, 2005.

154   *life sentence:* Ed Pilkington, "Fundamentalist Sect Leader Jailed for Life for Sex with Child Brides," *Guardian,* August 9, 2011.

154   *Samuel Bateman:* Associated Press, "FBI: Polygamous Leader in Colorado City Had 20 Wives, Many of Them Minors," *St. George News,* December 7, 2022.

Chapter Twelve: Arivaca

160   *Chris Simcox*: Associated Press, "Arizona Border-Watch Leader, Chris Simcox, Gets 19 Years for Molestation," *Arizona Daily Star,* July 11, 2016.

161   *"Shawna Forde killings"*: See Patrick Strickland, *The Marauders: Standing Up to Vigilantes in the American Borderlands* (Brooklyn: Melville House, 2022).

163   *Facebook Live video*: Eric Reidy, "Vigilantes Not Welcome: A Border Town Pushes Back on Anti-Immigrant Extremists," *Mother Jones,* May/June 2019.

163   *unwanted and unwelcome*: Reidy, "Vigilantes Not Welcome: A Border Town Pushes Back on Anti-Immigrant Extremists."

166   *"We did believe"*: Adelheid Fischer, "Documenting the Undocumented," *Places Journal,* February 2017.

Vignette: Bisbee Deportation

171   *Phelps Dodge Corporation*: Thomas E. Sheridan, *Arizona: A History* (Tucson: University of Arizona Press, 2012), 189–90.

171   *Bisbee deportation*: Sheridan, *Arizona: A History,* 192–95.

Chapter Thirteen: AR15ONA

177   *"Let's Go Brandon"*: Colleen Long, "How 'Let's Go Brandon' Became Code for Insulting Joe Biden," Associated Press, October 30, 2021.

178   *"We named it Crusader"*: https://www.spikestactical.com/collections/complete -rifles/crusader-2/.

180   *"America's rifle"*: Ali Watkins, John Ismay, and Thomas Gibbons-Neff, "Once Banned, Now Loved and Loathed: How the AR-15 Became 'America's Rifle,'" *New York Times,* March 3, 2018.

180   *Pastor Sean Moon*: Tim Dickinson, "Inside the Bizarre and Dangerous Rod of Iron Ministries," *Rolling Stone,* August 18, 2022.

181   *46 percent of the guns in the world*: "Americans Own Nearly Half World's Guns in Civilian Hands—Survey," Reuters, June 18, 2018.

Vignette: Howell Code

184   *"two out of every three"*: John S. Goff, "William T. Howell and the Howell Code of Arizona," *American Journal of Legal History* 11, no. 3 (1967): 221–33.

184   *"excusable homicides"*: Philip Bump, "Here Are Some Other Laws Arizona Had on the Books in 1864," *Washington Post,* April 10, 2024.

184 *"carnal knowledge of any female child"*: The Howell Code, Office of the Arizona Miner, Official Paper of the Territory, 1865, Section 45, 54.

184 *"No black or mulatto"*: The Howell Code, Section 14, 50.

184 *"the miscarriage of any woman"*: The Howell Code, Section 45, 54.

184 *This abortion ban stayed in place:* Jerod MacDonald-Evoy, "The History of Abortion Regulations in Arizona," *Arizona Mirror,* April 12, 2024.

Chapter Fourteen: Cities, Farms, and Water

186 *"a viciously overcrowded version"*: Hunter S. Thompson, *Generation of Swine: The Brutal Odyssey of an Outlaw Journalist* (New York: Simon & Schuster, 2011), 11.

186 *"The Blob"*: Edward Abbey, "The Blob Comes to Arizona," *New York Times,* May 16, 1976.

186 *harshest anti-immigrant law in the nation*: Alisa Reznick, "'Show Me Your Papers': A Decade After SB 1070," Arizona Public Media, July 30, 2020.

187 *cocaine and meth use:* Shelby Slade, "Dwayne 'The Rock' Johnson Claims Phoenix Is Top for Meth Use at WWE Smackdown. Is He Right?" *Arizona Republic,* March 2, 2024.

187 *downtown neighborhood that harvests rainwater:* Samuel Gilbert, "'A Living Pantry': How an Urban Food Forest in Arizona Became a Model for Climate Action," *Guardian,* March 21, 2023.

190 *water supply was going to be cut:* Tony Davis, "First Mandatory Cutback of CAP Water Now Likely in 2022," *Arizona Daily Star,* April 16, 2021.

190 *300 billion gallons:* Jake Bittle, *The Great Displacement: Climate Change and the Next American Migration* (New York: Simon & Schuster, 2023), 183.

190 *nearly 80 percent of Arizona's water:* George B. Frisvold, "Water, Agriculture, and Drought in the West Under Changing Climate and Policy Regimes," *Natural Resources Journal* 55, no. 2 (Spring 2015).

191 *Superstition Vistas:* Joshua Bowling, "Developers Are Building in the Massive Superstition Vistas Area Southeast of Phoenix, but Water Will Dictate How It Grows," *Arizona Republic,* February 9, 2022.

191 *over 370 irrigated golf courses:* Arizona Alliance for Golf, "The Economic Contribution of Arizona's Golf Industry," Arizona Alliance for Golf study, 2020.

192 *650,000 acre-feet:* Elena Saavedra Buckley, "One Tribal Nation Could Decide the Fate of Arizona's Drought Plan," *High Country News,* January 28, 2019.

Notes

193   *worst big city for traffic collisions:* Christina Estes, "How Phoenix Is Addressing Being 'The Worst Large City' for Traffic Deaths," kjzz.org, October 21, 2021.

193   *nearly a thousand billboards:* Elias Weiss, "How Rafi Became the Face of Phoenix," *Phoenix New Times,* May 27, 2022.

195   *Blacks were confined:* Thomas E. Sheridan, *Arizona: A History* (Tucson: University of Arizona Press, 2012), 269–70.

196   *Salado people fleeing drought:* Joseph K. Giddens, "Archaeologist Describes Migrations of Pre-Columbian Salado," *Sedona Red Rock News,* May 29, 2023.

196   *the world's least sustainable city:* Andrew Ross, *Bird on Fire: Lessons from the World's Least Sustainable City* (New York: Oxford University Press, 2011).

196   *The nights are roughly 9 degrees hotter:* Marguerite Holloway, "As Phoenix Heats Up, the Night Comes Alive," *New York Times,* August 12, 2019.

196   *another 2 million people:* Maricopa County, "Vision 2030, Maricopa County Comprehensive Plan," January 13, 2016.

196   *A recent study projected:* Brian Stone Jr. et al., "How Blackouts During Heat Waves Amplify Mortality and Morbidity Risk," *Environmental Science & Technology* 57, no. 22 (2023): 8245–55.

196   *most uninhabitable:* Keith Schneider, "Arizona's Future Water Shock," *Counter,* April 7, 2022.

197   *desalinization plant:* Christopher Flavelle, "Arizona, Low on Water, Weighs Taking It from the Sea. In Mexico," *New York Times,* June 10, 2023.

197   La Maravilla: Alfredo Véa Jr., *La Maravilla* (New York: Plume, 1994).

197   *Buckeye:* Alexandra Hardle, "A Report Confirms Buckeye Doesn't Have Enough Water. What Does the Growing City Do Next?" *Arizona Republic,* March 8, 2023.

198   *sweetheart deal:* Rob O'Dell and Ian James, "Arizona Provides Sweet Deal to Saudi Farm to Pump Water from Phoenix's Backup Supply," *Arizona Republic,* June 9, 2022.

199   *"xenophobic":* Isaac Stanley-Becker, Joshua Partlow, and Yvonne Wingett Sanchez, "How a Saudi Firm Tapped a Gusher of Water in Drought-Stricken Arizona," *Washington Post,* July 16, 2023.

Vignette: Evan Mecham

200   *a staggering 50 percent:* Thomas E. Sheridan, *Arizona: A History* (Tucson: University of Arizona Press, 2012), 339.

200   *fell and broke a leg:* Ronald J. Watkins, *High Crimes and Misdemeanors: The Term and Trials of Former Governor Evan Mecham* (New York: Morrow, 1990), 270–71.

200   *Martin Luther King Jr. Day*: Watkins, *High Crimes and Misdemeanors*, 62–63, 65.

200   *six felony charges*: Watkins, *High Crimes and Misdemeanors*, 238.

200   *strong second in the Republican primary*: Michael Oreskes, "The 1990 Elections: Primary Results Across U.S. Reflect Wide Outcry Against Politics as Usual," *New York Times*, September 13, 1990.

Chapter Fifteen: Monsoon Summer

207   *ranks among the bottom five states*: Bethany Blankley, "Arizona Earns D+ Grade for Education, Consistently Ranks in Bottom Five States," *Center Square*, September 17, 2019.

208   *Nathan Beaver*: Paul Ingram, "Man Arrested in Antisemitic Vandalism of Tucson Synagogue," *Tucson Sentinel*, June 24, 2021.

211   *Study after study*: Jordan Langs, "Poverty Impedes Children's Education Long Before They Enter the Classroom—Here's How We Can Change That," *Forbes*, April 4, 2022.

Vignette: Quartzite

215   *Hi Jolly*: Marshall Trimble, *Arizona Oddities: Land of Anomalies and Tamales* (Charleston, SC: History Press, 2018), 72–77.

Chapter Sixteen: Big Sandy

218   *"staunch citizens"*: Laurie Merrill, "In Arizona, Nothing from Nothing Equals a Ghost Town," ADOT Communications, September 2, 2020.

Vignette: AzScam

233   *Joseph Stedino*: Joseph Stedino with Dary Matera, *What's in It for Me? How an Ex-Wiseguy Exposed the Greed, Jealousy, and Lust That Drive Arizona Politics* (New York: HarperCollins, 1992).

233   *"There's not an issue in this world"*: Stedino with Matera, *What's in It for Me?*, 144.

Chapter Seventeen: The Lions of the Right

235   *the most politically corrupt*: Samuel Rubenfeld, "Study Names Arizona as Most Corrupt State," *Wall Street Journal*, December 4, 2014.

236   *Cyber Ninjas*: Dan Zak, "The Mess in Maricopa," *Washington Post*, May 21, 2021.

Notes

236 *a resolution commending:* Representative Holland, "House Resolution 90: A Resolution Commending and Congratulating Richard Grant upon the Successful Release of His Book, *Dispatches from Pluto: Lost and Found in the Mississippi Delta,*" Mississippi Legislature 2017, Regular Session.

236 *member of the Oath Keepers:* Charlotte Alter, "An Oath Keeper Could End Up in Charge of Arizona's Elections," *Time,* August 3, 2022.

238 *"heated exaggeration":* Richard Hofstadter, "The Paranoid Style in American Politics," *Harper's Magazine,* November 1964, https://harpers.org/archive/1964/11/the-paranoid-style-in-american-politics/.

238 *a $1.55 million house:* Tim Steller and Sam Kmack, "Political Notebook: Steve Bannon Buys Home in Oro Valley," *Arizona Daily Star,* February 25, 2022.

241 *"blatant white supremacist":* Martin Pengelly, "Republican Ex-Congressman Suggests Colleagues 'Had Serious Cognitive Issues,'" *Guardian,* September 27, 2022.

241 *"serious cognitive issues":* Pengelly, "Republican Ex-Congressman Suggests Colleagues 'Had Serious Cognitive Issues.'"

244 *giving a speech in the House:* Robert Draper, *Weapons of Mass Delusion: When the Republican Party Lost Its Mind* (New York: Penguin Press, 2022), 3–11.

244 *anime-style video:* Barbara Sprunt, "Rep. Paul Gosar Is Censured over an Anime Video Depicting Him of Killing AOC," *National Public Radio Morning Edition,* November 18, 2021.

244 *appearing at the white nationalist:* Melanie Zanona, "GOP Leaders Condemn 2 House Republicans for Associating with White Nationalist Event," cnn.com, February 28, 2022.

245 *contributions from retired individuals:* "Paul Gosar," federal congressional candidacy, summary, 2022 election cycle, campaign committee only, OpenSecrets, December 31, 2022, https://www.opensecrets.org/members-of-congress/paul-gosar/summary?cid=N00030771&cycle=2022.

245 *"He's just not fit":* Mihir Zaveri, "Six Siblings of a Republican Congressman Endorse His Opponent in Campaign Ads," *New York Times,* September 22, 2018.

246 *a legacy project:* Draper, *Weapons of Mass Delusion,* 235–38.

246 *Timothy McVeigh:* Tom Zoellner, *Rim to River: Looking into the Heart of Arizona* (Tucson: University of Arizona Press, 2023), 101.

247 *183 animals:* "Cops: Arizona Man Stuffed 183 Animals in Freezer, Some Alive," Associated Press, April 14, 2022.

Vignette: Place Names

251 *To get a post office:* Kira Caspers, "Headed to Puerto Peñasco? You May Pass Through Why, Arizona. How the Town Got Its Name," *Arizona Republic*, March 1, 2024.

251 *most common question asked by tourists:* Marshall Trimble, *Roadside History of Arizona* (Missoula, MT: Mountain Press, 2004), 153.

251 *Damfino:* Marshall Trimble, *Arizona Oddities: Land of Anomalies and Tamales* (Charleston, SC: History Press, 2018), 14.

251 *tall, bushy-haired bartender:* Trimble, *Arizona Oddities*, 13.

251 *"If you can show low":* Will C. Barnes, *Arizona Place Names* (Tucson: University of Arizona Press, 1988), 402.

251 *People Without Minds:* James L. Haley, *Apaches: A History and Culture Portrait* (Garden City, NY: Doubleday, 1981), 153.

251 *"people with high-pitched voices":* "About: Tonto Apache," DBpedia, https://dbpedia.org/page/Tonto_Apache.

Chapter Eighteen: Walk in Beauty

255 *90 percent of the people:* Marshall Trimble, *Arizona Oddities: Land of Anomalies and Tamales* (Charleston, SC: History Press, 2018), 11.

256 *not widely liked:* Robert M. Utley, *Geronimo* (New Haven, CT: Yale University Press, 2012), 1–4.

256 *only county seat:* Suzanne Hammons, "'No Place for Women and Children': A History of Holbrook, Arizona," *Voice of the Southwest*, September 19, 2014.

258 *"geology by day":* J. B. Priestley, *Midnight on the Desert: Being an Excursion into Autobiography During a Winter in America, 1935–36* (New York and London: Harper & Brothers, 1937), 3.

262 *Roughly 40 percent of people:* Laurel Morales, "For Many Navajos, Getting Hooked Up to the Power Grid Can Be Life-Changing," NPR, May 29, 2019.

Chapter Nineteen: Heatstruck for Trump

268 *Rapt devotees:* Steven Monacelli, "The Fringe QAnon 'Cult' Is Still Waiting for a JFK Jr. Miracle in Dallas," *Rolling Stone*, December 1, 2021.

270 *sixty people treated:* Cindy Barks, "Prescott Fire Dept.: 60 People Treated for Heat-Related Illness at Trump Rally," *Verde Independent*, October 24, 2020.

270 *fifty-six succumbed to the heat:* "56 People, Including Officers, Treated for 'Heat-Related' Issues at President Donald Trump Rally," abc15.com, August 22, 2017.

271 *"Let's all get together":* George Orwell, *Coming Up for Air* (New York: Harcourt Brace, 1950), 175.

Vignette: Pearl Hart

276 *Pearl Hart:* Marshall Trimble, *Arizona Outlaws and Lawmen: Gunslingers, Bandits, Heroes, and Peacekeepers* (Charleston, SC: History Press, 2015), 99–103.

Chapter Twenty: Forest People

281 *"I was born to be erased":* Charles Bowden, *Dakotah: The Return of the Future* (Austin: University of Texas Press, 2019), 5.

283 *"I'm going now":* Bowden, *Dakotah,* 165.

285 *mountain lion attacks:* Dr. Jim Keen, "The Economic and Ecological Value of Mountain Lions and Bobcats in the West: Part II," animalwellnessaction.org, January 10, 2024.